Betrayal at Pearl Harbor

How Churchill Lured Roosevelt into World War II

JAMES RUSBRIDGER
AND ERIC NAVE

A TOUCHSTONE BOOK
Published by Simon & Schuster
New York   London   Toronto   Sydney   Tokyo   Singapore

TOUCHSTONE
Simon & Schuster Building
Rockefeller Center
1230 Avenue of the Americas
New York, New York 10020

First Touchstone Edition 1992

Designed by Irving Perkins Assoc.

Manufactured in the United States of America

1   3   5   7   9   10   8   6   4   2

Library of Congress Cataloging-in-Publication Data
Rusbridger, James.
Betrayal at Pearl Harbor: how Churchill lured Roosevelt into World War II/James
Rusbridger and Eric Nave.
p. cm.
Includes bibliographical references and index.
1. Pearl Harbor (Hawaii), Attack on, 1941.   2. World War, 1939–1945—United
States.   3. World War, 1939–1945—Cryptography.   4. Churchill, Winston, Sir, 1874–
1965.   5. Roosevelt, Franklin D. (Franklin Delano), 1882–1945.   6. United States—
History—1933–1945.   I. Nave, Eric.   II. Title.
D767.92.R87   1991
940.54′26—dc20   91-696
CIP

ISBN 0-671-70805-8
ISBN 0-671-79231-8 (pbk)

Contents

Contents

Preface

THE FIRST EDITION of *Betrayal at Pearl Harbor,* published in July 1991, produced predictably polarized reactions from around the world. The vast majority of readers were fascinated by the previously undisclosed details of Britain's codebreaking work against Japanese naval codes from the early 1920s right up to December 1941.

However, a minority of readers, in particular some of those who had published books about Pearl Harbor and codebreaking in the past, were less than happy to see their work disputed. In Britain, the ever-active Churchill industry poured scorn on claims in the book that Churchill knew in advance, from his codebreakers in Singapore, details of the Japanese attack on the U.S. Pacific fleet.

Nevertheless, as sales of the book widened, so memories were awakened, including those of Mrs. Mary Burnett, the widow of Commander Malcolm Burnett, RN (see page 83), who had been Captain Nave's codebreaking colleague at the Far East Combined Bureau (FECB) in Singapore. Although Burnett never made any public comment about his codebreaking work, in 1980 he confided to a close family friend, the historian Dr. Andrew Gordon, that in the fall of 1939 (as Nave describes on page 87), he had brought out to FECB from London the solution for breaking the Japanese naval code JN-25.

Together with Nave and his wife Mary, who was also a codebreaker at Singapore, FECB continued reading JN-25 without difficulty right up to 4 December 1941 (the date of the last additive table change, see page 145). Burnett told Gordon that FECB had intercepted and read all the messages from Yamamoto to his Task Force both before and after it sailed and, by 26 November, Burnett had personally advised Churchill in London that the only logical target for the impending attack was Pearl Harbor.

In December 1991, Mrs. Burnett appeared on American television and confirmed what her husband had told Gordon, and that the same information he sent Churchill had also been sent to U.S. Navy codebreakers at Station Cast, at Corregidor and, FECB assumed, was automatically passed on to Washington and President Roosevelt.

However, Mrs. Burnett added that sharing the information with the Americans had not been sanctioned by London (who forbade the sharing of any codebreaking secrets, see page 93) and had been privately arranged by her husband. It follows that Churchill would *not* have expected Burnett's information to have been known to the Americans. Mrs. Burnett's testimony thus further confirms our contention that Churchill himself deliberately failed to inform the Americans of what he must have known was an almost inevitable attack on Pearl Harbor.

The Burnetts' statements not only confirm Nave's account but also that of Professor Harry Hinsley who, on page 53 of volume 1, *British Intelligence in the Second World War* (Cambridge: Cambridge University Press, 1979), states "it was not until September 1939 that . . . the [Japanese] Fleet cypher [JN-25] . . . began to yield to GCCS's [Government Code & Cipher School] attack." A footnote on the same page adds, "It remained possible . . . to keep track of her [Japanese] main naval movements."

An even more important development occurred during the Nimitz Conference, held in Hawaii on the fiftieth anniversary of the attack in December 1991. Among those attending was Mr. Frederick Parker, the National Security Agency's (NSA) historian, who was asked by many delegates to explain the inconsistencies in the official American account of breaking JN-25 with that detailed in *Betrayal at Pearl Harbor.*

As a result, Parker conferred with Britain's Government Communication Headquarters (GCHQ), who hold all the records of GCCS and FECB, and, with their approval (although without the agreement of the British government), issued a press release on 8 December 1991 admitting for the first time that both British and American codebreakers *had* broken JN-25 prior to the attack.

Because of the sensitive nature of this statement, which conflicts with everything that has been officially claimed by both governments in the past forty-five years (including the 1945 Congressional inquiry), the release was inevitably economical with the truth, and Parker asked not to be pressed further for fear of upsetting relations with Britain. However, Parker concluded his statement by saying, "In view of the full collaboration and exchange with FECB, Singapore, there is no reason to believe that the British exceeded the U.S. accomplishments." Parker revealed that, during 1941, 16,000 messages in JN-25 were intercepted by the Americans and, one must assume, also by FECB. Only when all these decrypts are made available for inspection will it be possible to evaluate the intelligence they provided, and who saw it.

While it is rewarding to us as authors that the publication of *Betrayal at Pearl Harbor* was responsible for this first break in the log-jam of official secrecy concerning JN-25, and thus also Churchill's role in the Pearl Harbor attack, it again raises the fundamental issue of why, and on whose orders, a vital part of American and British history has been deliberately concealed for so long. One can only hope that before long all JN-25 material for the period 1939 through 1941 will be placed in the public domain so a full evaluation can be made, and the official accounts properly rewritten.

James Rusbridger
Cornwall, 1992

Acknowledgments

THE STORY OF how this book came to be written has almost as many twists and turns as does the story of Pearl Harbor itself.

In 1984, I began investigating the bizarre tale of the secret Chiefs of Staff papers lost on the *Automedon* in 1940, which were passed by the Germans to the Japanese and thus informed them a year before Pearl Harbor that the British government had already abandoned any hope of saving Singapore and Malaya against a Japanese attack.

As this story had been deliberately concealed from both the British and American people by Churchill, and not a word about the disaster had appeared in his or any other official history of World War II, I wondered what other similar tales lay hidden in government archives.

Like many others, the story of the attack on Pearl Harbor had long fascinated me, but I was puzzled not only by the many inconsistencies in the official American account but also why the British government, although proud to acknowledge the success of its codebreakers at reading the wartime German Enigma messages, had refused to allow a word to be written about their equally important work against the Japanese. Churchill's own postwar memoirs gave the impression that he had received all his Japanese intelligence derived from codebreaking entirely from the Americans. This view was later repeated in the official histories of Britain's wartime intelligence operations written by Professor F. H. Hinsley and his team, who gave the impression that Far East codebreaking had been a matter solely for the Americans. This struck me as incorrect.

In 1985, when I asked the British Foreign Secretary—then Sir Geoffrey Howe—if I could see the Japanese Ultra material for the period 1939–41, I was refused access and told none of it would ever be released into the public domain. Why was the breaking of Japanese codes prior to 1941 so sensitive, especially when it was public knowledge since 1946 that the Americans had done this and shared their achievements with Britain?

In 1985, Melvin Lasky, editor of *Encounter,* encouraged me to write an article piecing together all that I knew about the Pearl Harbor attack, including some new information I had researched in Holland about the work of Dutch codebreakers in the Far East. Although the article went further than any previous accounts, I still lacked that final key to unlock the secrets surrounding the decryption of the most important Japanese code of all—the Japanese naval code JN-25.

However, the demographic distribution of *Encounter* ensures that in time what one writes will be read by a varied and erudite readership around the world, and one of those who saw the article was Howard Baker, who had been in Java before the war, where he married and with his family was later interned by the Japanese. Howard very kindly sent me his immaculate and fascinating diary (now fortunately in the safe-keeping of the Imperial War Museum in London), in which there was an intriguing reference to an Australian naval officer called Commander Nave, who had broken the Japanese naval codes before the war.

Attempts to find Commander Nave in Australia were protracted, because I wrote to the Royal Australian Navy (RAN) by airmail, and they replied by sea, eventually stating that no one of that name existed. I was about to abandon the search when, during a chance conversation with John Mackenzie, the RAN's extremely helpful historical officer in Canberra, he recalled the name of a Captain Nave, who, though an Australian, had served with the Royal Navy and was now living somewhere in retirement in Australia.

The staff at Australia House in London were extremely helpful and made available the telephone directories one by one until I eventually found a Captain T. E. Nave living in Melbourne. Since 1941 was a long time ago, I wondered who would answer as I pressed out the twelve digits in Cornwall, but twenty seconds later was rewarded by the resonant voice of Eric Nave himself. A week later, in 1988, I sat in Eric Nave's garden and listened with amazement as this eighty-nine-year-old naval officer quietly unfolded with perfect recall his career in codebreaking that started in 1925 at Britain's Government Code & Cipher School (GCCS), continued in Hong Kong and Singapore at the Far East Combined Bureau (FECB), and then throughout World War II at the Central Bureau in Australia. In simple terms, Eric Nave was the father of British codebreaking in the Far East.

As Eric Nave talked with me, the missing pieces in the jigsaw started to come together. The strange gaps in the American archives, the censored words in what little material has been released by the National Security Agency, and the almost total absence of any reference to Japanese naval codes in postwar histories and the eight Pearl Harbor inquiries.

So too the refusal of the Foreign Office to discuss any facet of the prewar work of FECB. The refusal of help from the Government Communications Headquarters (GCHQ) on even the simplest matter. The deliberate distortions in Churchill's memoirs. All these now made sense, because the tale Eric Nave had to tell not only rewrote the story of Pearl Harbor but also rewrote the entire history of British codebreaking in the Far East.

Over the next weeks, Eric Nave and his charming wife, Margaret, gave me a second home and allowed me to intrude into their life each day as I discussed and recorded Eric's fascinating story with all its amusing asides and anecdotes covering his forty-two years' service with both the Australian and British navies.

On my return home, I prepared a synopsis for two books, the first of which would tell the history of British codebreaking against the Japanese, starting with Eric Nave's early work in 1925 and continuing through to December 1941. The second would be of a more personal nature, covering Eric's thirty-two-year career as an officer with the Australian and British navies, and then after the war his ten years as a director of the Australian Security Intelligence Organisation (ASIO).

However, before any book contract had been signed, Eric Nave received a polite letter from the Ministry of Defence in London saying that they understood he was proposing to write his memoirs in conjunction with me and reminding him of his obligations under Britain's all-embracing Official Secrets Act. Australia is, however, a long way from London and, as the government had recently badly burnt its fingers trying unsuccessfully to interfere with the publication of another book, *Spycatcher* (ironically written by my cousin Peter Wright), also about intelligence affairs, Eric was in no hurry to reply.

With a contract for the book finally placed with a London publisher, work went ahead on the manuscript, and the first draft was ready by early 1989, just after the new and more draconian Official Secrets Act had been passed by a reluctant Parliament onto the statute book. The British publisher decided not to proceed with the book, and considerable confusion resulted as to the reason, causing Admiral William Higgins, chairman of the government's D-Notice Committee, that curious agency which in quaint British fashion unofficially tries to stop embarrassing material from reaching the public, was forced to write a rare letter to the press insisting he had not stopped the book's publication. As it transpired, he had not, and Michael O'Mara in London and James Silberman in New York decided they would see the story told.

To put Eric Nave's story into its proper context and show in hitherto unknown detail the prewar history of the British codebreakers against the Japanese prior to Pearl Harbor was a privilege and a challenge that I could not have achieved without the continuous support and encouragement from Michael O'Mara, James Silberman, Ann Meador, Carol Ratelle Leach, the production and copyediting staff at Simon & Schuster, and my kind and long-suffering editor, Robert Asahina, who turned a long technical manuscript into final concise print.

The epic scale of the attack on Pearl Harbor, and the war in the Far East and Pacific that followed, covered such a vast area that inevitably research for this book spanned many years and continents.

In Britain, Phillip Reed at the Imperial War Museum helped me track down many important documents, as did John Brown and David Ashby at the Naval Historical Library, and D. B. Inns of the House of Commons Library, all these sources providing invaluable material. Mrs. L. C. Unwin and Miss H. R. Martin at the Ministry of Defence were most helpful in supplying biographical information on many of Eric Nave's colleagues. Several other government archivists tirelessly trawled their records to assist me but later asked that they should not be identified as having helped with the book.

I am particularly grateful to Lieutenant Commander W. W. Mortimer RNR (Ret.), who, as one of the last surviving members of FECB during the period 1939–45, so willingly gave up his time to see me and provided a wealth of additional information about its work and his colleagues, which has added much invaluable detail to the book.

Others who kindly shared the products of their own research with me include Alan Stripp, who worked at GCCS during the latter stages of the war; Dr. John Chapman of Sussex University; Richard Deacon; David Irving, whose prodigious skills as a researcher I envy; Phillip Knightley; Ralph Erskine, whose knowledge of the Enigma cryptograph is unrivaled; Nigel West; D. A. Wall, who helped me piece together the history of Typex; Sir Stuart Milner Barry; Martin Gilbert; Michael Montgomery; Cedric Brown; Howard Baker; Dr. Toby Baker; Mrs. Jean Howard; and the late Professor G. C. McVittie, who sadly died while this book was in the course of preparation.

Elaine Jones, Martyn Thomas, and John Stevens, of the Cornwall library services tirelessly coped with requests for reference material and scoured the county and farther afield on my behalf without once failing to find what I needed; W. J. Hitchens of Sheffield University Library kindly made available the Malcolm Kennedy diaries for my inspection; and Dr. Christopher Woolgar at the Hartley Library, University of Southampton, extracted valuable information for me from the Mountbatten papers.

Amanda Moody, Sheila Venning, and Gail Gill used their skills and expertise to come to terms with the complexities of Japanese *kana* Morse code not normally seen in Cornwall, and their finished artwork is a tribute to their enthusiasm and adds greatly to the book.

In the United States, at the National Archives in Washington, D.C., I found myself on the thirteenth floor in the capable hands of my old friend John Taylor. His encyclopedic knowledge of the archives, which he willingly gives, is a shortcut to success so valuable that there can be few authors and researchers that have not benefited from his wisdom. His colleagues, Richard von Doenhoff, Wilbert B. Mahoney, Charlotte Seeley, Kathie Nicastro, Jo Ann Williamson,, Terri Hammett, and Amy Schmidt, all responded to my inquiries with the unfailing courtesy that is the hallmark of the National Archives and makes research there so profitable and pleasant.

At the Naval Historical Center at the U.S. Navy Yard in Washington, D.C., I renewed my friendship with Dr. Dean C. Allard and Bernard Cavalcante, who placed at my disposal their Pearl Harbor archives, which have provided much useful background material.

At the Federal Bureau of Investigation, Valerie Lynham, Helen Near, and Patricia Grant produced with tireless efficiency a wealth of hitherto unseen documents for me to study and copy. Also in Washington I had the pleasure of meeting Tom Kimmel, the grandson of Admiral Husband Kimmel, who was so shamefully treated in the aftermath of Pearl Harbor. Robert Haslach very kindly helped me understand the Dutch contribution to Far East codebreaking. Captain Roger Pineau, USNR (Ret.), was kind enough to correct and advise on my *kana* artwork, using his unrivaled knowledge of Japanese radio traffic.

Despite the high level of security prevailing at the U.S. Naval Security Group Headquarters, both Commander Newman and George Henriksen personally showed me over their fascinating museum devoted to cryptography containing many unique items that cannot be seen elsewhere. Despite the sensitive nature of my inquiries, Mr. Henriksen promptly responded to my Freedom of Information applications and declassified for the first time pages from the Red, Blue, and JN-25 codebooks, together with photographs of the special RIP-5 *kana* typewriters never previously publicly released. Mr. Henriksen's contribution to this book has been of immense value.

At the Franklin D. Roosevelt Library in New York, Raymond Teichman responded to my requests in his usual efficient and courteous manner. I am also particularly grateful for the help I received from David Kahn, Dr. Deavours, and Louis Kruh, who helped me understand some of the finer details of codebreaking techniques.

In Las Vegas, I was warmly received by Marie and Ralph Briggs, who put their lovely house at my disposal so that I could talk to Ralph about his experiences at length, thus enjoying the first interview he has ever given since leaving the U.S. Navy as to how he received the Winds message. I was pleased that I was able to show him the first documentary proof from the Australian archives that his story could now be confirmed after so many frustrating years.

In Phoenix, Arizona, I was welcomed by Colonel Abraham Sinkov (an old friend of Eric Nave's) to his cool and peaceful house, where we sat for several days discussing his incredible career as one of America's leading codebreakers. In San Francisco, I met with Bob Stinnett, with whom I had exchanged material about Pearl Harbor for several years. In Long Beach, I had the pleasure of meeting Captain Forrest Biard, USN (Ret.), who was a codebreaker at Station Hypo in Hawaii in 1941 and had much intimate knowledge of the pre-Pearl era, which he willingly shared with me.

In Honolulu, I felt privileged to be able to make the journey out to the wreck of the USS *Arizona,* which is one of the most moving experiences I have known and forms one of the cornerstones motivating this book. Later, Lieutenant Commander Garry Shrout, USN, and Dick Brady, the U.S. Navy's public relations officer, very kindly showed me over the naval base at Pearl Harbor and the offices in Number 1 Building, East Wing, including the basement where America's leading codebreaker, Commander Joseph Rochefort, USN, worked. They bravely held the naval security police at bay so that I could take my photographs and then persuaded them not to arrest me as a spy. David Lowman, who retired from the National Security Agency to Honolulu, gave me much useful information about the NSA's control over Japanese documents that are still unreleased and how those that were placed in the National Archives were censored and rewritten.

In Australia, my warmest thanks go to Moira Smythe of the Australian Archives at Mitchell in Canberra, who over the years with tireless efficiency has tracked down a vast hoard of documents for me, often letting me copy them only just in time before Britain's GCHQ insisted upon their reclassification. At the Australian Archives in Brighton, Victoria, Tim Bryant, J. M. Peterson, Nola Barnes, and Kathy Graham have been my staunch allies, despite the many pressures placed upon them by the British government to stop documents being released for my inspection.

Jim Stokes, the access director, and his assistant, Richard Summerrell, at the Archives Access Office in Canberra, with enormous patience and courtesy helped me wend my way through the bureaucratic maze of restrictions that surrounded my Freedom of Information applications. If they were not always successful in helping me completely achieve my goal, that was certainly not their fault.

Richard Pelvin and John Mackenzie at the Navy Office in Canberra produced a treasure trove of archival material concerning the early days of the RAN and other valuable information. I am particularly grateful to my good friend Creighton Burns, then editor of the Melbourne *Age,* for allowing me to use his offices for my Freedom of Information applications. Sir Charles Spry, Bob Swann, Lieutenant Colonel Courtney, Patricia Penrose, Geoffrey Slater, Lieutenant Colonel David Horner (the Australian Army's official historian), the author Richard Hall, David Sissons, Arthur "Jim" Jamieson (an old wartime colleague of Eric Nave), and Martin Clemens all generously gave me their time and provided fascinating material, for which I am most grateful.

At the New Zealand National Archives, which, apart from being the most relaxed and friendly in the world, are also the least censored by interfering bureaucrats, I was greatly helped by Ellen Ellis, Alison Midwinter, and Mary Neazor, who helped me trawl through many previously unknown intelligence files dealing with the work of GCCS and FECB. I am also most grateful to John Crawford of the Ministry of Defence, who over the years has been most helpful in providing information about surviving members of naval intelligence in their armed forces.

Because of the embarrassing nature of my research, understandably some people did not want to help. In London, the then Foreign Secretary, Sir Geoffrey Howe, twice refused to let me see any prewar Japanese intercepts and decrypts on the grounds that it would endanger Britain's "national security." He would also not let me see the messages passing between Churchill and Roosevelt in late November 1941 for the same reason. It is hard to take such excuses very seriously.

GCHQ at Cheltenham claimed they were so busy that they could not answer the simplest queries and even refused to identify markings on JN-25 material their predecessor GCCS had handled. The National Security Agency at Fort George Meade, in Maryland, was remarkably unhelpful and for a long time resorted to a curious form of convoluted obfuscation in their letters over the simplest of matters. However, just as the book was going to print, they finally agreed to confirm—after fifty years—that the Japanese naval code JN-25 did exist, and then kindly produced a set of new photographs of the Red, Purple, and Coral code machines.

In New Zealand, John Parker, director of the Government Communications Security Bureau (GCSB), their equivalent of the NSA or GCHQ, wrote me a weird letter using precise NSA terminology saying that he could neither confirm nor deny that the files I sought existed, and even if they did exist, I could not see them anyway.

Australia is a country one automatically associates with openness and absence of bureaucracy, and it had much enjoyed embarrassing the British government during the *Spycatcher* trial in 1986, pouring scorn on luckless Sir Robert Armstrong's claims of lifelong confidentiality. Yet Tim James, director of the Defence Signals Directorate (DSD), refused to let me see any files relating to Eric Nave's work with the Central Bureau in 1940–41, claiming that to do so would harm relations "with a foreign country" and endanger the security of the Commonwealth. When the DSD were finally obliged to release the files to me, every page relating to prewar codebreaking against the Japanese was blanked out. To believe that the defense of the Commonwealth relies on information contained in fifty-year-old files suggests that either the intelligence fraternity live in a bizarre world of mirrors or that future Pearl Harbors can be expected to happen again, as indeed has been the case in the Falklands in 1982, and with Iraq in 1991.

Refusals of this kind are naturally a disappointment to an author and historian interested only in telling the truth about events fifty years ago. They also show how strong is the paranoia that still grips these agencies that they cannot bear the truth to be told about what happened half a century ago. Inevitably this makes one wonder what it is they have to hide. Sad though such refusals and their pathetic excuses were, they did not prevent the story from being told, and I am therefore all the more grateful to those who gave up their time and information so willingly.

James Rusbridger
Cornwall, 1991

Glossary of Terms and Abbreviations Used and Main Characters in the Book

TERMS AND ABBREVIATIONS USED

A MACHINE	Japanese cryptograph, Alphabetical Typewriter 91, codenamed Red by the Americans
ADB	American-Dutch-British
AN CODE	American codename for JN-25
ANB	Australian Naval Board
ANLO	Australian Naval Liaison Officer
ASA	American Army Security Agency, forerunner of the NSA
B MACHINE	Japanese cryptograph, Alphabetical Typewriter 97, codenamed Purple by the Americans
BAMS	British Allied Merchant Shipping Code
BJ	British-Japanese (colloquially Black Jumbos), codename for British Purple intercepts
BLUE BOOK	Japanese naval code introduced in 1930 and broken by OP-20-G and GCCS in 1932
BONIFACE	Early British codename for Ultra decrypts
BRUSA	British-United States of America Security Pact
BSC	British Security Coordination, cover name for MI6 offices in New York
CAST	American Navy codebreaking office in Cavite, Philippines
CIA	American Central Intelligence Agency
CID	British Committee of Imperial Defence

CINCAF	American Commander-in-Chief, Asiatic Fleet
CINCPAC	American Commander-in-Chief, Pacific Fleet
CNO	American Chief of Naval Operations
COIC	New Zealand Combined Operational Intelligence Centre
COIS	British Chief of Intelligence Staff, cover name for head of FECB
COM-16	Another name for CAST
COMINT	Communications intelligence
CORAL	American codename for Japanese cryptograph used for naval attaché messages
COS	British Captain on Staff, cover name for FECB
COS	British Chiefs of Staff
DMI	British Director of Military Intelligence
DNI	British Director of Naval Intelligence
DSD	Australian Defence Signals Directorate
ELINT	Electronic intelligence
ENIGMA	Rotor cryptograph used by Germans before and during World War II
FBI	American Federal Bureau of Investigation
FECB	British Far East Combined Bureau
G2	American Army Intelligence
GAF	German Air Force, or Luftwaffe
GCCS	British Government Code & Cipher School
GCHQ	British Government Communications Headquarters
GCSB	New Zealand Government Communications Security Bureau
GPO	British General Post Office
HOLLERITH	British punched-card system similar to that made by IBM
HUMINT	Human intelligence or spying
HYPO	American Navy codebreaking office at Pearl Harbor
IBM	International Business Machines Corporation
J-19	Japanese consular code
JCS	Joint Chiefs of Staff

JIC	British Joint Intelligence Committee
JN-25	Japanese naval code D, *Kaigun Ango-sho D,* also known by Americans as AN code
KAMER 14	Dutch codebreaking center in Batavia
KANA	Condensed form of Japanese alphabet enabling messages to be sent over western telegraph systems
MAGIC	American classification for all intelligence derived from decrypted Japanese signals
M-1	American codename initially given to Red machine but later discontinued
M-5	American codename initially given to Purple machine but later discontinued
MI5	British Security Service
MI6	British Secret Intelligence Service
MI8	America's first codebreaking agency in World War I
MS-5	American Army radio monitoring station in Hawaii
NEGAT	Alternative name for OP-20-G
NEI	Netherlands East Indies (Indonesia)
NID	British Naval Intelligence Division
NSA	American National Security Agency
NSG	American Naval Security Group
OIC	British Operational Intelligence Centre
OP-20-G	American naval codebreaking headquarters in Washington, D.C.
ONI	American Office of Naval Intelligence
OPERATION Z	Japanese codename for Pearl Harbor attack
OPNAV	American Chief of Naval Operations
ORANGE	American prewar codename for Japan
OSA	British Official Secrets Act
OTP	One-time pad (code system)
PA-K2	Japanese consular code
PERS-Z	German codebreaking agency
PRO	Public Record Office, Kew, England
PURPLE	American codename for the Japanese Type B cryptograph

RAF	Royal Air Force
RAN	Royal Australian Navy
RCA	Radio Corporation of America
RED	American codename for the Japanese Type A cryptograph
RED BOOK	First Japanese naval code broken in 1926 by OP-20-G and 1930 by GCCS. Initially called Code B and JN-1 by OP-20-G
RIP-5	Radio Intelligence Publication 5, codename for a special Underwood typewriter used at OP-20-G to convert *kana* messages into *romanji*
ROMANJI	Roman format of *kana* ideographs
ROOM 40	British naval codebreaking center in World War I
SIGINT	Signals Intelligence
SIO	Australian Special Intelligence Organisation
SIS	American (Army) Signal Intelligence Service
SLU	British Special Liaison Unit
TYPEX	British rotor cryptograph copied from the Enigma
UK-USA	United Kingdom–United States of America Security Agreement
ULTRA	British secret classification for intelligence derived from codebreaking, called Top Secret Ultra in America
ZEAL	British security classification
ZYMOTIC	British security classification used by FECB, similar to Ultra, to denote intelligence derived from codebreaking

PRINCIPAL CHARACTERS

America

Franklin D. Roosevelt, *President of the United States*
Cordell Hull, *Secretary of State*
Sumner Welles, *Under Secretary of State*
Henry L. Stimson, *Secretary of War*
Frank Knox, *Secretary of the Navy*
Admiral Harold R. Stark, *Chief of Naval Operations*

Rear Admiral Royal E. Ingersoll, *Assistant Chief of Naval Operations*
Rear Admiral Richmond K. Turner, *Chief, Naval War Plans Division*
Rear Admiral Leigh Noyes, *Chief, Communications Division*
Commander Laurence E. Safford, *Chief, OP-20-G*
Mrs. Agnes Driscoll, *Senior Cryptologist, OP-20-G*
Commander Arthur H. McCollum, *Far East Section Intelligence*
Lieutenant Lester R. Schulz, *White House Communications Duty Officer*
Rear Admiral Theodore S. Wilkinson, *Chief, Office of Naval Intelligence*
Lieutenant Commander Alwin Kramer, *Chief Translator, OP-20-G*
Lieutenant Commander Egbert Watts, *Chief, Japanese Desk*
General George C. Marshall, *Army Chief of Staff*
Brigadier General Leonard T. Gerow, *Chief, War Plans Division*
Brigadier General Sherman Miles, *Chief of Intelligence*
Colonel Rufus S. Bratton, *Chief, Far East Intelligence*
Colonel Otis K. Sadtler, *Chief, Signals Intelligence*
William S. Friedman, *Chief Cryptographer, SIS*
Abraham Sinkov, *Cryptographer, SIS*
Frank Rowlett, *Cryptographer, SIS*
Admiral Kichisaburo Nomura, *Japanese Ambassador*
Captain Johan E. Ranneft, *Dutch Naval Attaché*
Ralph T. Briggs, *Senior Radio Operator, Cheltenham Intercept Station*
Daryl Wigle, *Chief Radioman, Cheltenham Intercept Station*
William Stephenson, *Head of BSC, New York*
Herbert O. Yardley, *America's First Cryptologist*

Hawaii

Admiral Husband E. Kimmel, *Commander-in-Chief*
Lieutenant Commander Edwin T. Layton, *Fleet Intelligence Officer*
Lieutenant Commander Joseph J. Rochefort, *Chief Cryptographer, Station Hypo*
Lieutenant General Walter C. Short, *Commanding General*
Nagao Kita, *Japanese Consul*
Ensign Takeo Yoshikawa, *Japanese Naval Spy*
Fritz Kuehn, *Japanese Spy*

Britain

Winston S. Churchill, *Prime Minister*
Anthony Eden, *Foreign Secretary*
Sir Stewart Menzies, *Chief, Secret Intelligence Service, MI6*
Major Desmond Morton, *Churchill's Personal Assistant*

Alastair Denniston, *Head of GCCS*
Paymaster Commander Eric T. Nave, *Chief Cryptographer, Japanese Section GCCS, and later FECB*
Lieutenant Commander Malcolm Burnett, *Chief, Japanese Section GCCS*
Joseph Kennedy, *American Ambassador until April 1941*
John Winant, *American Ambassador from April 1941*
Averell Harriman, *Roosevelt's Special Envoy*

Singapore

Sir Shenton Thomas, *Governor*
Air Vice Marshal Sir R. Brooke-Popham, *Commander-in-Chief*
Captain F. J. Wylie, *Administrative Chief,* FECB
Captain Purvis Shaw, *Assistant Chief, FECB*
Captain W. W. Mortimer, *Analyst, FECB*

Netherlands East Indies

General Hein ter Poorten, *C-in-C, Netherlands East Indies Army*
Lieutenant J. A. Verkuyl, *Cryptographer Kamer 14*

Japan

Admiral Isoroku Yamamoto, *Commander-in-Chief*
Sir Robert Craigie, *British Ambassador*

I went up to my father's bedroom. He was standing in front of his basin and was shaving with his old-fashioned Valet razor. He had a tough beard and as usual was hacking away. "Sit down, dear boy, and read the papers while I finish shaving." After two or three minutes of hacking away he half turned to me and said: "I think I see my way through."

I was astounded and said: "Do you mean we can avoid defeat or beat the bastards?" He flung his Valet razor into the basin, swung round, and said: "Of course I mean we can beat them." I replied: "Well, I'm all for it, but I don't see how you can do it."

By this time my father had dried and sponged his face and turning round to me said with great intensity: "I shall drag the United States in."

—Randolph Churchill's recollections, 18 May 1940
Martin Gilbert, Finest Hour (London: Heinemann, 1983), page 358

Introduction

IN THE EARLY hours of Thursday, 4 December 1941, Lieutenant Longfield Lloyd[1] of the Australian Special Intelligence Organisation (SIO) was duty officer at the Park Orchards radio interception station, just outside Melbourne. At 4 A.M., while Park Orchards was monitoring the Japanese news broadcast from Tokyo's powerful transmitter known as JAP, operating on 11,980 kilocycles, one of Lloyd's operators heard the words *Higashi no kaze ame* ("East wind—rain"), included in the weather forecast.

Lloyd grabbed the telephone and woke Lieutenant Commander Eric Nave, an Australian codebreaker serving with the British Royal Navy at the Far East Combined Bureau (FECB), the British codebreaking agency in Singapore, who had been assigned to the SIO. "It's in," Lloyd told him. "The second part. It's just come in. No doubt about it." Nave thanked him and told him to see that a copy was with Commodore J. W. Durnford in the morning. As Nave had been expecting the message, having decoded the first part contained in message #2353 sent in the Japanese consular code on 19 November, there was nothing more for him to do, and he turned over and went back to sleep.

THREE DAYS later, in Singapore, on Sunday morning, 7 December, which was to be the last day of peace, Captain W. W. Mortimer was working at FECB when the telephone rang, and the duty Royal Air Force (RAF) officer asked if he knew anything about an aircraft flying over Singapore. Mortimer went outside and picked it up with his binoculars and saw it was Japanese. Mortimer telephoned the RAF and told them this and asked if they were going to intercept it. But he was told that was impossible because it was a Sunday. Mortimer reported the sighting to London and also—he assumed at the time—to the Americans and the headquarters of Commander-in-Chief Pacific Fleet (CINCPAC). However, the governor of Singapore, Sir Shenton Thomas, ordered that no one was to be told about the incident. But by now the clock was ticking away, and there was nothing anyone could do to stop it.

AT 5:30 A.M. on the morning of 7 December 1941 (8 December in Tokyo), two seaplanes were launched from the Japanese cruisers *Tone* and *Chikuma* some 200 miles north of Hawaii with orders to make a cautious reconnaissance of Pearl Harbor to ensure that the Pacific Fleet was in harbor. Half an hour later, without waiting for their report, the six aircraft carriers in Yamamoto's Task Force turned into the wind and, led by Commander Mitsuo Fuchida, the first wave of aircraft began taking off. In the next fifteen minutes, with the loss of only one aircraft, 183 aircraft, comprising forty-three fighters, forty-nine high-level bombers, fifty-one dive-bombers, and forty torpedo planes, had struggled off the pitching decks into the murky dawn for their ninety-minute flight. It took just forty-five minutes to bring the second wave of fifty-four bombers, thirty-six fighters, and seventy-eight dive-bombers up on deck and launch them, so that by 7 A.M., a striking force of 350 aircraft was on its way to an unsuspecting Pearl Harbor.

As dawn broke over the Pacific, Fuchida saw this vast armada of aircraft spread across the skies, with the bombers at 10,000 feet, the dive-bombers at 11,000 feet, the torpedo bombers just below at 9,000 feet, while high above at 14,000 feet were the Zero fighters watching for any signs of the American defenders. At 7:35 A.M., Fuchida tuned in to the local Hawaiian radio station and heard the weather forecaster promising a warm, clear, sunny Sunday. He continued listening to his station using the transmitter as a radio beacon.

In fact, Fuchida's first wave had already been spotted. At 7:02 A.M., Privates Joseph L. Lockard and George E. Elliott were about to shut down the Army's Opana mobile radar station, situated 230 feet up on Kahuku Point, on the northern tip of Oahu, when Elliott noticed his screen cluttered with so many blips that he and Lockard assumed the RCA SCR-270B set was malfunctioning. But a check proved otherwise, and the two operators plotted a flight of more than fifty planes approaching Hawaii from the north 132 miles away. As normal operating hours had ended, the pair were reluctant to contact the information center at Fort Shafter, but as the plot showed the aircraft getting closer, they eventually called and spoke to the duty officer, Lieutenant Kermit Tyler.

Tyler was new to the job of assistant controller, having had only one day's experience; and since his plotters had left the center for breakfast at 7 A.M., he was now on his own. Recalling that twelve B-17 bombers were flying into Hawaii from the mainland that morning. Tyler assumed the two radar operators had picked them up, and he told Lockard not to worry and to shut down the station. Unfortunately, Lockard forgot to tell Tyler that there were at least fifty planes showing on his screen. Had he done so, even an inexperienced officer like Tyler would have immediately realized it could not have been the flight of the B-17s.

At 7:20 A.M., the Opana radar showed Fuchida's aircraft only seventy-four miles away. But, despite their orders to shut down, Lockard and Elliott were so fascinated at what their set was showing, they continued to watch the blips until they were blocked by the mountains at 7:30 A.M., with the aircraft twenty miles away. The last chance of any warning had long passed.

A few minutes later, as the clouds parted over Kahuku Point, Fuchida had his first glimpse of his prize. There lay Pearl Harbor with every detail clearly visible in the crisp morning light and, right in the center, the entire U.S. Pacific Fleet with the ships looking just like the models he and his crews had been studying these past weeks. Across the harbor, alongside Ford Island, lay Battleship Row, their main target.

Amazingly, everything had gone according to plan, and there was still no sign of the enemy. At 7:49 A.M., just off Lahilahi Point, Fuchida ordered the attack signal—*To, to, to*—the first syllable of *totsugekiseyo* ("charge") to be sent. As the first wave of torpedo bombers swept in toward the battleships at 7:53 A.M., Fuchida sent out the now famous codeword *Tora! Tora! Tora!* ("Tiger! Tiger! Tiger!"), the signal that told Yamamoto, over 5,000 miles away, that the attack was under way and surprise was complete.

At the naval base, the leisurely Sunday morning peacetime routine was just beginning. On board the ships, breakfast was just starting, while on the fantails, color parties were lined up waiting for the 8 A.M. bugle call to hoist ensigns. At 7:55 A.M. the silence was shattered as the Japanese torpedo bombers roared in across the harbor, their cannon fire shredding the half-hoisted ensign on the battleship *Nevada*. While the crews stood open-mouthed in astonishment, some believing this must be a practice attack that had gone wrong, bombs started to explode on the hangars and among the tightly packed rows of aircraft, at Wheeler Field. At 7:58 A.M. the naval radio station flashed out the message "Air raid Pearl Harbor. This is not a drill" that told a stunned President, his colleagues, and the rest of the world that the Japanese had gone to war.

Within thirty minutes, the first attack was complete, and the battleships of the U.S. Pacific Fleet lay in ruins. The second attack swept in forty-five minutes later while the defenders were still bewildered and disorganized. By 10 A.M. it was all over, and as the Japanese withdrew from Hawaii, it seemed that within less than two hours they had achieved a victory unparalleled in history, for the loss of only twenty-nine aircraft and fifty-five crew.

Pearl Harbor was ablaze and the airfields at Hickam, Bellows, Wheeler, and Kaneohe were in ruins, with 177 Army and Navy aircraft destroyed, although the majority of ships destroyed were elderly battleships that would have played no significant role in the war.

SHORTLY BEFORE 9 P.M. (11 A.M. in Hawaii), Winston Churchill was at Chequers, his official country house, some forty-five miles north of London in the Chiltern Hills. Mrs. Churchill was unwell and had gone to bed, while Churchill was dining with his guests,[2] Averell Harriman, Roosevelt's special envoy, and John Winant, the American ambassador in London. Then Churchill's butler, Saunders, appeared and told the three that the staff had heard on the radio that the Japanese had attacked the Americans at Pearl Harbor. The trio looked at each other incredulously.[3] Churchill jumped to his feet saying, "We shall declare war on Japan," and immediately went to his office and asked for a call to be put through to Roosevelt. Winant was surprised that Churchill accepted such momentous news so readily, simply on what his butler had told him, without even bothering to contact either Downing Street or the Foreign Office. "Don't you think you'd better get confirmation first?" he asked. "You can't declare war on a radio announcement." But Churchill had no need for that. He had known all the time what had happened. Joyfully he spoke to Roosevelt and assured him that Britain's declaration of war would follow immediately.

For Churchill it was the grand finale of an enormous gamble. "So we had won after all!"[4] Churchill was later to write. With the benefit of hindsight, Churchill could claim nine years later that he knew the attack on Pearl Harbor assured Britain victory. But it was much more than that. Churchill was jubilant at having won his battle to let Japan drag America into the war.

CHAPTER 1

The Broadway
Eavesdroppers

FROM THE EARLY 1920s, the British Government Code & Cipher School,[1] known as GCCS, had shown particular interest in Japanese diplomatic and naval attaché messages and were always on the lookout for naval officers who could speak the language. Although Japan had been an ally in World War I, that did not stop her from becoming a GCCS target, especially as the Admiralty wanted to know what naval developments in Britain and Europe might be of interest to Japan's fast-expanding Navy.

One of those who caught the attention of GCCS—although he was unaware of it at the time—was young Paymaster Sub Lieutenant Eric Nave, then serving in Australia with the Royal Australian Navy (RAN). Nave had joined the RAN in 1917 at the age of eighteen, and two years later was due to sit for his examination for promotion to sub lieutenant, which required him to learn a foreign language. Upon discovering that proficiency in Japanese entitled him to an extra five shillings a day pay, Nave took courses in the language from a local tutor and subsequently sat for the official examination.

On 1 September 1919, the results came in, and Nave received 90 percent out of a possible hundred, a first-class pass that sent him to the top of the group of newly promoted sub lieutenants. For a year nothing happened, until on 11 September 1920 the Naval Board decided to send him to Japan for two years to become proficient in the language.[2] On 28 February, aged only twenty-one, Nave set sail for Japan via Hong Kong on the SS *Eastern,* with twenty-six golden sovereigns for his advance pay and expenses strapped around his waist in a money belt.

During his stay, Nave was looked after by the British Embassy in Tokyo (because Australia had no diplomatic links with Japan), where he met Harold (later Sir Harold) Parlett, who had taken over from Ernest Hobart-Hampden as Japanese counselor. Both Hobart-Hampden and Parlett had tenuous connections with GCCS in London, and at the end of Nave's two-year stay, Parlett and Colonel Piggott, the military attaché, examined Nave for his grasp of Japanese.

On 3 April 1923, Nave received his results, which showed that he had scored 910 marks out of a possible total of 1,000. Since 60 percent was required for a pass, in their report Parlett added the comment: "The Board feel they should emphasise the fact that this officer's knowledge is on a higher plane of practical utility than is usually obtainable in two years. The three Royal Navy officers who left last November, Lieut Cdr Shaw, Lieut R Leeds, and Lieut D Tufnell obtained 810, 750, and 610 respectively after two years' stay."

On his return to England, Lieutenant Commander Shaw[3] had joined GCCS, so it was not surprising that Parlett also passed back to London details of Nave's linguistic achievements. Nave knew nothing about any of this and returned to Australia in May. He was able to use his skills the following year, when the Japanese Training Squadron visited Australia and New Zealand[4] and he acted as personal interpreter to Admiral Saito. Nave impressed the admiral so much that in his farewell letter[5] to the Australian Naval Board he wrote:

> I tender my sincerest thanks to you for attaching Lieutenant T E Nave RAN to me during the cruise . . . there was hardly a person who was not astonished to hear that his masterly grasp of Japanese language has been acquired in so short a time as two years' stay in Japan, which, I think, clearly shows that he is a genius at it and I can assure you that through my speeches, which were delivered in Japanese and most of them impromptu, he never missed the points and conveyed the shade of meaning of what I said.

For Nave it was rather anticlimactic to return to his normal duties in HMAS *Sydney*, but meanwhile Parlett's information from Tokyo had made an impression on GCCS. The next year, in May 1925, the RAN unexpectedly received a signal from the Admiralty in London asking if they would be willing to lend Nave to HMS *Hawkins* on the China Station, to be based in Hong Kong, as an interpreter. The RAN thought about this and then received a second and more urgent message from London: "My 786.[6] Admiralty press for appointment Nave on staff Commander in Chief for interpreter's duties."

At the time, the RAN was very much under the control of London, so no one asked why Nave was in such demand by the Royal Navy. Reluctantly it was agreed, and Nave eventually arrived to join the *Hawkins* in July 1925, which by that time was at Shanghai. The admiral, Sir Edwin Alexander-Sinclair, was not pleased to have a young Australian naval officer appointed to his staff and even less so when he was told that Nave would get his own orders direct from London.

When Nave opened these orders, he discovered that he would not be on the staff of the admiral at all but was to begin gathering information about Japanese radio traffic and their call signs, and to start intercepting as many messages as possible for naval intelligence in London. Nave then established a small Sigint[7] (Signals Intelligence) operation, using the various ships' radio operators throughout the China Station. Thus GCCS entered into the codebreaking war against the Japanese.

BRITAIN'S CODEBREAKING activities owe their origins to the work of the Foreign Office, which as early as 1650 had begun intercepting and opening postal packets arriving and leaving England in order to discover "dangerous and wicked designs against the commonwealth." For this work they established a Secret Office, where teams of specialists would break open diplomatic mail and other interesting letters and then reseal them so that no evidence of tampering showed.

The legality for doing this was obscure, since the original statute that had established the British postal service was supposed to guarantee absolute confidentiality. However, later acts, such as those in 1660 and 1663, conveniently gave government officials the power to open mail under warrants they had themselves issued.

In 1844, an unexpected public scandal[8] resulted in a House of Commons select committee examining this practice. They concluded that the principle of opening mail "was of value to promote the ends of justice" but—just as today[9]—carefully avoided giving any opinion as to whether the Foreign Office had any legal authority to do so. In fact it had none. It was simply something that had been going on for a long time, which, in Britain, is often the basis for such activities that operate in the twilight world of secrecy and illegality.

But all this was a very small affair, and since many foreign governments did not trust the British Post Office and used private couriers instead, a great deal of information could not be intercepted anyway. However, that same year of 1844, Samuel Finley Breese Morse erected the world's first telegraph line between Washington, D.C., and Baltimore and, using his own code system, sent the famous message "What hath God wrought!" The telegraph system spread rapidly around the world, to be followed by Alexander Graham Bell's invention of the telephone in 1876 and the first wireless transmissions sent by Guglielmo Marconi twenty years later, in 1896. Thus, in a space of about a half century, international communications had reached the speed of light.

Britain, with its far-flung empire, immediately recognized the importance of the telegraph system, and the government established Cable & Wireless, which began to lay a network of undersea cables around the world connecting the colonies and dominions to London. Because messages sent over the system were charged per word, a number of commercial codebooks were produced containing thousands of phrases which could be sent as a single word.

In theory, messages sent by telegraph cable, unlike those sent by wireless, were totally secure because, unless the cable was physically tapped (which in those days[10] would have meant hauling it up from the seabed and cutting into it), there was no other way messages could be intercepted.

Progress in developing international communications proceeded at a leisurely pace until the outbreak of war in 1914. Radio now made it possible for a headquarters to maintain instantaneous contact with any number of units in the field or ships at sea, irrespective of distance, time, terrain, or weather. But this sudden ease of communications was itself an open invitation to the enemy eavesdropper, and thus was born the art of signals intelligence, or what today is called Sigint.

In 1912, the Committee of Imperial Defense (CID) had decided that in the event of war with Germany the Royal Navy would cut their underwater telegraph cables. Accordingly on 5 August 1914, the cable ship *Telconia* cut the five main cables that entered the North Sea near Emden, on the German-Dutch border, and ran down the English Channel to France, Spain, Africa, and North and South America. This forced Germany to use either radio or other countries' telegraph systems, and as a result a flow of raw intercepts began reaching the Admiralty. But neither they nor the War Office had any codebreakers to handle them.

As a result, Sir Alfred Ewing, the Director of Naval Education at Dartmouth Naval College, was asked by the Admiralty to put together a team of codebreakers[11] to start work on this German cipher traffic. Ewing recruited Alastair Denniston—who was then aged thirty-two and a foreign language teacher at the Osborne Naval College—together with two other teachers at Dartmouth, E. J. Green and G. L. Hope. The four of them founded Britain's first properly organized Sigint and codebreaking operation, which became known as Room 40[12] at the Admiralty, under the control of the Director of Naval Intelligence, Admiral Reginald "Blinker" Hall.

Apart from a knowledge of German, none of the four had any experience of codes or codebreaking. To begin with, all they could do was study every available commercial codebook to see if they provided any clues to help them penetrate the systems being used by the Germans.

More gifted amateurs were recruited from the universities, the church, and other obscure non-military backgrounds, until Room 40 eventually had a staff of more than fifty. However, their individualistic styles and personal eccentricities were viewed with considerable concern by the established naval hierarchy, which refused to believe that battles could be successfully fought on information supplied by such curious outsiders.

After making little progress, the team acquired three German codebooks[13] captured at sea, which enabled them to understand the basic principles of superencipherment. Gradually the fortunes of Room 40 changed, and they were eventually able to read most German naval messages throughout the rest of the war.

But decrypting the coded messages was only half the task. The other was to assess the correct value of the information exposed and pass it on to the naval commanders. The problem for Room 40 was that because it was a totally secret organization known to only very few senior officers, it was not allowed to communicate directly with the fleet. Instead, Room 40 had to give its decrypts to the Operations Division, which was supposed to decide on the significance of each message and whether to pass it on to Admiral John Jellicoe, C-in-C of the Grand Fleet. Unfortunately, the officers in the Operations Division knew nothing about intelligence or the German fleet.

It was this division or responsibility that led to the fiasco over the Battle of Jutland,[14] when on 30 May 1916, Vice Admiral Reinhard Scheer led the German fleet out into the North Sea in an operation designed to lure the British Grand Fleet into a trap where they could be attacked by his submarines. Through intercepted messages, Room 40 learned that the German fleet was putting to sea. But the director of Operations Division, Captain Thomas Jackson, RN, misread one of Room 40's decrypts and assumed the German fleet was still in port; and without telling Room 40, he radioed Jellicoe that the German fleet was still in harbor, whereas in fact it had been steaming north for over ten hours. As a result, a few hours later Jellicoe found himself fighting the entire German High Seas Fleet instead of a handful of battle cruisers he had been led to anticipate. Both sides claimed a victory, but the Germans had sunk three battle cruisers, three cruisers, and eight destroyers for the loss of one battleship, one battle cruiser, four cruisers, and five destroyers.

Although the German Fleet did not venture out again into the North Sea for nearly two years, Jutland was nevertheless a British intelligence disaster of the first order and showed the need for a properly coordinated operational intelligence center rather than odd pieces of fragmented information being handled by different people.

World War I was therefore the watershed for integrated Sigint on a global basis and shaped the pattern for today's vastly more elaborate agencies. But at the end of the war in 1918, intelligence organizations were among the first to be consigned to the scrap heap of victory, and since they were secret agencies, their demise went unnoticed. Tales of wartime spies like Edith Cavell, executed by the Germans in 1915, and Mata Hari, executed by the French in 1917, had caught the public's attention, but in general the secret war of intelligence had remained secret.

With budgets pruned, it was hardly surprising that British intelligence operations were soon consigned to a bureaucratic backwater. However, the success of Room 40, though known to only a few, was sufficient to ensure that some attempt be made to allow its function to continue. On 24 October 1919, the Cabinet secretly authorized Admiral Sir Hugh "Quex" Sinclair,[15] then Director of Naval Intelligence, to recruit twenty-five officers from the remains of Room 40 and MI 1(B), the army code-breaking team at the War Office, and form the Government Code & Cipher School, a meaningless name invented by Courtenay (later Sir Courtenay) Forbes of the Foreign Office's communications department, which was to be a civilian agency under the control of the Admiralty.

In simple terms, GCCS had two functions. The public one was "To advise as to the security of codes and ciphers used by all government departments and to assist in their provision." The secret one was "To study the methods of cipher communications used by foreign powers."

GCCS opened for business with Alastair Denniston as its chief in offices at Watergate House on London's Strand, not far from the Savoy Hotel, with a staff of twenty-five codebreakers and forty-six office juniors. The annual budget was to be less than £22,000.

The immediate task facing GCCS was to find some work to do. Military activity had come to a halt around the world following the 1918 Armistice, so the only other potentially useful material was diplomatic traffic, and the problem was how to get hold of it. This was solved when the government agreed to GCCS's request that all cable companies operating in Britain should be ordered to hand over copies of all their messages to GCCS for examination.

At the time, there were three cable companies involved: Cable & Wireless[16] (which was owned by the government, so there was no difficulty getting their messages), and two American companies, The Commercial Cable Postal Telegraph Company and Western Union. These latter companies did not acquiesce so readily, because they feared their clients in America would not take kindly to having their confidential messages read by a foreign government. However, when they were told their operating licenses might be taken away if they did not cooperate, both reluctantly agreed.

Unfortunately, GCCS's instructions accidentally became public knowledge on 16 December 1920, during a U.S. Senate subcommittee hearing[17] in Washington. Western Union's president, Newcomb Carlton, explained that his company had protested to the British government about this order and that they had told him: "Messages in their original form—ninety percent of them are in code—are taken to, I think, the British Naval Intelligence Bureau. They hold them not more than a few hours and then return them. They do not hold them long enough for anything like deciphering."

The chairman of the subcommittee intervened to point out that "Though it may take several hours or perhaps weeks or months to decipher a document, only a few seconds are required to make a copy. Once the telegrams are copied, the cryptographers can take their time solving them."[18]

Carlton continued: "They wanted those messages only for such supervision as might give them an inkling of pending disorders within Great Britain, I assume having to do with Irish unrest[19] and also to do with Bolshevik propaganda."

Carlton further told the committee that he had been assured by the British government that "The messages would not be deciphered. The reason why they [GCCS] wanted the messages was to keep general track of who was cabling."

Highly embarrassed by this revelation, the British government denied that any such order had been given to cable companies in London. But at the same time it swiftly amended the 1920 Official Secrets Act[20] so that, in the future, cable companies in Britain would be required to hand over their traffic on the basis of a warrant signed by the Secretary of State.

When hearings resumed after Christmas 1920, Carlton begged the subcommittee not to press him further on the matter, because it was embarrassing Western Union's position in Britain, where they did much business with the government. He did, however, confirm again that "The British government was desirous of supervising in and out cable messages to certain European countries in the interest of British peace and quiet."

In fact, the British explanations were untrue. Had GCCS been cleverer —and used today's procedures—the American cable companies would never have known anything, since all their messages went over leased Post Office lines and could have been intercepted by GCCS at the Central Telegraph Exchange in Moorgate. But that would have meant GCCS having to run banks of teletypes monitoring each circuit. It was obviously cheaper and simpler to have copies of the original messages sent to them.

The American Embassy was well aware that the British were intercepting and trying to decipher their messages. An assistant secretary later recalled how "a message had been sent to Washington one evening but through inadvertence we had not kept a copy. We telephoned the cable company and asked them to return the original and evidently a new clerk answered and replied 'That message isn't here. It's over at the Admiralty.' "[21]

GCCS was monitoring not only cables going in and out of Britain and telephone conversations throughout the country, but was also able to read cables sent over many other circuits around the world. Cable & Wireless had slowly built up, with secret British government subsidies, the largest cable network in the world, which by 1939 totaled nearly 200,000 miles out of the 350,000 miles of international cable networks. It also operated 140 permanent radio circuits carrying international telegrams. The network spanned the globe, with repeater stations at various key points like Gibraltar, Malta, Bermuda, Aden, Cocos Islands, and Hong Kong, all of which were safely under British colonial rule and thus not answerable to any inquisitive legislature. Although the primary task of Cable & Wireless was to provide a secure Empire communications service, it also had an equally important secondary intelligence role.

Despite the keen competition for business prevailing among the world's cable companies, Cable & Wireless were always willing to let their competitors use its circuits at extremely favorable rates. Naturally this proved extremely popular, because few other countries could afford the enormous cost of laying their own undersea cables across the oceans, and Cable & Wireless enjoyed a high reputation for speed and accuracy. But this generosity was not all that it seemed, for in those days it allowed Cable & Wireless to intercept any or all of this traffic and send it back to GCCS in London for analysis without the other cable companies or their clients knowing.

For example, a message sent from Berlin or Paris to Tokyo would initially be carried by the local cable company of that country but at some convenient point—usually Malta[22]—would for reasons of economy be switched to Cable & Wireless for the rest of its journey to Tokyo. The reverse would happen to messages from the Japanese Foreign Ministry in Tokyo sent to Europe. The same thing could happen anywhere in the world where similar exchange arrangements existed. Another advantage was that at Cable & Wireless stations abroad there was no need for GCCS to go through any pretense of getting a warrant to inspect messages. They were simply sent back to London without question.

There were, however, times when it did not work in favor of GCCS. During the 1921 Washington Naval Conference (see Chapter 2), GCCS was able to read the Japanese messages passing from Berlin and Paris to Tokyo but could not read any of the more important messages between Washington and Tokyo because these went west across America and then on across the Pacific without passing through any Cable & Wireless station.

The growth of telex was to come later, and although the first private telex service had started operating over American Telephone & Telegraph (AT&T) circuits in America for United Press in June 1917, it was not until 21 November 1931 that the first public service was introduced in America. This was followed by a similar service inaugurated in Britain by the Post Office on 1 August 1932. But as telex used the same international circuits as did cables, the messages were no more secure from interception by GCCS.

As a result of this international exchange of cable traffic, GCCS was able to read all the Japanese diplomatic and naval traffic, not only from their London mission but also from their other embassies throughout Europe that unwittingly used Cable & Wireless circuits to Tokyo. And of course it applied to other countries' diplomatic traffic as well. For example, American diplomatic traffic from Germany to the United States would pass over Cable & Wireless circuits for part of its journey. Although the primary target of this operation was foreign governments' messages, GCCS was also able to target economic messages from large foreign companies involved in banking, mining, shipping, oil exploration and refining, and even specific individuals, all of which was passed on to the relevant government department, providing them with a unique insight into international business affairs that might affect British interests.

Effectively, therefore, Cable & Wireless had secretly become the largest, most efficient, and cheapest eavesdropping organization in the world. It was not to be eclipsed until the advent of American satellite monitoring technology in the 1960s.

GCCS's liaison officer with the Post Office and Cable & Wireless was Henry Maine, who had served in King George V's private secretary's office at Buckingham Palace, joined the Grenadier Guards in 1916, and transferred to military intelligence in 1917 before moving to GCCS in 1919. He had an office on the fourth floor of GCCS's offices, with a number of Post Office sorters specially selected for this work.

After three years, the Foreign Secretary, Lord Curzon, pointed out that, as virtually all GCCS's work was concerned with diplomatic messages (since there was no military traffic worth intercepting), he recommended that GCCS be transferred to the Foreign Office. As the Admiralty was under pressure to reduce costs, they readily agreed, and GCCS therefore became part of Britain's Secret Intelligence Service, MI6, which is also controlled by the Foreign Office. By 1925, it had moved into MI6's offices of Broadway Buildings near St. James's Park, taking over the third and fourth floors for its forty codebreakers and other staff. For security reasons the elevator only stopped at the fourth floor, and staff had to identify themselves to the formidable porter called Godfrey, who knew everyone by sight, before being allowed to walk down to the third floor, where the codebreaking work took place.

GCCS concentrated its early codebreaking efforts on the diplomatic codes of America and France, even though both these countries had been recent wartime allies, which only goes to show how friendships and alliances mean nothing in the world of cryptography. The American State Department had introduced a new diplomatic code shortly after the war, and it took GCCS about a year to read it, while the French diplomatic code took only a month to break.

In both cases, GCCS was helped by the fact that, because of their cable interceptions, they had a lot of material to work on, and by the fact that all diplomatic traffic contains a great deal of material culled verbatim from newspapers and parliamentary reports, which immediately provides an excellent clue to the contents of the message.

GCCS also kept watch on German traffic, but in the aftermath of the war and the internal turmoil, there was very little material of any value. As Germany did begin to re-establish its foreign relations around the world, their Foreign Office at first used the one-time pad (OTP) system because the volume of traffic was sufficiently small. Later they turned to machine enciphering. These messages were monitored by GCCS but could not be broken.

The OTP code system remains to this day the only method of enciphering plain text that, if properly used, is completely unbreakable. The system is in two parts, the first of which is a basic dictionary or codebook containing the alphabet, numbers, and any frequently used phrases. Each is given a five-digit number.

The second part consists of pads containing sheets of random five-digit numbers. The German Foreign Office in the 1920s used sheets containing forty-eight five-digit groups per page, but modern copying technology allows many more groups per page, which can be photographically reduced to the size of a credit card and still be readable. Only two copies of each sheet are produced—one for the sender and the other for the recipient.

To send a message, the code clerk writes out the plain text and then looks up in the basic codebook the various numbers relevant to each letter, word, or phrase. So the message [23] ALEK HAS ARRIVED might look like this:

A	L	E	K	HAS	ARRIVED
03152	13415	05789	12141	81324	14287

The code clerk would then take his first sheet on the random pad and note the page and column number, which would be transmitted as part of the cipher text to identify the starting point. Starting with the first five-digit group, the clerk would add these to the codebook numbers thus:

03152	13415	05789	12141	81324	14287
+74932	+44734	+65277	+53865	+00118	+54968
77084	57149	60956	65906	81432	68145

The clerk used the Fibonacci system or what is sometimes called Chinese arithmetic, in which numbers greater than 9 are not carried forward so as to avoid non-random distribution.

Having prepared the final cipher text and sent it, the clerk then destroys the random sheets, so that each is used only once (hence the name of the code). On receiving an OTP message, the reverse procedure is used, whereby the random number is subtracted from the cipher text, thus exposing the basic number, which is looked up in a reverse order codebook which gives the plain text.

The obvious disadvantages of the OTP code are that it requires a different set of random pads for each pair of correspondents, making it very laborious and therefore unsuitable for use where there is a lot of traffic to many different places. Furthermore, if at any time the random sheets get out of sync, the message is unreadable.

Yet the system has many advantages. Because it is totally random, it produces no repetitive characteristics; even if a code clerk defects, provided the used random sheets have been destroyed, he cannot bring with him any information that will yield retrospective decryption. Even if the contents of one message become known, that will not help decrypt another; and even if the codebook is captured,[24] that will not reveal past messages, because the random pages still provide protection.

Another country that was to make much use of the OTP system was Russia, although the reasons for this were to cause great misgivings within GCCS. In 1920, Liberal Prime Minister Lloyd George had established diplomatic relations with the new Bolshevik regime in Russia and later that year invited a trade delegation to London to begin talks about an Anglo-Russian trade treaty. On 16 March 1921, the Anglo-Russian trade agreement[25] was signed, and three months later the Russians opened their trade delegation's offices and also established a new £1 million company called the All Russian Co-Operative Society, or Arcos.[26] Using trade delegations as a cover for espionage activities is one of the oldest tricks of the intelligence game and goes on to this day.

To communicate with Moscow, the Russians used a number of different codes that they had constructed following the revolution. As these messages were intercepted, they were passed to Felix Fetterlein at GCCS, who had been formerly employed working on British codes in the Russian cipher office in the days of the Czar and had been forced to flee the country in 1918. A somewhat eccentric figure who wore a high stiff collar and glasses with very thick lenses, Fetterlein was assisted by two women assistants who were also Russian emigrés, and together they managed to break all the codes over the next six years, which was hardly surprising, since Fetterlein had devised most of them. As a result, the British government was able to follow in detail the covert espionage operations being planned through the Russian trade delegation and Arcos in London.

Eventually, on 11 May 1927, the police raided the offices of Arcos, believing they would find a secret RAF document that had been planted on the Russians by a double agent working for MI5. In fact, the operation was unsuccessful, and although MI5 took away truckloads of incriminating material, the RAF report was not found. This placed the Conservative government in a dilemma when called upon to explain the purpose of the raid in Parliament. The Labour Party in opposition claimed that the raid would lose Britain much needed exports to Russia at a time of high unemployment and that the whole affair had been politically motivated, designed to discredit the Labour Party's proposals for trade union legislation.

At first, the government tried to claim that sufficient documentary evidence had been found in the Arcos offices to justify the raid. But when they could not produce this and exchanges became more heated, Prime Minister Stanley Baldwin read out the texts[27] of three intercepted messages between the Russian Embassy in London and Moscow. Later in the same debate, the Home Secretary read out four more intercepted messages between the trade delegation and Moscow to prove their subversive nature.

GCCS was appalled. The Russians immediately realized their codes had been compromised and at once switched to the OTP system, so GCCS could no longer read any of their traffic. On 24 May, the British government broke off diplomatic and trade relations with Russia, expelled all their diplomats and officials, abrogated the Anglo-Russian trade treaty, and closed down the trade delegation's offices. But the damage was done. GCCS lost the traffic they had previously been able to read. Overall, the loss of information was devastating. On balance it would have been far cleverer to have allowed Arcos to continue and to read all its cables, which were far more valuable than the material recovered in the raid.

The government's revelations in Parliament and also the Labour Party's attitude toward the Arcos affair soured relations between GCCS and politicians. As a result, GCCS concluded that most politicians were unreliable and would use sensitive information for their own ends rather than for the nation's security. From that moment onward GCCS never fully trusted politicians who had any grand ideas of unilateral disarmament. Some years later, in June 1929, Ramsay MacDonald formed Britain's second Labour government and decided to resume diplomatic and trade relations with Russia while at the same time announcing his intention to pursue all opportunities for disarmament.

"Quex" Sinclair had a meeting with Prime Minister MacDonald, who told him he was in favor of open international diplomacy and no secrets between nations. Sinclair was appalled and returned to GCCS, where he told Nave, "This new Prime Minister MacDonald. Just been having a talk with him. Tells me's in favor of cards on the table, no secrets, all that sort of thing. Won't do at all. Can't have that. In future he isn't to get any of our information without my permission." Sinclair feared secrets would be revealed at the conference table and compromise GCCS's sources.

In truth, Sinclair had no right to do this, and it was a good example of how easily intelligence agencies become politicized against certain types of politicians. Some years later, when GCCS again felt that the government in power could not be trusted, they began leaking highly secret material to Winston Churchill, then in the wilderness of opposition, so that he could taunt the government with accusations that they were neglecting Britain's defenses.

The first task in GCCS's codebreaking war against the Japanese was to identify the different types of messages being sent and the frequencies used. This is called traffic analysis and is just as important as codebreaking itself. One of the great advantages for a codebreaker working on military traffic is that the bureaucratic and hierarchical nature of armed services throughout the world betrays the nature of their messages, because there is such a proliferation of standardized daily reports, listing numbers of personnel, casualties, ammunition, fuel stocks, and other routine information. Such messages have to be sent each day at the same time and to the same number of recipients. Even when there is nothing to report, it is customary to send a nil return. Simple analysis soon shows which ones these messages are, and their text lengths can be compared daily.

One batch of coded messages that were intercepted in the early days was very short. The radio operator in one of the Royal Navy's gunboats stationed on the Yangtze River thought they might be connected with the sailings of Japanese ships. The traffic was carefully monitored, and it was soon found that every time one of their warships sailed, a routine signal was sent back to base. It was not difficult to work back through earlier messages and extract those of similar length and compare them with the sailing notices of Japanese ships at the time. In this way it was possible to break that part of the code very easily. In codebreaking jargon this is known as a crib.

After a while, Nave discovered that DA meant *Daijin,* Minister of Marine, and *Shichi-Shireichokan* meant Commander-in-Chief. Destroyer squadrons were indicated by a preceding numeral, so that *12 Kuchiku Tai* meant 12th Destroyer Division, or *12 Sesuta* the 12th Submarine Division. The ships themselves each had a call sign, and gradually as reports filtered in from the various operators at the China station, it was possible to build up a list of all the commands and ships in each division. For example, Nave soon discovered that the destroyer and submarine divisions 1 to 10 were home-based at Yokosuka, 11–20 at Kure, and 21–30 at Sasebo. Simple though this may sound when set against more exotic tales, this is the first essential first step in any codebreaking operation.

Obviously the heart of any Sigint operation is good interception facilities, for unless the message is read perfectly it cannot be decrypted. In the Far East, there were only the ships' radios to work with at the beginning, but by 1936 the Admiralty built and operated for GCCS a very powerful intercept station, known locally as Q (Q being a symbol denoting something secret), on Stonecutters Island at Hong Kong. This station was able to eavesdrop on any transmission from Japan, no matter how faint. Later, another equally powerful station was built at Singapore. The radio messages were sent in shortwave on the 10–100 meter band and reflected off the ionosphere, often called the Heaviside Layer, with the result that they could be received at very great distances, particularly at night. However, atmospheric disturbances sometimes play curious tricks on such signals, with the result that they cannot be heard nearby but are picked up clearly on the other side of the world. These are known as skip transmissions.

Radio was still in its infancy, and the Japanese were not very security-conscious at the time. Some messages were sent in code, but other routine messages were sent in plain language and contained much useful peripheral information. The history of codebreaking is full of examples of how the intelligence jigsaw can be built up from seemingly innocuous pieces of routine information sent in low-grade codes or plain language. The whole art of Sigint is to suck up everything so as to catch those brief lapses of radio security. One bored operator at the end of a long shift who carelessly transmits a single message without using the proper procedures can jeopardize an entire code system.

To begin with, the volume of intercepted traffic was quite small, because the Japanese Navy was not very active except for its regular annual exercises. But gradually the material began to accumulate, enabling greater in-depth analysis.

Sometimes Nave was helped by an unexpected bonus, such as one that occurred around Christmas 1926, when a sudden flurry of messages between Tokyo and all their diplomatic missions and military headquarters around the world announced the death of Emperor Yoshihito and the succession of his son Hirohito. At an elaborate ceremony, Hirohito pledged himself to work for "the moral and material improvement of his beloved subjects." From his knowledge of the Japanese, Nave knew that everything the new Emperor said would automatically be relayed around the world, and so it proved to be. Throughout the days following, it was an easy task to match the cipher texts of the long coded messages with the various statements that had appeared in the sycophantic Japanese press with all their repetitive flowery introductions, and this made it very simple to reconstruct the messages.

At the end of each month, Nave sent a summary of his work back to the Admiralty in London, showing the parts of the current codebook he had been able to reconstruct, call signs, and copies of all the intercepted and decrypted messages. Unknown to Nave at the time, his summaries were sent on to the naval section at GCCS, which was gradually able to build up a complete picture of the Japanese Navy and how and where it operated. Some months later, the Commander-in-Chief China Station received a message stating that "Lieutenant Nave had an expression of their Lordships' pleasure placed on his service record," which meant nothing to the C-in-C, as neither he nor any of Nave's colleagues knew what he was doing.

At the end of two years, in 1927, Nave's Sigint work in Hong Kong had laid bare the entire Japanese naval radio organization, so that London now had a complete list of all their call signs and radio frequencies, right down to individual ships. Additionally, all the Japanese naval codes then in use had been broken, so that GCCS could read every message sent from Tokyo and those sent from one warship to another.

As the result of Nave's success, GCCS decided to have him transferred to London. So the Admiralty asked the Australian Naval Board (ANB) if they could retain his services for a further period. The Admiralty did not tell the ANB why they wanted to retain Nave's services nor what kind of work he was doing. The RAN showed no curiosity either and apparently did not think it odd that this young officer whom they had sent to Japan to learn the language was in such demand by the Royal Navy. At the time the RAN had only a small intelligence department of its own, which relied almost entirely on the Royal Navy for its information. It had no Sigint facilities or any codebreakers and knew nothing about the existence of GCCS in London.

Nave arrived in London in January 1928 and reported to Rear Admiral Sir Barry Domvile, Director of Naval Intelligence (DNI), who then told him that in fact he would not be working at the Admiralty but for GCCS, an organization Nave had never heard of. And so that afternoon Nave took the creaking elevator up to the fourth floor of Broadway Buildings, where, having passed Godfrey's inspection, he met the director, Commander Alastair Denniston, who introduced him to William Clarke, head of the Japanese section.

Clarke was a barrister by training (the son of Sir Edward Clarke, a leading king's counsel who had been involved in the 1895 trial of Oscar Wilde), and had worked in Room 40 during World War I and afterward written an official history about its work, which was never published. Clarke introduced Nave to his old friend Harold Parlett, who by then had returned from Japan to work at GCCS on Japanese diplomatic material, and then took Nave farther down the passage and showed him into a small shabby office containing an old desk, two chairs, a cupboard, and a safe. Without any further formalities, the Japanese Naval Section at GCCS was in business.

CHAPTER 2

Other Gentlemen's Mail

ALTHOUGH THERE HAD been no cooperation or exchange of information between Washington and London, by 1925 both had simultaneously achieved identical penetration of Japanese codes. The battle of the codebreakers was about to begin.

In the years before World War I, the American government had obtained all its foreign intelligence from its diplomatic missions around the world and by analyzing reports in the foreign press and radio. It operated no spies[1] in other countries, nor did it indulge in any form of covert Sigint.

Geographically and politically isolated from Europe and without an overseas empire, America had not during its early history become involved in the intrigue that encouraged the development of codes and codebreaking throughout Europe. During the Civil War,[2] there had been a limited use of various forms of secret writing to convey information around the country, against which there had been rudimentary attempts at codebreaking.

But internationally, America felt supremely confident and secure, well able to defend itself in the unlikely event of an attack, and able to produce within its borders all the vital necessities needed to ensure an increasingly prosperous standard of living. Second, America had no desire to become the world's policeman. Third, the population of America contained large numbers of immigrants who had fled to the New World in order to escape governments that indulged in all manner of repressive activities, and America prided itself on having a written Constitution that prohibited any such secret and illegal behavior. Finally, Congress refused to provide funds for any foreign covert intelligence operation.

This was undoubtedly the most significant reason for America's limited capacities, because subsequent experience has shown that whenever funds have been made available for American covert intelligence operations, whether secretly or accountably, the question of legality has been swiftly and quietly consigned to the scrap heap of morality.

The main source of military intelligence[3] came from the military, naval, and, later, air attachés who, as is the normal custom, were allowed to see whatever their host nation wanted them to see. Nevertheless, some of these attachés cultivated personal contacts which, for example, in Germany[4] were to provide a surprisingly accurate and valuable amount of information about Hitler's intentions, the bulk of which was ignored by the State Department.

In Japan, attachés and other observers were far less successful. The Japanese had a mania for secrecy and distrusted all foreigners; it was impossible for a westerner to pass unnoticed in sensitive areas; the Japanese social culture precluded all but the briefest of contacts with outsiders; and loyalty to the state was so strong that at no time was there any anti-government movement to cultivate.

A further problem affecting accurate intelligence gathering in Japan during the interwar years was an automatic assumption by the white race of superiority over the Oriental. Both Americans and the British looked upon the Japanese as comical buck-toothed little yellow men wearing spectacles who went around the world making notes and taking photographs of everything they saw so that they could manufacture inferior copies back home.[5] As a result, attachés and other experts developed the common intelligence syndrome of cognitive dissonance, whereby they refused to believe any information about Japanese prowess that did not match their preconceived ideas.

All sorts of stories abounded about the failings of the Japanese. One naval expert wrote: "Every observer concurs . . . that the Japanese are daring but incompetent aviators. Four main theories have been advanced . . . according to the first . . . the Japanese as a race have defects of the tubes of the inner ear just as they are generally myopic. This gives them a defective sense of balance."[6]

On the quality of their flying boats[7] the same writer commented: "Japanese builders copied the Short hull, attached it to a pair of German-type wings, and mounted a homemade copy of the Pratt & Whitney motor atop." The writer added that "nothing is much stupider than one Japanese, and nothing much brighter than two." Other claims propagated the belief that the Japanese could not see in the dark and could not close one eye at a time and thus were unable to fire a rifle accurately, that their warships would overturn on launching because they were so poorly designed, and that their army would run away at the first sight of a white soldier.

Laughable though such stories may seem now, they dramatically affected the quality and significance of intelligence emerging from Japan because so many Americans underrated Japanese abilities and thus attuned their own defense strategy accordingly. (It has to be added that these beliefs persisted long after World War II, so that in 1957 a prestigious American producer was able to make *The Bridge on the River Kwai,*[8] a popular and award-winning film, based on an equally popular novel, depicting a Japanese railway-building battalion incapable of erecting a wooden bridge across a hundred-yard-wide river without the skill and help of the white man.)

Although it is true that informed military attachés, diplomats, businessmen, or a well-placed spy can sometimes produce startling information of enormous importance, for long-term knowledge about another nation's innermost thoughts and plans there is nothing to supplant good continuous Sigint. It was not until America entered World War I in 1917 that it began to take a serious interest in international cryptography and was able to reap the rewards.

America's—and without doubt one of the world's—most famous codebreaker[9] was Herbert Osborne Yardley, born on 13 April 1889 at Worthington, Indiana. In 1912, at the age of twenty-three, Yardley joined the State Department code room in Washington, D.C., as a clerk, with an annual salary of $900. In his spare time Yardley tried breaking the State Department's codes, which he soon found he could do without difficulty. What alarmed Yardley was that if he, a young clerk with no special training, could break these codes so easily, who else was doing it?

On one occasion Yardley got hold of a 500-word message from Colonel Edward House, who was reporting direct to President Woodrow Wilson from Berlin after a meeting with the German Emperor. Yardley broke the message in less than two hours, and since he knew that it had gone via London, he was quite sure British codebreakers at the Admiralty had done the same. Yardley became so concerned at the State Department's lack of cipher security that over the next few months he set out his worries in a 100-page report entitled *Solution of American Diplomatic Codes,* which he gingerly showed to his superiors.

Shocked State Department officials were forced to realize their codes were insecure. As a result, Yardley was commissioned into the U.S. Army at the age of twenty-seven and authorized to set up America's first codebreaking agency, known as Section 8 of U.S. Military Intelligence, or MI-8. Like all such organizations, MI-8 began to grow, because manpower is the key to successful codebreaking, and soon spawned five divisions:

1. Code and cipher compilation
2. Communications
3. Solutions of intercepted shorthand material
4. Secret ink laboratory
5. Code and cipher solutions ·

Ignoring shorthand and secret ink, these divisions are remarkably similar to those in today's giant organizations like the NSA and GCHQ.

In August 1918, Yardley was sent over to Europe, going first to London, to learn more about the Allies' codebreaking achievements. However, MI6 agents operating out of the British Embassy in Washington had warned the War Office in London of Yardley's visit and its purpose, with the result that on his arrival he was met with much politeness but little cooperation. The breakthrough came when Captain Brooke-Hunt of the War Office asked Yardley if he would examine a new code they intended introducing and test out its security. Yardley took a few sample cipher texts away and shortly returned with the answers. The War Office was so impressed by his skills (and for having stopped them from introducing an insecure code) that they became much more forthcoming and helpful.

The Admiralty gave Yardley a copy of a German naval code they had captured, which he took back to Washington, but they absolutely refused to let him see Room 40 and how it worked or speak to any of the codebreakers there. Yardley then moved on to Paris, where he hoped to see how the French codebreakers worked. Although he was courteously received by Captain Georges Painvin, France's leading codebreaker, who even allowed him to sit in his office and look through various files, Yardley never got to see the French codebreakers at work. However, he stayed on in Paris after the Armistice and attended the peace talks, where from two rooms in the Hotel Crillon he sent enciphered messages back to Washington for the American team and also decrypted some of those passing between other delegations. Yardley eventually returned to Washington on 18 April 1919 and found, just as Room 40 had, that with the war at an end, there were no more military funds to keep MI-8 going.

Both General Churchill, director of the U.S. Army's Military Intelligence, and Captain John Manly, who had been running MI-8 while Yardley was in Europe, recommended that MI-8 be allowed to continue its work. In the end a compromise was reached whereby the State Department put up $40,000 a year out of special funds and Military Intelligence the balance of $60,000 (on the strict understanding that the Navy Department was to be totally excluded) to establish a new codebreaking bureau. Acting Secretary of State Frank L. Polk approved the deal, and the order was signed on 20 May 1919 by the U.S. Army's Chief of Staff, General Peyton C. March. For legal reasons, the State Department's funds could not be spent within the District of Columbia, so Yardley had to move to New York, where on 1 October 1919 he opened an office at 3 East 38th Street, moving a year later to 141 East 37th Street.

Having got his codebreaking agency, or Black Chamber, established, Yardley's next problem—like that of GCCS in London—was to find some raw material to work on. He solved this by quietly approaching Western Union and asking if he could be given copies of their international messages. This was quite illegal and strictly against the terms of the Radio Communications Act of 1912, which prohibited any disclosure of such traffic and had been reinforced by the International Radio-Telegraph Convention of 8 July 1912, which had been ratified by America and Britain. Although Britain had no scruples about ignoring the Convention, it was a different matter in America, which, in those days at least, took the matter of its citizens' secrets seriously.

After much thought, Western Union's president, the same Newcomb Carlton who had testified about GCCS's similar orders to his company in Britain, agreed, and Yardley's team concentrated their efforts on Japanese diplomatic messages passing between the Foreign Ministry in Tokyo and their embassy in Washington, D.C., which had to use American commercial cable systems.

As Japan began to enter the commercial world of the twentieth century, the first problem it faced was the development of a common means of communicating with other countries. To most people outside Japan, the Japanese language, which was based on ninth-century Chinese ideographs, was totally incomprehensible. Furthermore, there was absolutely no way Japanese writing could be sent over modern telegraph systems.

Ironically, the complexity of the language was its weakness, because to adapt to international commercial requirements a form of shorthand called *kana* had been invented, which expressed the Japanese alphabet or syllabary in seventy-three ideographs representing Japanese and Chinese sounds. Subsequently, in order to express Japanese *kana* in roman letters that could be printed out on western typewriter fonts used by commercial telegraph systems, these *kana* ideographs were romanized [10] and became known as *romanji*.

It was not a perfect system, because without the sound of the speaker's voice to show the hard and soft sounds, a single *kana* ideograph might have several different meanings, the correct one only becoming clear when the text of the message was exposed. Furthermore, some letters like L, Q, V, and X, are not used, which makes the spelling of some western words very odd. For example, the word "Ireland" in *kana* comes out AI RU RA N DO. A message in Japanese sent by radio had first to be phonetically converted into *kana* groups, each of which had its Morse code equivalent. A full list of *kana, romanji,* and their Morse code equivalents is given in Appendix 1.

Having no previous material to provide any help, and unable to speak any Japanese, Yardley set about his task by breaking the cipher texts down into groups of *kana* characters so that their frequency could be statistically analyzed. Each *kana* combination was typed onto a separate card, and the first twenty-five messages Yardley worked on produced 10,000 separate cards.

Eventually, with the aid of a Japanese linguist, Frederick Livesey, they began to recognize a number of *kana* groups that regularly appeared. The final breakthrough came when Yardley woke in the middle of the night and: "Out of the darkness came the conviction that a certain series of two-letter code words absolutely *must* equal *airurando* (Ireland). Then other words danced before me in rapid succession: *dokuritsu* (independence), *Doitsu* (Germany), *owari* (stop). At last the great discovery! My heart stood still, and I dared not move. Was I dreaming? Was I awake? Was I losing my mind? A solution? At last—and after all these months!"

This rather dramatic account was written by Yardley several years later and has perhaps benefited from hindsight and dramatic license, because at the time the code was far from broken, and a great deal more work was needed before complete messages could be read. What Yardley had done, and many codebreakers were to do after him, was to make an educated guess at certain words,[11] for example, that "independence" was likely to follow "Ireland," and if they fitted, then to work backwards. Another way into the code was through the flowery salutations and valedictions the Japanese bureaucrats repeated in each message.

The final translations were made with the help of a retired missionary who had lived and worked in Japan for many years and thus understood not only the various inflections [12] of the language but the mentality of those sending the messages. The first complete translation of a Japanese diplomatic message from Tokyo to Washington was made on 12 June 1920.

But there was no time for Yardley and his team to rest on their laurels. The Japanese employed a Polish code expert, Captain Jan Kowalefsky,[13] to help them improve their codes, since the Poles had always been in the forefront of codemaking and breaking. Ten years later they were to begin breaking the German Enigma cryptograph, the details of which they eventually gave Britain in 1939.

Kowalefsky adopted a very scientific approach in constructing new codes for the Japanese, doing away with the haphazard fashion in which the early systems had been constructed. The Japanese assumed this made their codes more difficult to break. In fact it did quite the reverse, because once Yardley's codebreakers understood how Kowalefsky's mind worked they could anticipate his next development. For example, Kowalefsky designed a new system whereby a message would be encoded in several different codes, each one having its identifying indicator. The idea was to make the codebreaker's work harder, but in fact once Yardley had identified the indicators it made it simpler.

Likewise Kowalefsky split messages up into several parts which would be transposed with the beginning and the end (always the most useful parts of the text with their repetitive phrases), hidden in the middle of the cipher text. To identify the sections, each was given a letter. If there were two sections, they were lettered Y and Z; if three, then X, Y, and Z; if four, then W, X, Y, and Z. The code clerk then transposed them so that Y-Z became Z-Y, X-Y-Z became Z-Y-X, and so on. But Yardley's team quickly identified these indicators, and since the same arrangement was used with other codes, it helped break them also.

The Japanese made lots of elementary errors in their codes. For a start, they assumed their language alone was a formidable barrier that few westerners could penetrate, without realizing that by having to use *kana*, which drastically reduced the total number of characters, they had unwittingly stripped away much of their language's incomprehensibility. They also assumed that the more scientific they made them, the better they became. Again this was untrue. And perhaps most important of all, they could not bring themselves to believe that their codes had been broken even when they were presented with irrefutable proof.[14] But of course they were not alone in this.

It was fortunate that Yardley's team had mastered the Japanese codes when they did, for the following year in July 1921 Japan started negotiations with Britain about the possibility of holding a Pacific Conference. The first Yardley knew about it was when the Japanese ambassador in London sent Telegram #813 on 5 July 1921 to the Foreign Ministry in Tokyo. The ambassador reported meeting with Britain's Foreign Secretary Lord Curzon and sounding out British views about such a conference. Curzon and the ambassador had a further meeting on 8 July, summarized in Telegram #825 to Tokyo, which explained that the British preferred the idea for the conference to come from the Americans.

Both these messages went by Western Union from London to Tokyo via America, so they were first intercepted and read by GCCS and then by Yardley. GCCS had begun breaking Japanese diplomatic codes about the same time as Yardley, using the services of Hobart Hampden, who had come to work for them in London after thirty years in Japan.

On 10 July, the Japanese ambassador sent Tokyo message #386 saying that the American Secretary of State "Desired to hold in America a conference on the question of reducing armaments, but before issuing formal invitations wished to know the attitude of Japan, England, France, and Italy." There then followed a flurry of diplomatic telegrams from Japanese embassies in Paris, London, and Washington that urged Tokyo to agree. As the volume of coded traffic increased, so the task of the codebreakers became easier as they became more familiar with the code routines and inevitable repetitions. However, this euphoria suddenly evaporated on 14 July, when Tokyo suddenly changed the code system.[15] It took Yardley and his team several weeks before they discovered that the Japanese had altered the code words from two- and four-letter groups to odd three-letter groups. But by now they knew enough about the basic principles of Japanese codes to overcome this change, and from then on all messages between Tokyo, Washington, Paris, and London, were read with ease once more.

The Washington Conference was formally opened by U.S. Secretary of State Charles Evans Hughes on 14 November 1921 in Washington's Pan American Building. Hughes represented America, Arthur Balfour was there for Britain, Admiral Tomosaburo Kato for Japan, and Aristide Briand for France. The Hughes plan called for the size of the delegates' navies to be matched on the basis of ratios. America on parity with England, and a 10:6 ratio with Japan. This became known as the 5:5:3 agreement. In truth, it was 5:5:3:1.67:1.67. The two 1.67s represented France and Italy. Each point in the ratio meant 100,000 tons, or three battleships.

As the conference proceeded, both sides fenced for the best deal. But the Japanese were completely unaware that their every move was known in advance by their adversaries. On 22 November, Tokyo sent its delegation the following message:

From Tokyo
To Washington Conference
#44 November 22

Very confidential. Urgent.

Referring to your #28, importance is attached to the fact that at the meeting of the Diplomatic Advisory Council, Minister of Navy Kato said that the ratio of 10 to 7 between the America Navy and our Navy should be the limit. We understand that you will work to maintain this limit without any change.

Kato then told the media that this was the bottom line as far as Japan was concerned, so everyone assumed the conference had stalled. There then followed a series of long messages back and forth in which the Japanese delegation impressed upon Tokyo the need to find a compromise. Tokyo began to yield. The Americans sat tight, reading every message. Eventually, on 28 November 1921, the first cracks began to appear:

From Tokyo
To Washington Conference
#13 November 28

Secret.

Referring to your conference cablegram #74, we are of your opinion that it is necessary to avoid any clash with Great Britain and America, particularly America, in regard to the armament limitation question. You will to the utmost maintain a middle attitude and redouble your efforts to carry out our policy. In case of inevitable necessity you will work to establish your second proposal of 10 to 6.5. If, in spite of your utmost efforts, it becomes necessary in view of the situation and in the interests of general policy to fall back on your proposal No. 3, you will endeavor to limit the power of concentration and manoeuvre of the Pacific by a guarantee to reduce or at least to maintain the status quo of Pacific defences and to make an adequate reservation which will make clear that this is our intention in agreeing to a 10 to 6 ratio.

As Yardley was later to write: "With this information in its hands, the American government . . . could not lose. All it need do was to mark time. Stud poker is not a very difficult game after you see your opponent's hole card."

On 10 December, the long awaited capitulation came:

From Tokyo
To Washington Conference
#155 December 10

Very confidential. Urgent.

Referring to your #142 and #143. We have claimed that the ratio of strength of 10 to 7 was absolutely necessary to guarantee the safety of the national defence of Japan, but the United States has persisted to the utmost in support of the Hughes proposal, and Great Britain has supported it. It is therefore left that there is practically no prospect of carrying through this contention. Now therefore in the interests of the general situation and in a spirit of harmony, there is nothing to do but accept the ratio proposed by the United States.

Japan felt badly let down by Britain. After having been such a loyal ally during World War I, when it suited Britain to have the help of Japan's Navy in the Far East, they had now failed to renew the alliance when it suited them, simply to placate America. To Japan it meant that Britain had joined America against Japan's future interests. In fact this was untrue. There was no political agreement between America and Britain on their joint role or responsibilities in the Far East and Pacific.

Britain had not renewed its alliance with Japan simply because it was the only way of reducing military spending at a time of great economic misery back home, where the most important battles to be fought were at the polling booths and not on the high seas. But if Japan felt spurned, it had, nevertheless, gained much in the long term. For accepting the lower ratio, Japan obtained agreement that there would be no fortified American base west of Hawaii and no British base north of Singapore. As for new warships, Japan soon learned how to build much larger vessels than permitted under the treaty and to conceal the truth from the world.

For Britain the reduction in the size of their Navy ended the dream that they controlled the high seas of the world. No longer would the Royal Navy be able to send a fleet out to the East to protect Singapore and the vital trade routes. Although at first sight the 1921 Washington Conference was an achievement for peace, in reality it became a signpost for war and sowed the first seeds of the Pearl Harbor attack.

Yardley and his team had produced some 5,000 decrypts during the conference. As a result Yardley's health collapsed and he was off sick for several months. And, ironically, it was the success of the conference that spelled the end for Yardley. After all, the bureaucrats argued, with peace ensured, who needs codebreakers?

By 1924, Yardley's budget was cut, and he was forced to halve his staff. He even had to move to smaller and cheaper offices. Much more serious was the decision by Western Union not to allow him to have any more copies of their messages.

But worse was to come. In March 1929, the newly elected thirty-first president of the United States, Herbert Hoover, with peace and disarmament being talked about everywhere around the world, told an eager audience in March 1929, "I have no fears for the future of our country, which is bright with hope." Hoover appointed Henry L. Stimson as his

Secretary of State, and four months later, in May, Yardley sent Stimson some original decrypts he had just made of some particularly important Japanese messages so that Stimson would appreciate the quality of his work.

> For a few weeks no bulletins from the cryptanalytic bureau in New York were given him [Stimson] the intention being to "go slow" until he had become sufficiently well oriented in the duties of his office to warrant bringing to his attention the highly secret activities . . . early in May 1929 the time was deemed ripe for this measure but it was with some trepidation that a few translations of Japanese code messages were placed on Mr. Stimson's desk.[16]

It was a very unwise thing to do and certainly would not have happened in Britain. There the custom was—and still is today—that politicians neither inquire nor are told how intelligence information has been obtained.[17] What the politicians receive through their civil servants are carefully paraphrased summaries that give no indication as to sources. Back in the 1920s, it was unlikely that many British politicians had ever heard of GCCS, and there was certainly no question of them being allowed any direct contact with the organization, as happened in America.

Stimson's reaction was quite extraordinary, and he immediately branded Yardley's organization as illegal, believing that codebreaking was a dirty sort of business akin to peeping through keyholes. He stated that "gentlemen do not read each other's mail."

As the official history explained: "To put teeth into his decision he gave instructions that the necessary State Department funds would be withdrawn at once. It was only after considerable pressure that he was dissuaded from this course which might have had serious consequences."[18]

Nevertheless, on 31 October 1929, Yardley's team of codebreakers was quietly disbanded. For over a decade they had ignored the legislation enacted after the International Radio-Telegraph Convention of 8 July 1912, which, unlike Britain, the American government had ratified and which guaranteed absolute secrecy of American domestic and international communications. Undaunted, Yardley had secretly and illegally scooped up all the cable traffic entering and leaving America and broke with ease every coded message that interested him. The total cost of these ten years to the taxpayer had been $300,000, a bargain[19] by any standards.

Yardley was so upset by Stimson's action that the deep anger inside him finally boiled over. In 1931, he wrote about his experiences in a book,[20] parts of which were serialized in the *Saturday Evening Post.*[21] Rather in the manner of Peter Wright, author of *Spycatcher,*[22] half a century later, Yardley justified his actions by claiming that Stimson's behavior had placed America's intelligence operations in jeopardy, and he believed his fellow countrymen should know the truth.

The government tried to stop the book's publication but could find no easy way to do so. A trial was thought unwise, since it might allow even more embarrassing secrets to emerge, and there was no legal basis in peacetime America to suppress the book. As a result, on 1 June 1931, *The American Black Chamber* appeared and was an immediate success, selling nearly 18,000 copies in America alone, greatly helped by the controversy surrounding it. In England, the book was retitled *Secret Service in America* and sold a respectable 5,480 copies and gave GCCS their first knowledge as to the extent and success of their counterparts in America during the 1921 conference—for, unlike today, when all such work is more or less shared,[23] in those days there was no contact at all between the two organizations. But it was in Japan that it went to the top of the best-seller list, with a total of more than 33,000 copies sold, causing some in America to believe it might have been deliberately subsidized[24] by the Japanese government.

In the book Yardley gave a vivid description of how the Japanese codes had been broken and how this had enabled the Americans to outmaneuver their delegation at the Washington Conference. He also revealed details of how GCCS in Britain was intercepting cables and how the Americans had radio intercept stations on the East Coast powerful enough to eavesdrop on messages passing between Berlin and Spain.

Having failed to stop the book, the American government had to deny that they had ever read any Japanese diplomatic traffic, or that of other countries either, and Stimson publicly stated that he had never heard of the Black Chamber, although a few days later he changed this denial to "no comment." The more the government denied the story, the better the book sold.

Encouraged by his literary success and the size of his royalty check, Yardley decided to write another and even more revealing book entitled *Japanese Diplomatic Secrets: 1921–1922.* This time the American government decided to act and, after persuading his original publisher, Bobbs-Merrill, not to handle it, then put pressure on Macmillan, who were considering handling it. On 20 February 1933, the manuscript was seized in New York from Macmillan's offices by U.S. marshals and taken before a grand jury by Chief Assistant U.S. Attorney General Thomas E. Dewey.[25] As a result, the manuscript was impounded under Title 50, Section 32, of the United States Code, the espionage law. To this day it remains the only book officially banned in America by the federal government.[26]

For the Japanese, Yardley's revelations were a severe shock and loss of face. They now knew they had been tricked into accepting the lower tonnage ratio, although by then it hardly mattered, since they had decided to ignore their treaty obligations anyway. As a result they immediately began a frantic search for new and even better ways of protecting their secrets in the future.

Stimson's claim that America would not read gentlemen's mail was more political rhetoric than fact, for as Yardley's organization closed, its work was quietly switched to the U.S. Army's Signal Corps, which on 24 April 1930 fostered a new codebreaking agency known as the Signal Intelligence Service (SIS),[27] whose chief was William F. Friedman.

Yardley may have been a brilliant codebreaker, but he was also a maverick. Friedman was a pragmatist and dedicated scientist. An immigrant from Russia born in 1891, Friedman was brought to America by his family a year later and in 1896 became an American citizen. Friedman had intended to be a farmer but changed his mind and decided science was more interesting. On 1 June 1915 he had the good fortune to be taken under the wing of Colonel George Fabyan,[28] a philanthropist and heir to a cotton fortune, who ran his own laboratories on his estate, Riverbank, in Geneva, Illinois. Fabyan was interested in codes and allowed Friedman to establish his own codebreaking department. In May 1917, he married a fellow cryptologist, twenty-three-year-old Elizebeth Smith, and thus forged what was to become the most famous husband and wife team in the history of codebreaking.

In order to staff his tiny organization, Friedman was always on the lookout for new recruits and used to comb through the results of those taking the U.S. Government Civil Service examination. One name that caught his eye was that of Abraham Sinkov.

Sinkov's background[29] was very similar to Friedman's, for his father had come to America from Russia at the turn of the century and had set himself up as a house painter. Eventually he was able to bring his wife and their two daughters to Philadelphia, where in 1907 Abraham was born, to be followed by three more sisters. In 1912, the Sinkovs moved to New York, and Abraham Sinkov was educated at a local high school, where he demonstrated an early skill for mathematics.

Upon graduation, Sinkov became a mathematics teacher at his old school, but in 1921 his father was fatally mugged on the streets of New York and young Sinkov found himself responsible for supporting the entire family. Unhappy with teaching, Sinkov took the Civil Service examination in 1929 and did so well that Friedman offered him a job at SIS at an annual salary of $2,000 a year, a considerable reduction from his teacher's salary of $2,600. Nevertheless Sinkov accepted, and he and his family moved down to Washington in 1930 and Sinkov became a codebreaker. While working at SIS, he was able to take his doctorate at George Washington University. Shortly afterward, Friedman hired two more young men—Frank Rowlett and Solomon Kullbach.

At first there was not much to work on, for they were not allowed access to any of the commercial cable traffic. A young army lieutenant Joseph O. Mauborgne (later to become the U.S. Army's Chief Signals Officer) did some Sigint work privately on the West Coast and intercepted a few messages, which he passed on to Friedman's team. Eventually Sinkov was able to make a private—and strictly illegal—arrangement with the cable companies so SIS could see some of their traffic. Gradually SIS began to read some Japanese, Latin American, and Italian traffic. In July 1936, Sinkov went to Panama, where he supervised the establishment of a Sigint station. Similar stations were built in Hawaii and the Philippines.

Apart from breaking the few coded messages that came their way, Friedman's SIS also established a training school. One of the early pupils was Lieutenant Preston Corderman, who later became a general commanding the Army Security Agency (ASA), forerunner of today's NSA.

Besides Friedman's SIS, the U.S. Navy had its own codebreaking organization, dating back to its first radio transmissions in 1899.[30] It was small and suffered from endless internecine rivalries with the U.S. Army. World War I offered the U.S. Navy few codebreaking opportunities, and instead they had concentrated on establishing a network of medium-frequency direction-finding (DF) stations along the East Coast to track German submarines operating in the western Atlantic.

During the war, the Admiralty's Room 40 had passed on to the U.S. Navy some decrypted material from German naval messages. But despite being allies, the Americans were never allowed to learn any of Room 40's secrets or have a liaison team there or with the naval section at GCCS after the war.

Friedman later wrote:

> Cryptanalytic activities in our Navy Department were practically non-existent until after the close of the last war [World War I] during which whatever problems they had were referred to MI-8. But in 1921 the Navy recognizing the important role which cryptanalysis was bound to play in the future began building up a large unit with echelons afloat . . . until by 1939 . . . the Navy had considerably outstripped the Army. However, it may be said, with some justifiable pride that while they were ahead in quantity we were ahead in quality,

for all the important developments in both the cryptographic and cryptanalytic fields must be credited to Army personnel.[31]

In July 1922 the Code and Signal Section of the U.S. Naval Communications Service was reorganized and given the title of OP-20-G, headed by thirty-one-year-old Lieutenant Laurence F. Safford, USN, a nervous and somewhat eccentric figure who did not fit the conventional image of a peacetime polished naval officer at all. However, like so many other codebreakers, Safford was not interested in his appearance or social graces but was immersed in his love of mathematics and mechanical coding machines, which made him a genius in his field and led the U.S. Navy to eventual cryptographic victory over the Japanese.

Safford set up office with just four civilians and two U.S. Navy radiomen (hardly the large unit Friedman claimed) in Room 2646 in the Navy Department's offices on Constitution Avenue in Washington, D.C.[32] To conceal the true nature of its work, it was referred to as the Research Office. Although next door to the Munitions Building, where Friedman had his SIS, there was little cooperation between the two organizations. That was to prove one of the primary causes of the Pearl Harbor disaster. Had America adopted an integrated codebreaking agency like GCCS, things would have been very different.

The next problem facing OP-20-G was that they only had two radio operators capable of receiving and transcribing *kana* texts from Morse code transmissions. Safford solved this by designing a typewriter which he called a special code machine.[33] On 26 November 1924, he sent details to John T. Underwood of the Underwood Typewriter Company, who examined Safford's specifications with his chief designer, Charles A. Joerissen. Two weeks later, on 10 December, they offered to build Safford four such machines for $645. The makers called them the Underwood Code Machine, and the U.S. Navy CSP-602, which designation was changed to Radio Intelligence Publication 5 (RIP-5) on 24 July 1930.

The machine's keyboard was the same as the regular typewriters supplied throughout the U.S. Navy to radio operators, except that the typefaces on the typebars printed *kana* characters in Japanese brush-stroke form instead of normal roman letters.

When an operator heard a Japanese cipher message sent in international Morse code, he would depress the key of the Morse combination, which then printed out the relevant *kana* character. This took care of twenty-six of the seventy-three main *kana* characters normally used (see Appendix 1) and greatly reduced the time needed to train a radio operator to intercept Japanese transmissions. *Kana* characters not in the standard Morse code were positioned on the upper case sections of the keyboard, while numerals were the same in both *kana* cipher text and its roman equivalent. Thus the *kana* symbol I was transmitted as the Morse letter A, so all the operator had to do was to press his A key and the equivalent *kana* brush stroke was printed out. The Morse letter C produced the *kana* symbol NI, and so on.

So successful were these machines that on 25 September 1925, five more were ordered, two of which were retained by Safford, while three went to Friedman's SIS next door. In June 1926, the Underwood Company further improved the machine so that it would automatically print out the romanized equivalent, or *romanji,* for the *kana* symbol. This made it possible for an operator with no knowledge of the Japanese language to intercept Japanese *kana* transmissions and reproduce them in roman letters ready to send to the codebreakers.

Thus a simple machine based on a normal typewriter and costing $156[34] had stripped away much of the incomprehensibility of the Japanese language. Fortunately, the Japanese did not discover this during the following twenty-five years.

So in 1924–25, Friedman's team at the SIS were in a position to read foreign—but primarily Japanese—diplomatic traffic, always provided they could circumvent the restrictions on intercepting American cable traffic, while Safford's team at OP-20-G had begun reading Japanese naval signals.

CHAPTER 3

Straws in the Wind

BRITAIN FIRST BROKE Japanese naval codes on a regular basis following Nave's arrival at GCCS in London in January 1928. The U.S. Navy's OP-20-G codebreaking team, headed by Laurence Safford, had begun work slightly earlier, in October 1924. Neither knew the details or extent of the other's work,[1] as there was no exchange of any information between the two organizations.

There was, however, a very important difference between the two agencies. GCCS was a fully integrated Sigint and codebreaking organization working on diplomatic material for the Foreign Office and military messages for the Army, Navy, and Air Force. In America, the U.S. Army's Signal Intelligence Service (SIS) worked separately from the U.S. Navy's OP-20-G. This led to some curious divisions of responsibilities and trust.

To begin with, OP-20-G handled both Japanese diplomatic and naval messages.[2] During the crisis caused by the sudden disbandment of Yardley's codebreaking team in October 1929, the U.S. Navy was the only source of diplomatic decrypts for the State Department. When the U.S. Army's SIS was created in April 1930, it began work again on Japanese diplomatic messages and eventually took over the entire task, leaving OP-20-G free to concentrate on naval traffic.

However, by 1940, the volume of Japanese diplomatic traffic had increased to the point where the SIS asked OP-20-G if they could take over half the workload. According to Safford:

> After studying and rejecting two earlier proposals it was agreed to divide all Japanese Diplomatic (JAP DIP) "processing" (decrypting or decoding) plus translation on a daily basis, the Navy taking the odd days and the Army the even days. . . . A few months later Naval Intelligence and G-2 [SIS] arranged for the dissemination of JAP DIP to the

White House and State Department on a monthly basis, the Navy taking the odd months and the Army the even months.[3]

Bearing in mind that the two agencies were not working together in the same office, it is hard to think of an arrangement likely to cause more mistakes and misunderstandings. Furthermore, the sharing of information between the two was strictly limited, as Safford starkly describes: "The collaboration between the Army and Navy on Japanese diplomatic crypto-systems did not extend to Jap military (Army and Navy) crypto-systems. A secret divulged to a third party is no longer a secret. The US Navy withheld all details of its success with Japanese naval crypto-systems from the Army."[4]

If Safford seriously believed it was unsafe to share OP-20-G's work on Japanese naval material with the U.S. Army, then it raises the fundamental question of how the Army's SIS could correctly analyze the diplomatic material it was handling, since any Japanese attack would initially have to be seaborne. Here the seeds of distrust and rivalry were sown that helped lead to the ultimate disaster at Pearl Harbor.

Initially the Americans had the advantage over the British. In 1921, the Office of Naval Intelligence (ONI), together with the Federal Bureau of Investigation (FBI) and the New York police, burgled the offices of the Japanese consul in New York, picked the lock of his safe, and inside found a copy of the current 3-*kana* naval code. The burglars and their locksmith returned to the offices over the next few weeks and carefully photographed each page of the book until they had a complete copy.

This was given[5] to Dr. B. C. Haworth[6] and his wife, who, although expert Japanese linguists, required the next four years to translate it into English and then have it typed up by Miss Castleman and Mrs. DuVerger. As each set of pages was completed, it was passed on to OP-20-G so that they could begin to decrypt the few messages they were starting to get from their intercept stations in the Far East as early as October 1924. It was 1926 by the time the Haworths had finished their work and the complete code was available to OP-20-G in the form of ten 8-by-13-inch loose-leaf binders entitled *Imperial Japanese Navy Secret Operations Code—1918.*

In 1926 and 1927, the ONI burgled the consul's office in New York on several further occasions and photographed the various updates that had been added to the code. Dr. Haworth incorporated these in the copy at OP-20-G. In 1929, Miss Feather, Mrs. Wedding, Miss Calman, Mrs. Wilson, and Mrs. Tulley typed up four new copies on 12-by-18-inch paper, which were bound into two volumes in red leather binders. Accordingly the code became known as the Red Book, although it was also sometimes known as Code B.[7]

One copy of the Red Book code was sent by courier to the USS *Pittsburgh*, the flagship of the U.S. Asiatic Fleet in the Far East, responsible for coordinating the interception of Japanese naval signals there. Another copy was kept at OP-20-G, while the remaining two were locked away in a vault.

According to Safford:[8]

> This code was not too difficult and we were literally surfeited with blessings. The one or two available translators could not possibly go through all the intercepted messages so it was necessary to sort out the high priorities . . . and thus skim off the cream. The Japanese used this code until December 1930 thus giving US naval authorities a complete picture of the Japanese naval manoeuvres of 1930 and Japanese naval war plans and strategic concepts.

This was confirmed in a secret letter[9] (Serial #081420) sent by the Chief of Naval Operations in Washington to the C-in-C's of the U.S. Asiatic and Pacific fleets in October 1940, which said:

> During the past ten years Orange [the U.S. Navy's codename for Japan] intelligence has been provided by solution of Orange cryptographic systems. . . . Every major move of the Orange fleet has been predicted, and a continuous flow of information concerning Orange diplomatic activities has been made available.

The general naval code (the Red Book) required much more work in order to build up the 97,336 groups of 3-*kana* letter groups, and the speed of this was largely determined by the volume of intercepted traffic and the types of messages involved. A great weakness with the Red Book code was that the basic dictionary was arranged in alphabetical order, so that as the code was built up so the missing pieces automatically fell into place.

Safford's assistant at OP-20-G was Mrs. Agnes Driscoll,[10] who in June 1918 at the age of twenty-nine, then Miss Agnes May Meyer, joined the U.S. Naval Reserve and in July the following year accepted a job as stenographer for the Director of Naval Communications in the Code and Signal section at an annual salary of $1,400. Miss Meyer had graduated from Ohio State University in 1911, where she qualified in four languages —German, French, Latin, and Japanese—and became head of the mathematics department of a high school in Amarillo, Texas, before joining the Naval Reserve during World War I. Her incredible mathematical skill attracted the attention of Edward Hebern, who was then developing his cryptograph that he hoped to sell to the U.S. Navy, and in 1923 he persuaded her to leave OP-20-G and come to work for him. However, a year later, in 1924, Miss Meyer married a Washington lawyer, Michael B. Driscoll, and on 1 August 1924 returned to work for the Navy at a salary of $1,860, where her first task was to teach Safford the basic principles of codebreaking.

Mrs. Driscoll, or Miss Aggie as she was known to her colleagues, was a tall, slender, and unusually quiet woman (although one fellow codebreaker[11] recalls she could swear like a deckhand when the occasion demanded), totally dedicated to her work, and one of America's most brilliant codebreakers whose genius continued right through World War II. In the 1930s, Mrs. Driscoll testified before the Senate Naval Affairs Committee that she had assisted the late William P. Gresham in developing a secure cryptograph for the U.S. Navy and was awarded $15,000.

In February 1926, Safford left OP-20-G to resume sea duties as part of his normal career, and his place was taken by twenty-eight-year-old Lieutenant Joseph J. Rochefort, who had joined the Navy in World War I after attending the University of California. Rochefort stayed as head of OP-20-G until 1929, when he went to Japan for two years to learn the language, and Safford returned to take over again. In May 1941, Rochefort took charge of the codebreaking team at the 14th Naval District at Pearl Harbor, which he renamed the Combat Intelligence unit.

LIFE AT GCCS was very different. Although Nave was an Australian naval officer, GCCS itself was a civilian organization run by Britain's Foreign Office. Nave's two tasks were the breaking of the Japanese naval attaché code and continuing to penetrate the Japanese general naval 3-*kana* code (what OP-20-G called the Red Book), which he had been working on in the Far East since 1925. Of the two, the naval attaché's code was far more important, because the Japanese Navy was not very active at the time outside Japanese home waters, except for annual maneuvers, and consequently the amount of radio traffic intercepted was small and unimportant.

The naval attaché's signals were a useful way of knowing what things in the west interested the Japanese, particularly in respect of new naval technology, what they were telling Tokyo about their observations and contacts, and what orders Tokyo was placing with naval suppliers. Each morning, Nave received copies from Cable & Wireless, Western Union, and the Commercial Cable Company of all messages that had been sent and received between the Japanese diplomatic missions in Europe and Tokyo. If Nave was interested in some other matter connected with naval affairs, for example, messages passing between a naval supplier in Britain or on the Continent and Tokyo, he only had to ask Henry Maine in the sorting office on the fourth floor of GCCS to look out for them.

At the same time, the telephone lines to the Japanese Embassy in London were tapped by the General Post Office (then responsible for the British Telephone system and forerunner of today's British Telecom) at the Central Telegraph Exchange at Moorgate and brought back by land-line to GCCS's offices, terminating in a small booth where Nave could sit and listen to their calls. Since intercontinental calls were extremely rare, these were usually of a local nature, so the amount of information gleaned was very limited compared to the cable traffic. And, because no recording facilities existed, it was a time-consuming task listening to them. All the other embassies in London were treated in exactly the same way by GCCS, although its activities were completely illegal and in breach of the Vienna Convention [12] on the diplomatic privileges that are accorded to foreign embassies.

Solving the naval attaché code was greatly helped by the fact that all attachés felt it necessary to show their superiors in Tokyo how efficient and observant they were by sending back any important article [13] or political statement about maritime affairs they saw in a newspaper, magazine, or parliamentary report. Such messages were frequently copied verbatim, and if there had been an important speech or political debate about naval affairs in London, Berlin, or Paris, it was very easy to look for a message whose cipher text length matched it. Sometimes the naval attaché in London would be sent an official press statement by the Admiralty which Nave knew would at once be sent back to Tokyo in code, thus providing a perfect crib, exactly as Yardley had discovered in Washington several years earlier.

Reading the naval attaché's cables in London sometimes produced an unexpected bonus. In 1928, one of the messages Nave decoded gave details of an arrangement whereby the Japanese in London were paying a Labour member of Parliament, Cecil Malone, [14] a quarterly retainer for providing any information he could acquire about defense matters. Malone had joined the Royal Navy in 1905, had become assistant to the director of the fledgling Air Department at the Admiralty in 1912, later was air attaché at the British Embassy in Paris, and then in 1914 joined the Royal Naval Air Service.

After World War I, Malone entered politics and was elected as the

Liberal member for East Leyton, in London, in 1918. But in November 1919, he had switched sides to the Socialist Party and in 1920 joined the Communist Party but had somehow managed to be re-elected as Labour member for Northampton in January 1928. Altogether, Malone was an odd person, but he nevertheless had contacts in the aircraft industry. GCCS advised MI5 of this development, and they kept Malone under surveillance while GCCS continued reading the scraps of information he gave the Japanese that were passed on to Tokyo by the naval attaché. It was wiser to let the matter run rather than arrest Malone and compromise GCCS's ability to read the attaché's code.

Malone was not the only spy the Japanese had in London. Reading through the intercepts, Nave discovered that the Japanese had also recruited a British officer, Major Frederick Joseph Rutland,[15] to work for them. His first contact with the Japanese had been in Manchuria, where plans had been made for him to meet the Japanese naval attaché on his return to London. GCCS should have told MI5 about this, but instead kept Rutland under surveillance themselves with the help of MI6 and followed him to the middle of Richmond Park in south London. Shortly afterward the Japanese naval attaché arrived in his car and the pair went off for a walk.

When the attaché got back to the embassy, he sent off a long coded message to Tokyo detailing the arrangements he had made, which included the plan that Rutland should go to California. Nave read the entire message before it had even reached Tokyo and gave the only copy personally to Sinclair at MI6. "We'll handle this ourselves," decided Sinclair. "If we tell MI5, they'll only make a balls of it." Strictly speaking, this was an MI5 affair,[16] since they were responsible for counterintelligence operations in Britain. "Anyway, if we arrest Rutland now," continued Sinclair, "the Japs will know we're reading their code and then Nave won't get anything more. Let Rutland go to America as planned and I'll have a quiet word with the FBI to keep an eye on him."

Rutland was kept under observation, and an MI6 officer booked a passage on the same ship. When Rutland arrived in America, he opened an investment brokerage company as cover, and the FBI took over surveillance.

In the summer of 1930, after Nave had been working at GCCS for two and a half years, the Australian Naval Board (evidently unaware[17] of his work in London) asked the Admiralty when Nave was likely to return to Australia, as they intended appointing him secretary to Admiral E. R. G. Evans, who had been selected to become the RAN's next C-in-C. The Admiralty acted quickly, and the Director of Naval Intelligence explained to Nave that they wished to retain his services on a permanent basis because he was their most experienced Japanese codebreaker, and he invited him to transfer from the RAN to the Royal Navy.

Nave was guaranteed promotion at least to commander and full Royal Navy pension rights based on the date of first joining the RAN in 1917. Nave realized that the transfer would mean the end of any future sea-going duties, but the work fascinated him and the offer was financially generous. So in the end he accepted. On 2 December 1930, *The London Gazette* carried on its front page the official statement that, by special order of King George V, Nave was transferred from the RAN to the Royal Navy, effective 27 November 1930.

On 1 December 1930, the Japanese introduced a new 4-*kana* version of their general naval code, which, continuing the use of American nomenclature, was called the Blue Book[18] because it was bound in a blue binder as it was reconstructed at OP-20-G. The first that GCCS knew about the new code was when a series of messages defied decryption. After Nave had worked on them for a while, he realized that it was a new 4-*kana* system. Unlike the previous code (the Red Book) that had been in operation since 1918 and was arranged in alphabetical order, this new code was a "hatted" code, which means the order in the codebook was totally random, or pulled out of a hat. The Blue Book consisted of 85,184 code groups, each representing a word or phrase, and was used with superencipherment. Since the code was a random one, there were two code books needed, one to encode and the other to decode.

At OP-20-G, they too had discovered the introduction of this new code when Lieutenant Tommy Dyer suddenly found he could no longer break the incoming intercepts. It was Mrs. Agnes Driscoll who looked at some of his work sheets and said, "Of course you're not getting anywhere. This is a new 4-*kana* code." And so in September 1931 she began the slow reconstruction of the Blue Book, without on this occasion any assistance from stolen copies of the code itself.

Eventually Mrs. Driscoll and Dyer discovered, as did GCCS, that although the Blue Book differed from the previous Red Book version in several important respects (its random nature and superencipherment being the two most important), it used the same basic dictionary and phraseology. Once this was appreciated, the speed of reconstruction quickly increased.

APART FROM British and American codebreaking, Holland was equally intent on breaking Japanese diplomatic and naval codes,[19] in order to anticipate any plans to attack the Netherlands East Indies (NEI) and their important oil fields. The Dutch had also sent officers to Japan to learn the language, one of the first being Lieutenant Commander J. A. L. Muller. On 7 March 1933, the Dutch Navy established a monitoring station in Batavia to eavesdrop on British, French, Japanese, and American naval signals.

In early 1934, the Japanese cruiser *Kuma* paid a visit to the NEI (now Indonesia), and the radio operators in Batavia began to copy its signals. These intercepts were sent back to Holland and shown to a Professor Krieger of Leiden University, a former naval officer fluent in Japanese. But he could not break them down into plain language. Krieger contacted Lieutenant (later Rear Admiral) J. F. W. Nuboer, who was about to be posted to the new intelligence section, Afdeling 1, at the naval headquarters in Batavia, where he arrived in August 1934. Nuboer's previous experience had been with the German Enigma cryptograph. The Dutch, at his suggestion, had bought several copies of the original commercial version, and Nuboer had written the Dutch operating instruction handbook for them.

The Dutch codebreaking center in Batavia, known as Kamer 14, was staffed by two expert codebreakers, Lieutenant J. A. Verkuyl and Lieutenant W. van der Beek, who concentrated their efforts on Japanese diplomatic traffic passing between their consulate in Batavia and the Ministry of Foreign Affairs in Tokyo. They had originally broken into this code in 1932 and now with the help of their expert translator, Mr. van de Stadt, were able to read all these messages. As with GCCS, the Dutch codebreakers obtained their intercepts by getting copies of the Japanese consular cables from the local telegraph office, which was controlled by the Dutch government.

ALL THESE different codes being used around the world had one thing in common: They were all book codes, using a basic dictionary with words, phrases, and numbers, and then separate superencipherment or additive tables. But as the pace and scope of radio transmissions increased, so too did the number of messages, placing great strain on operators, sometimes working under difficult conditions in battle, with systems that required cumbersome codebooks and endless calculations to add or strip away the superencipherment tables. The slightest error could make a message unreadable, not only causing mistakes on the battlefield but also leading to endless requests for repetitions, which gave Sigint operators more opportunities to eavesdrop. Frequently, frustrated and tired operators would repeat an entire message in plain language.

Furthermore, if a codebook was captured in battle or stolen by a traitor, the entire system was compromised and complete new sets had to be distributed to every unit. Apart from being a protracted task, this often meant that messages continued to be sent simultaneously in the old system and the replacement version.

The idea of making a machine that would automatically turn plain text into cipher text and then reverse the procedure at the other end was not new and had fascinated inventors for hundreds of years. (A brief history is included in Appendix 8.)

Japan's code systems had been greatly influenced by the Polish expert Jan Kowalefsky, whose original book codes had been broken by Yardley (see Chapter 2). One of Kowalefsky's pupils was Commander Risaburo Ito. The Poles knew a lot about Enigma and were already trying to break the German commercial version, so it was not surprising that when Ito saw an Enigma he decided to incorporate its basic rotor principle into a cryptograph he called the Type A machine or 91-Shiki O-bun In-ji-ki, or Alphabetical Typewriter 91, the 91 being an abbreviation for the Japanese calendar year 2591, which corresponds with 1931.

During 1932, GCCS had begun intercepting some new Japanese naval attaché messages that defied decryption by the old system. Nave soon deduced that the Japanese had started using a cryptograph. The Americans at OP-20-G noticed the same thing, and it was Mrs. Driscoll[20] who realized they had introduced machine enciphering. At first OP-20-G called it the M-1, but later, to maintain the custom of using colors, it was called the Red machine,[21] which was confusing since there was already a Red Book code.

Fortunately, the Japanese never realized that *kana* has its own statistical peculiarities and frequency characteristics, just like any other language, so the *romanji* equivalents inherit these same patterns, which were easily identifiable over long messages. Despite its seeming complexity, romanized Japanese has a greater index of coincidence[22] than any major European language. Therefore the Red machine was not very efficient, and both GCCS and OP-20-G had little difficulty in breaking it.

At first the Red machine was used only for naval attaché traffic, and soon after OP-20-G had broken it, they decrypted a message—almost identical to those Nave had broken in London—which referred to someone called Tomimura,[23] or Thompson, who was evidently supplying the Japanese with secret information that included the performance of U.S. Navy warships and the Model D-4 bombsight. A lengthy investigation by the ONI and the FBI revealed that Harry H. Thompson was a radioman second class who was working with a cashiered naval officer, John S.

Farnsworth. Together they had passed on their information to Lieutenant Commander Akira Yamaki and Lieutenant Toshio Miyazaki of the Japanese Navy, who were in America posing as students. Farnsworth and Thompson were both sentenced to long terms of imprisonment, but great care was taken at their trial in 1937 not to give any hint as to how their spying activities had been uncovered.

After a few years, naval attachés stopped using the Red machine and reverted to book codes. But in late 1940, the Japanese Navy introduced another cryptograph called 97-Shiki In-ji-ki san Gata, invented in 1937, known to OP-20-G as Coral, which was used exclusively for naval attaché traffic. By the time Coral was fully in service, the number of Japanese naval attachés abroad had dwindled, and so too had the amount of traffic that could be intercepted. As a result Coral was not broken until 1943.

Neither the Red machine nor Coral was ever used by the Japanese Navy itself, whose code systems remained non-machine throughout the war—still one of the greatest puzzles of Japanese cryptographic history. By the time Yardley's book appeared in 1931, the Japanese naval cryptographers in the 4th Department (Communications) of the General Naval Staff headquarters were well aware that their most complex book codes had been broken by the Americans and, they would have to assume, by other nations, like Britain, with similar codebreaking talents. Yet their Navy never benefited from this knowledge and continued using the same old-fashioned book codes from 1918 right through World War II to 1945—first the Red Book from 1918–30, then the Blue Book from 1931–39, and finally JN-25. At no time did the Japanese Navy experiment with any of the smaller cryptographs then on the market—like Hagelin's M-209—which they would have had no problem copying and which would have been ideal for shipboard use, just as the Enigma was to be found on every vessel in the German Navy.

It is easy to understand that in the euphoria of victory after 7 December 1941, as the Japanese swept across the Far East, cipher security did not seem particularly important. But the Navy soon found its lines of communications stretching far away from Tokyo, causing long delays as new additive tables had to be circulated to every ship and shore station. As a result, some units continued using the old tables, while others received the same message in the new table. In some cases the ships delivering the new tables were sunk, so the delay in replacing them grew even longer. By contrast, a cipher machine's key settings can be distributed very easily. It was not until September 1942, long after the Battle of Midway in June, as the result of being shown captured Ultra material[24] from the Combined Operations Intelligence Centre (COIC) in New Zealand, which included details of the planned movements of Japanese warships prior to Midway that could only have come from reading JN-25, that the Japanese reluctantly accepted that their book code JN-25 was insecure. But by then it was too late, and the task of re-equipping the entire Japanese Navy with cryptographs was beyond the technical resources of either Germany or Japan.

Nave was also helped in breaking the new attaché code by a series of breaches in security that occurred when the Japanese naval attaché in Rome sent a long message in code, which he then repeated verbatim in plain language. The officer was under great emotional stress at the time, having had an affair with a local girl, only to discover that she was an employee of Italian intelligence. Having so disgraced himself and betrayed his country, the officer calmly told his superiors in Tokyo that he would pay for his indiscretions with his life. And this he did. It was very poignant to read all this from afar, but it nevertheless gave GCCS the key to the current edition of the code.

By 1934, the naval section at GCCS had grown considerably, while the volume of traffic being intercepted increased monthly as the Japanese Navy became more active. As the Royal Navy had built an intercept station at Stonecutters Island in Hong Kong, which would be able to monitor any message transmitted from Japan, GCCS also decided to open an office in Hong Kong, so that some of the work could be done on the spot. Captain Tait, then deputy director of Naval Intelligence at the Admiralty, visited Hong Kong to make the necessary arrangements, and later that year Captain Arthur Shaw[25] was sent out to start up this new operation, which was called the Far East Combined Bureau (FECB).

Among the Japanese attaché traffic that Nave intercepted on the Berlin-Tokyo circuit in 1936 was a series of messages concerning a German who had been engaged by the Japanese to spy for them in Honolulu. There was an enormous amount of detail about his salary, expenses, and life insurance, for him, his wife, and their two children. As cover he would establish a steel furniture business in Hawaii. The only thing GCCS did not know was his name, because the messages referred to him only by his Japanese codename, "Jimmy." Eventually they picked up details of his sailing arrangements from Hamburg to Hawaii via Japan, and it was not hard for MI6 to trace the family. He turned out to be forty-one-year-old Otto Kuehn, a former officer in the German Navy during World War I whose ship had been sunk by HMS *Lion.* Kuehn had spent some years as a prisoner of war in Britain. He and his family finally reached Honolulu on 29 October 1936 aboard the *Tatuta Maru* from Yokohama.

All this information was so sensitive that handwritten translations were given personally only to Sinclair. Set against the background of the earlier discovery of Rutland and his work for the Japanese in California, these were very significant straws in the wind of impending war and demonstrated Japan's growing interest in naval operations in the Pacific and especially Hawaii. Sinclair passed on the information about Kuehn to the FBI, who did little about the matter. The FBI's 683-page file on Kuehn [26] is still so heavily censored (so as to remove any reference to British intelligence) that whole sections are unreadable, but it was not until early 1939 that the the FBI began to investigate Kuehn and his wife.

Meanwhile technology at GCCS was constantly improving. As well as the Japanese and German embassies, more diplomatic missions and the homes of diplomats had their telephones tapped and monitoring circuits brought back to their offices. There was also a special booth set aside for eavesdropping on Hitler's radiotelephone conversations with his chancellery in Berlin when he was traveling around Germany in his special train. Whenever Hitler started out on one of his travels, the German section at GCCS manned this listening booth constantly so that all the conversations could be monitored.

As far as Japan was concerned, by the end of 1937 GCCS could read all its naval attaché messages passing between Europe and Tokyo, diplomatic traffic sent on the Red machine (this was handled by Hobart-Hampden and Parlett), and signals sent in the general naval code (the Blue Book), used by all the ships of the Japanese Navy in home and foreign waters.

America's neutrality received a nasty setback on the morning of 12 December 1937, when the USS *Panay* was deliberately bombed by Japanese aircraft, killing two seamen and an Italian journalist. But though at long last the American people were outraged to the point where it seemed the incident might lead to war, Roosevelt quite deliberately decided not to provoke the Japanese—and even had newsreel pictures of Japanese aircraft attacking the *Panay* censored—and instead accepted the Japanese apology and compensation check for $2,214,007.36.

Whether the *Panay* incident was a genuine mistake or a Japanese test of America's response is unclear, but their motive made no difference to their overall objectives in China. Immediately after the incident, Japanese troops captured Nanking and in the next few weeks raped and butchered over 250,000 Chinese men, women, and children. As news of the atrocities spread across America, attitudes slowly began to change. Though isolationism remained strong, America began its inexorable course toward the inevitable war with Japan.

CHAPTER 4

A Touch of Magic

BY THE AUTUMN of 1937, the international situation had become so serious that it was decided that Nave should go out to the Far East Combined Bureau (FECB) in Hong Kong and continue his codebreaking work there. By now, GCCS in London had a large Japanese section that took care of the tedious work of reconstructing the codebooks. But an expert Japanese-speaking codebreaker with the right naval qualifications was needed on the spot to understand the jargon used in the more important messages.

Officially, Nave was listed as an interpreter on the Commander-in-Chief's staff, but this was a cover for his real duties with FECB, which was located in the naval dockyard. Although in theory a combined services organization, in practice all the interception and decoding was done by the Navy (with its powerful monitoring station on nearby Stonecutters Island), while the Army and Air Force only had liaison officers because there was very little traffic that concerned them.

One of Nave's first tasks was to visit the local office of the Eastern Telegraph Company, a subsidiary of Cable & Wireless, and have a talk with the manager and ensure that FECB was getting copies of all the cables sent and received by the Japanese consul general. Unlike London, it was not necessary for FECB to go through a charade of producing warrants to justify the request. "No problem," the manager replied cheerfully, "just send someone along each morning and you can collect any you want. Bring them back the next day and we'll change them over for the next lot." It was as simple as that.

Almost immediately the alarm bells began to ring when one of the first cables Nave decoded was from the consul general advising Tokyo that a Japanese-speaking expert called Nave had arrived in Hong Kong and that there had been an increase of staff at the Stonecutters Island station. How was the consul so well informed about an operation that was supposed to be top secret?

In a small place like Hong Kong, service gossip circulates quickly, and it was always possible that the consul had heard something from sailors working at Stonecutters intercept station or the local Chinese cleaners employed there. But the quality of his intelligence indicated a leak at a much higher level, which was particularly worrying. Nave kept the information to himself, locking the decrypts away in his safe, and then started to feed some "barium meals" into the system at FECB. A "barium meal" is a counterintelligence trick whereby different bits of seemingly accurate information are fed to suspected people and then a watch is kept to see which piece turns up in the wrong hands. As the result of decrypting further messages from the consul, Nave was able to narrow the suspects down to an Italian woman married to a business-man working in Hong Kong. What was particularly embarrassing was that this woman was a close friend of the unsuspecting wife of Captain E. G. N. Rushbrooke, who was in charge of administration at FECB. Nave carefully rechecked all his facts and then had the unpleasant task of confronting Rushbrooke, who was naturally most upset and refused to believe him.

The only way to prove it was to wait until the businessman and his Italian wife went off to Europe on leave. Immediately the reports from the Japanese consul general stopped. Even then Rushbrooke argued it might just be a coincidence. But when the couple returned to Hong Kong after their holiday, the Japanese consul's reports based on the wife's information began again. Naval intelligence later discovered that the Italian woman had been recruited as a spy by Edda Ciano,[1] Mussolini's daughter, when the Cianos were in Shanghai. Nave realized this woman was extremely active when the wife of an army officer also questioned Nave closely about his work at a dinner party one night shortly after his arrival. She too was a friend of the same Italian woman.

Plainly she had been instructed to target people connected with military and naval intelligence. But it was also quite possible that Nave's name had been in some Japanese intelligence file ever since he had gone to Japan to study the language and later acted as official interpreter during the Japanese visit to Australia in 1924. Rushbrooke was highly embarrassed by the affair, but no official action was taken, because FECB did not want to compromise its ability to read the consul's cables. As a result, Rushbrooke's career[2] was not affected, and in 1942 he was promoted to commodore and became Director of Naval Intelligence in London, taking over from Rear Admiral Godfrey.

The volume of traffic being intercepted by FECB was growing daily, because Japan was now engaged in an all-out war in China. On 7 July 1937, there was a brief outbreak of fighting between Chinese and Japanese troops guarding the Marco Polo Bridge, near Peking. This was a minor skirmish based on a misunderstanding,[3] but it was sufficient to provide the long-awaited catalyst that within a few weeks had erupted into full-scale war, euphemistically called the China Incident, the start of eight years of hostilities that were to engulf Japan and eventually the rest of the Far East.

The situation for the Chinese had become so serious that Chiang Kai-shek was forced to come to an arrangement with his hated rival Mao Tse-tung. At a meeting in Nanking on 29 September, the two leaders agreed that their armies must now unite to fight the Japanese. Only a few months earlier, Chiang had ridiculed such a suggestion, but now events were overtaking the Chinese faster than anyone could have imagined.

In August, Japanese reinforcements began to arrive at Shanghai, and on the sixteenth Japanese Navy aircraft carried out the world's first trans-oceanic air attack[4] by flying the 1,250-mile round trip from Formosa to attack Chinese positions in Shanghai. At first the Japanese bombers suffered disastrous losses from the defending Chinese fighters. But the Japanese learned quickly from their mistakes and ordered the carrier *Kaga* in with fighters to protect the bombers. Soon the Japanese had the skies to themselves.

FECB read all the Japanese messages with ease and had prior knowledge of every operation they planned. The first advice usually came after a War Cabinet meeting in Tokyo and would be sent in the Commander-in-Chief's code. A typical message would read, "Instructions have been issued for the capture of Canton. This will be known as Operation Y. Further details will be given by Chief of Naval Staff." This immediately helped FECB identify the much longer messages that would shortly be intercepted in the Blue Book code. These would give precise details of the number of transports, escorting warships, the Army units involved, landing place, route to be taken, and so forth. Not a single message escaped the listening post in Hong Kong. The powerful intercept station at Stonecutters sucked up everything transmitted from Japan and by any ship at sea. However, none of this information was passed on to the Chinese, who were Britain's allies, presumably because GCCS could not risk letting the Japanese become aware their codes were compromised. China was the first major overseas military operation the Japanese had embarked on, and for FECB and GCCS in London it was the perfect Sigint training ground that was to serve them so well in the years ahead.

Aside from these local crises, the inexorable march toward war continued. In America, despite the tide of isolationism, Roosevelt persuaded Congress to pass the Naval Expansion Bill, which would raise the U.S. Navy's strength by 20 percent over the old treaty limit. But the race to match Japan's new Navy was a slow one, and already Japan had six operational aircraft carriers against America's three, with another three under construction. Over the years, history books have created a mythology that President Roosevelt tried to spend more money on the armed services but was always vilified and defeated in his attempts by the isolationist movement and Congress. But a study of the American national defense budget for the years 1934 through 1941 shows a different story.[5] During that period the Army and Navy jointly asked the Bureau of Budget for $26,580,145,093. In the same period Roosevelt recommended to Congress that they be allocated $23,818,319,897, but Congress actually made available $24,943,987,823, or $1,125,667,926 more than Roosevelt's recommendations.

The American codebreaking picture remained far less well organized[6] than that of GCCS and FECB. By 1938, there were three U.S. Navy codebreaking groups at work: Station Negat, the original OP-20-G office in Washington; Station Cast, at Cavite in the Philippines; and Station Hypo, in Hawaii.

Station Cast had begun life at Olongapo in the Philippines in 1927 and then later transferred to Cavite. In its early days, the station staff was so small that all they could do was to intercept Japanese signals and send them to OP-20-G for breaking, and attempt some rudimentary traffic analysis. By 1934, Lieutenant T. A. Huckins, USN, and his assistant, Lieutenant E. S. L. Goodwin, USN, were in charge. Since Goodwin had done some codebreaking work while at OP-20-G, he began doing the same at Cast.

Station Hypo, in Hawaii, was far more recent and had only started in 1936 under the command of Lieutenant Thomas Dyer, USN. It was located on the second floor of Building No. 1 in the main naval yard of the 14th Naval District at Pearl Harbor. Later, in 1941, it moved down into the basement of the building.

In 1937, Risaburo Ito decided to improve upon the Type 91 cryptograph, or Red machine, and build an even more secure machine. This he called 97-Shiki O-bun Injiki, or Alphabetical Typewriter 97, after the year 1937, according to the ancient Japanese calendar, although it was also referred to by the Japanese Foreign Ministry as the Type B machine. The U.S. Navy codebreakers first gave it the name M-5, then used the Japanese designation B Machine, and eventually adopted the codename Purple.[7] The decrypts produced from it were distributed under the codename Magic. Together with Enigma, Purple is without doubt the best-known encoding machine in the world. But unfortunately this publicity has generated a wealth of inaccurate information, which over the years has obscured the truth about its design and use.

The first indication the Americans had about this new machine was in late 1938, when SIS decoded a message sent on the earlier Red machine giving travel details of a Japanese communications expert called Okamoto, who was to visit the diplomatic missions in Washington, Berlin, London, Paris, Moscow, Rome, Geneva, Brussels, Ankara, Shanghai, and Peking to install a new cipher machine called Type B, which was to replace the earlier Type A or Red machine. On 19 February 1939, SIS intercepted another message sent on the Red machine stating that the new machine would start operation the next day, although some smaller diplomatic missions would continue using the earlier Type A cryptograph. The first Purple messages intercepted by SIS were from Tokyo to Berlin in March 1939.

On 14 October 1940, Friedman wrote an account of how the Type B machine was solved.[8] (This was eventually released by the NSA into the National Archives on 10 March 1982.) Although the report runs to ten pages, six of them still remain censored in 1991, and the only part of the report publicly available merely says that breaking the Type B cryptograph "took 18 months of intensive study by a group of cryptanalysts" and then lists the names of those involved.

Fortunately, one of those involved in this work was Abraham Sinkov, so it is now possible to fill in[9] the censored portions of the report. Alongside Sinkov were Frank Rowlett, Leon Rosen, and Robert O. Ferner, who did much of the initial work, also helped by several others, including Delia Ann Taylor. (She caught Sinkov's eye, and in 1942 they were married.) Purple was broken because very foolishly the Japanese also sent the same messages via the earlier Red machine; and because SIS was reading everything sent in Red, it was extremely easy to match the text lengths and obtain a perfect crib. This type of back-door codebreaking is as relevant now as it was then, which is why the NSA continues to censor this fifty-year-old report. It is not anxious to remind those responsible for code security around the world today, upon whom the NSA eavesdrops, of the dangers of sending exactly the same message in both a high- and low-grade code system.

But being able to read the messages from a Red machine crib did not automatically explain how Purple worked, although the Army and Navy codebreakers were able to identify part of the encoding system and realized that it was not the rotor system hitherto used in Red. In the summer of 1940,[10] Safford's team at OP-20-G were withdrawn from the

Purple project to work on Japanese naval code systems, leaving SIS to go it alone. So in August 1940, Friedman asked a newly arrived code-breaker, Larry Clark, to take a look at the problem. He suggested that the Japanese were using Strowger rotary selector switches used in automatic telephone exchanges. Friedman immediately got some Strowger selectors from Western Union and asked OP-20-G to help reconstruct a copy of the Type B machine. Within a month, Safford and a team of naval engineers with the Radio Laboratory at the Washington Navy Yard had reconstructed its switching mechanism. And on 25 September 1940, their rickety Purple machine spewed forth its first decrypt.

Better copies followed, and from then onward Army and Navy code-breakers had no problems in reading all messages encoded in Purple. The achievement of building a copy of the Type B cryptograph without ever having seen it remains one of the world's greatest cryptographic achievements. Eventually, toward the end of the war in 1945, a Type B machine was captured, and the codebreakers had the satisfaction of finding that they had matched the original Japanese design wire for wire.

The Japanese built a total of twenty-five Type B machines, which were distributed to their most important diplomatic missions around the world, while the smaller missions continued using the Red machine. By October 1941, the Americans had built only eight copies of Purple. The U.S. Army and Navy each had two in Washington, one had gone to the U.S. Navy at Cavite (Station Cast), and three were given to GCCS in Britain in 1941. No Purple machines were ever sent to Hawaii (Station Hypo).

As soon as the first Purple decrypts began to appear, it was decided by General George C. Marshall, the Army Chief of Staff; Captain Leigh Noyes, director of naval communications; and Rear Admiral Walter S. Anderson, of the Office of Naval Intelligence (ONI), that the codeword Magic would be used to cover the entire operation of decoding Japanese diplomatic systems. This included the Type A or Red machine, the Type B or Purple, the J series or TSU, and the PA system. Magic was to be a security classification higher even than Top Secret, with the aim of re-stricting distribution to as few people as possible.

However, Magic did not cover the Japanese naval code, then the Blue Book, because OP-20-G had never told the Army or indeed anyone else, including Roosevelt, that they had been breaking these codes since the 1920s. So once again the divided nature and unnecessary secrecy—which was in reality jealousy—of America's Sigint operations was to prove its ultimate downfall.

General Marshall and Admiral Harold R. Stark, Chief of Naval Operations, decided that within the Army, the secret of Magic would be shared only with Henry Stimson, Secretary of War (no longer concerned about reading other people's mail); Brigadier General Leonard T. Gerow, chief of the General Staff Operations Division; Brigadier General Sherman Miles, assistant chief of intelligence, and Colonal Rufus S. Bratton, chief of intelligence, Far Eastern Section.

In the Navy, Magic would only be seen by Secretary of the Navy Frank Knox; Rear Admiral Richmond K. Turner, chief of the War Plans Division; Captain Royal E. Ingersoll, Director of Naval Intelligence; Commander Arthur H. McCollum, head of the Far East Section at ONI; and Lieutenant Commander Egbert Watts, chief of the Navy's Japanese desk.

Including Marshall and Stark, a total of only eleven people were allowed to see Magic. Two names absent from the list were Roosevelt and Cordell Hull. On what basis Marshall and Stark believed they had the authority to deny such vital intelligence to their Commander-in-Chief and his Secretary of State has been discreetly glossed over in the postwar inquiries. And when we realize that Roosevelt also knew nothing at all about the Navy's ability to read Japanese naval codes, we can understand how badly he was served. However, after four months, Stimson and Knox concluded that it was illegal under the Constitution to continue denying the President Magic. So on 23 January 1941, Roosevelt and Hull began to receive Purple decrypts. The decision was a reluctant one, because neither Marshall nor Stark liked or trusted many of those who surrounded the President, considering them to be "long-haired New Dealers"[11] who would be unable to handle Magic properly. As a result, really important Magic material was frequently withheld from Roosevelt.

Roosevelt and Hull did not appreciate any of this, because both were too preoccupied with other matters of state. In addition, they lacked the expertise[12] to ask direct questions of either the Army or Navy codebreakers or to challenge the quality of material they were getting. Had they been able to do so, they might then have realized how internecine squabbling between SIS and OP-20-G and the contempt in which senior commanders held White House staff was fouling up the flow of vital intelligence to those who had to make the ultimate decision.

One of the greatest sources of mythology and misunderstanding about Pearl Harbor stems from the belief still held to this day by many people, as the result of inaccurately researched books and articles, that the Magic decrypts from the Purple machine enabled the Americans to read the Japanese operational plans for the attack. This is completely untrue. Neither the Purple machine nor the earlier Red machine was ever used by the Japanese Navy, Army, or Air Force. Both were solely used for sending diplomatic messages between the Foreign Ministry in Tokyo and its various missions around the world (although for a limited period, naval attachés did use the Red machine).

Diplomats may know that war is near and be told to deliver an ultimatum at a specific date and time. But they are never given any information about the military plans for commencing hostilities. Consequently Purple and Red decrypts never contained any operational orders at any time either before or after Pearl Harbor.

A further complication about the Magic decrypts was that when it was the Army's SIS monthly turn to handle the material, they had no knowledge of the naval operational signals in the JN-25 naval code that OP-20-G were also decrypting, so their analysis of the Magic material was incomplete. This state of affairs again highlights the dangers of a divided Sigint organization.

The success of the American codebreakers with Purple was not shared by GCCS, which although able to intercept the messages and to realize it was a totally new form of machine, could not break it. Because in those days there was no cooperation between Britain and America, GCCS was unaware of the progress the Americans had made against this new cryptograph until late in 1940.

As Europe drifted toward war with Germany during the last days of 1938, Britain hoped that America would come to its aid by taking over the responsibility for guarding the Pacific against Japan and sending in its fleet. But Roosevelt was in no position to act and had no more wish to provoke a conflict with Japan than did Britain. Japan exploited this political stalemate to its own advantage by consolidating her gains in China, while in Europe Hitler was about to call Britain's bluff for the third time as he turned his eyes toward Poland.

At the beginning of 1939, Roosevelt at last pushed his domestic problems onto the back burner, and the administration shifted its priority to America's long-neglected foreign policy.[13] Although Roosevelt was well aware of the dangers Japan posed, both he and his Chiefs of Staff agreed that the primary threat now was Germany. Consequently a new set of war plans—codenamed Rainbow—were drawn up. The most likely of these was Rainbow 2, which assumed America's going to war together with Britain and France against Germany to prevent further military expansion and protect Poland. In the Pacific, Roosevelt's planners accepted that they could do no more than buy time and might have to concede the loss of the Philippines. They still had insufficient naval forces to send a fleet to Singapore to reinforce the supposed fortress. But Roosevelt continued to tread carefully because the forces of isolationism at home were strong and vocal. And the President was well aware that in November 1940 he would have to run for re-election almost certainly on an anti-war ticket.

In May 1939, an event occurred that was to play the crucial role not only in the attack on Pearl Harbor but also in how the history of the event was subsequently recorded for posterity. It began when FECB and OP-20-G both intercepted a number of messages in the current Blue Book code, which revealed that the Japanese Navy was about to introduce a new code system to be called Kaigun Ango-sho D (Navy Code D). Subsequent messages indicated that the changeover to this new code would take place on 1 June 1939. But as so often happened with the Japanese, some naval units had not received their new codebooks by that date and were obliged to continue sending and receiving messages in the Blue Book code.

This overlap proved extremely valuable because it enabled Nave in Hong Kong and his counterpart at GCCS, Lieutenant Commander Malcolm "Bouncer" Burnett,[14] who was in charge of the expanding Japanese section, to compare cipher texts in the two systems and thus identify the principle of the new code,[15] which FECB called the Five-Figure Operational Code.

At OP-20-G, the new code was first called the AN Code, or the Five-Numeral Operations Code. Later, breaking the tradition of using color codenames, it was called Japanese Navy Code 25, or JN-25. As with the previous Japanese codes, the attack on the new code was led by Mrs. Driscoll and Ensign Prescott Currier, USN,[16] who soon discovered, in November 1939, that although JN-25 differed materially from the two earlier naval codes (the Red and Blue books), it was in fact a very old type of book code system[17] that had first been used by the American Army and Navy during the Spanish-American War in 1898 and by the British and French navies in World War I. The Americans had abandoned it in 1917 because Friedman considered it insecure.

A year later, in October 1940, Mrs. Driscoll and Ensign Currier had made sufficient progress to turn over the work of reconstruction to Lieutenant Bayley, USN, and Lieutenant Chisholm, USN, who would also instruct Lieutenant Lietwiler, USN, and Lieutenant Brotherhood, USN, in codebreaking at the same time.[18] Mrs. Driscoll and Ensign Currier then turned their attention to breaking the German naval Enigma that was baffling the U.S. Navy as much as Purple was GCCS. But again, because there was no cooperation between the two, OP-20-G were unaware of the progress GCCS had made.

Because the JN-25 code plays such a crucial part in the Pearl Harbor story, it is important to understand how it worked. Like every previous Japanese naval code, it was in two parts. The first was a dictionary of

78630	國ゝ	[Koku]	26865	黒色	[Koku]	47403	今夕(…時)	[Kon]

78630 国ゝ [Koku]	26865 黒色 [Koku]	47403 今夕(…時) [Kon]
17682 国体	75537 黒色火薬	74286 今週
51753 国法	53964 黒人	57642 今朝(…時)
82992 国威	31626	74484 今朝来
77100 国家	95259 臨	68259 今夜(…時)
60027 国権	10344 臨案	42504 今次(ノ)
01872 国際	73656 臨兵	30051 今次(ノ)行動
75117 国庫	97542 臨時ニ	52017 今次(ノ)作戦
59775 国交	53925	79701 今次(ノ)事件
63649 国交断絶ス	26571 穀物ゝ	04026 困
75858 国境	94854 穀物	99231 困苦(ス)
37404 国境線	84510 穀物	52602 困却(ス)
19059 国民	18603	74316 困却(ス)
83898 国民学校	59124 故	88935 困難(ス)
37467 国民政府	31905 駒 [Koma]	70449 困難ナリ(ル)
94704 国務	72267 細か物	49356 困憊(ス)
51468 国務大臣	27438 田ゝ	52884
93273 国内	31605 濃ゝ	87912 坤
47664 国幹	67230 米	06261 昆
88131 国丁	96627 込ゝ	84096 晋[晉]
11874 国力	17565 込人ゝ	31233 昏睡(ス)
97389 国債	85071 駒	77559 昏倒(ス)
81834 國際	92463 低包ゝ物	51264
15012 国際法	45015 交	75912 金
44373 国際関係	37281 難ゝ	96333 金剛石
56088 国際問題	84660 今 [Kon]	21660 慎
15342 国際科学	72186 今晩ゝ時	78219 恨事(ス)(ス)
97053 国際通信法	90540 今度	95730
42348 国際通信者	26157 今月	16317 根
35190 国地	69168 今月中	07980 根元
11913 国産	76455 今後	83811 根源
35892 国情	25068 今後ノ方針	05937 根幹
46617 国防中央	94365 今後ノ行動	59085 根気
25734 国防	79002 今後ノ電波	45750 根絶
72462 国運	42105 今後ノ状況	87543 根拠地
64290 国足	36720 今晩	17355 根拠地部隊
80997 国事	42252 今回ノ	65022 根拠地隊
15810 国情	79014 今期	71211 根拠地隊司令官
24501 国際(ス)(ス)	26388 今朝	50169 根本
09714	17370 今朝日	61482 根紙
57570	43626 今年	08757 根絶(ス)
94692 斜	78459 今年度	10419 根治(ス)
58134 黒	47868 今日	07932 婚
75693 平橋	15386 今日中	75489 混(ス)
47430 平褐色	62751 今較	11055 (ト)混同(ス)

91599 ゛	43197 ゜	73902 ノ	82410 ヲ

Code	Word		Code	Word		Code	Word	
92940	(ト)混合[3]	[Kon]	15072	蠶		20817		[Kono]
60981	混淆[3]		09240	粉	[Kona]	00048		
35925	混入[3]		71064	粉微塵[...]		62583		
03849	混亂[3]		90933	此方(コナタ)		15777	近衞	
76131	混載[3]		00078	捏[3]		36054		
90402	混成[3]		18003			05091	好[3]	
88557	混戰		68106	此(ノ)	[Kono]	47940	好マレ[3]	
55485	(ト)混信[3]		95319	此ノ間		80652	体[3]	[Kora]
22134	(ト)混信其レ[3]		19005	此ノ場合		07143	闢[3]	
15684	混雜[3]		47946	此ノ分(ニテ)		66003		
73389	混燒爐		80580	此ノ儀		38028	之	[Kore]
19854	混池[...]		00006	此ノ枝		99189	之ヲ	
64446	混用[3]		44745	此ノ項		72330	之ヲ為	
35958	混部[3]		03072	此ノ方面		28392	之ニ	
72381			73443	此ノ程		09678	之ニ	
20682	痕		31788	此ノ外		32427	之ニ反[3]	
46137	痕跡[...]		95184	此ノ附近		49515	之ニ關シ[X××]	
74898	紺		10590	此ノ限ニ在ラズ[ザル]		85233	之ニ關[X××]	
29127	紺色		74445	此ノ件		30258	之ニ對[X××]	
82821	紺青		00597	此ノ期間		24135	之ニ要[X××]	
23499	棍		98211	此ノ様		07389	之ヲ	
47742	渾		55683	此ノ場合		66600	之ヲ歐退[3]	
98955	渾身		85838	此ノ儘		12219	之ヲ歐離[3]	
67830	渾池[...]		61137	此ノ旨		81024	之ヲ攻撃[3]	
29025	壼		18204	此ノ旨…薄達(セリ)		23940	之ヲ行[3]	
82386	壺		39741	此ノ旨…電報(セリ)		47109	之ヲ變スルモ	
65268	綑		76083	此ノ旨取敢ズ		62031	之ヲ實施[3]	
34050	綑綑[3]		46254	此ノ趣		22428	之ト	
52902	綑		11532	此ノ際		68433	之ニヨリ	
62844	綑		72834	此ノ際成ルベク		80748	有之[3]	
00810	綑		03915	此ノ際至急		09963	無之[3××]	
79722	魂		24204	此ノ針路		79674	之等	
51054	残骸[...]		57705	此ノ速力		30987	之ヲ歐比[3]	
98589	艫		74736	此ノ楓		85149	之ヲ殲滅[3]	
70350	艫		12759	此ノ度		38001	是	
30006	舩輪		50445	此ノ對勢		09294	是ヲ	
84411	懇		06930	此ノ點		67926	是ニヨリ	
00786	懇		45861	此ノ點		88032	是ニヨリ先	
48291	懇談[3]		29400	此ノ時		34914	是応	
90714	懇泣		57471	此ノ上		07761	是等	
78828	懇願[3]		96633	此ノ事件		49776		
93270	懇願[3]		46335	此ノ事情		74832	樹(ニ)	
49695	懇切[3]		65364	此ノ狀況		33093	樹[3]	
23166	懇篤[3]		89943	此ノ情勢		56022	檻[3]	
35823			22200	此等		70869	檻[3]	

96699	アリ	68520	ナレ	48561	一依リ	34152	セリ

(107)

(呂貳ノ三)　　　072

	91	50	24	73	56	39	02	15	44	81	54	70
16	14929	35628	80562	00147	88137	93504	21580	58665	97820	17326	56653	01076
85	23183	63454	07541	65826	38803	42393	94804	78478	04047	33917	36748	52211
32	36831	78346	37569	43223	01494	14713	46236	32552	58667	91712	08545	94676
17	71819	48704	11557	81078	90567	25006	84864	67611	40964	47620	97947	17795
98	61324	58431	96434	33724	57582	75984	54976	16316	30250	52377	49357	06013
05	44635	95883	21137	67209	29321	98312	05937	89563	74978	00156	87674	34542
33	53252	04722	58423	82158	76806	49301	39186	77288	20120	72090	15782	63648
95	97453	22039	61220	56471	41787	34328	78153	46194	85468	25594	78566	25839
07	84961	70850	44526	18789	60024	54267	10645	09150	62621	65227	16912	93190
52	02843	83298	74802	03172	15648	26854	02163	92218	13055	84914	64117	11285
46	85513	62153	95276	31374	06282	80618	63245	36922	86983	45706	08607	71953
11	90492	41881	52291	99366	70718	61941	88117	12267	73010	19542	88902	40963
04	13767	23648	72023	48762	52050	12805	49358	28994	07034	37760	20805	56921
72	27364	30867	87101	28450	32180	68543	93360	58470	69311	98487	38189	89513
69	09317	52569	19755	76921	24866	45705	27023	69809	22984	59410	76035	64610

33,333 words and phrases, each of which was given a five-figure number. The second was an additive table book comprising random five-figure number groups. Each page of the additive table was numbered, and so too were the columns of numbers, both across the top and down the side, so that the location of the additive groups being used could be identified. Because the additive tables were changed every six months, OP-20-G gave the code a suffix so that the second edition, introduced on 1 December 1939, was known as JN-25b, the third, on 1 June 1940, JN-25c, and so on. But the principle of the code and its basic dictionary remained unchanged throughout the war to 1945.

To encode a message, the plain text was converted into five-figure groups using the dictionary (pages 84–85). A starting place in the current additive table was then chosen. The first random group was added to the first five-figure group using the Fibonacci system, or Chinese arithmetic, where numbers greater than 9 are not carried forward. Then the next five-figure group is added to the next additive group in the table, working down each column in turn and across the page from left to right.

To decode a JN-25 message, the reverse procedure was used. The recipient looked up the relevant place in the additive table, subtracted the five-figure number from the enciphered group, and thus exposed the basic code number, which could then be looked up in the reverse order part of the dictionary.

Nave and Burnett agreed that the best way to break JN-25 was through the additive table. The method by which additive tables are penetrated is complex and still considered highly secret by some agencies. Nevertheless, since JN-25 is the vital key in understanding the Pearl Harbor story, it is essential to include a very simplified account of how this is done.

Additive tables for JN-25 came in books of 100 pages, and a typical page is shown on page 86.[19] There were fifteen vertical and twelve horizontal columns of five-figure groups, giving 180 groups per page, or 18,000 per book. On the face of it, that sounds like a large number of groups, but in fact is not when traffic volumes start to rise sharply, as happens when a huge navy is preparing for war around the Pacific Ocean. The next problem is that the work of code clerks is extremely boring and repetitive, requiring them to cope with piles of messages, each of which with JN-25 had to be laboriously hand-encoded word by word, requiring endless additions and subtractions. Add to that the unsocial hours code clerks work and the frustrations caused by indecipherable groups being received due to poor radio reception, and it is not hard to see how boredom intervenes.

Human nature being what it is, clerks soon tire of randomly searching through the additive table book and start going back to the same pages over and over again because it makes life easier for them to use familiar groups.[20] In order for the recipient to decode a JN-25 message, the page number and starting point in the additive table have to be sent in plain language at the start of the message; the page we show is 072. For simplicity we will assume the starting point chosen for one message is the first group at the top left-hand corner (14929), which is identified as 9116. So the prefix would read 0729116, while for the next message the clerk chooses a point midway across the same page (21580) which is identified as 0216, so that message's prefix would be 0720216.

The codebreaker looks for all messages that have used the same page prefix (072) and then those using the same starting point—9116 and 0216—and sorts these out into matching piles. When the codebreaker has accumulated enough messages bearing the same prefix, he knows that the five-figure groups in each message have used the same portion of the additive table. The codebreaker then looks for cribs that give him an insight into the plain text, usually starting with the stereotyped flowery introductions so beloved by the Japanese.

If the codebreaker believes the first groups in different messages represent the phrase "We have the honor" or "It is reported that," then he knows that, although the coded totals are different, they represent the same words in the basic code dictionary and that the difference between them is the additive table group. By calculating this difference in the various messages, the codebreaker exposes the additive groups on various pages of the tables, which he can recognize in future messages, and at the same time starts building up the basic dictionary of words and phrases.

Fortunately, as war drew nearer, the British government had relaxed financial controls, and GCCS at Bletchley Park[21] were able to recruit large numbers of clerks who laboriously started to reconstruct the JN-25 additive tables—a task that was later taken over by punched card systems, which were admirably suited to matching up additive group differences at great speed. JN-25 was therefore not a difficult code to break. As Nave described it: "It was a tedious one but once GCCS had deployed enough manpower the dictionary was built up at a terrific rate because, oddly enough, it was not a hatted book, as the previous [Blue Book] code had been, but a simple alphabetical one. This was an unexpected bonus because it meant, for example, if you could identify a date in January and another in September you could fill in the rest of the year without difficulty."

By the autumn of 1939, GCCS, which had moved to its wartime home at Bletchley Park some fifty miles north of London, had reconstructed the JN-25 codebook, and Commander Burnett flew out to FECB to give Nave the reconstructed dictionary and current keys. Thereafter, JN-25 offered no problems, and FECB/GCCS were able to reconstruct the six monthly key table changes without difficulty. "For the first three or four weeks into the new table change," recalls Nave, "there was a slight delay, but we soon overcame this. As with all Japanese codes, JN-25 started off very simply and only later did the Japanese try and make it more complicated, by which time GCCS had completely mastered it."

So by the end of 1939, GCCS and FECB could read JN-25, used between Navy headquarters in Tokyo and all their ships and shore stations; the naval attaché traffic, which was still using the Red machine; the Commander-in-Chief's code; and several other low-grade codes, such as the Appointments Code, which contained little of importance.

CHAPTER 5

The Nail in the Horse's Shoe

ON 1 SEPTEMBER 1939, ignoring all ultimatums and pleas for peace, Hitler's armies smashed their way into Poland. Two days later, Europe was at war, and within less than twenty-four hours the British liner *Athenia*,[1] full of refugees fleeing to the safety of America, had been torpedoed and sunk by a German U-boat, with terrible loss of life.

War came as no surprise to Roosevelt, who throughout 1939 had been unsuccessfully trying to get Congress to repeal the Neutrality Act in order to be able to help Britain and France with military supplies. But isolationism was still a powerful force, and the President had to keep his eye on the election the following year. Nevertheless, secret links with Britain were beginning to be forged. During the state visit[2] of King George VI and Queen Elizabeth to Washington in June, Roosevelt felt sufficiently secure to privately assure the King that America's neutrality would not stop it from sending naval patrols far out into the Atlantic if war with Germany began.

One of the first acts of British Prime Minister Neville Chamberlain was to bring Churchill back from his long political isolation during the interwar years and appoint him First Sea Lord of the Admiralty. Churchill immediately began to cultivate a direct personal friendship with Roosevelt.

In 1939, Churchill was sixty-five, a time when most men are thinking of retirement. He had had a disastrous political career, constantly frustrated by such failures as the Dardanelles expedition of 1915, where the loss of life was to play heavily on his memory throughout the next war, and his equally disastrous adherence to the gold standard as Chancellor of the Exchequer. Always the opportunist throughout the interwar years, Churchill changed political sides whenever he saw an opportunity to advance his career. Unable to find a genuine political role, he set himself up as the voice of doom, warning Parliament and the nation of Britain's lack of defenses. Mythology and postwar hubris have created the impression that Churchill became Britain's Prime Minister because of popular appeal. This is not so. Churchill was not voted into office at an election but became leader[3] only when Chamberlain yielded the premiership after a series of military reverses.

Churchill and Roosevelt were never great friends, and prior to 1941 had only once met briefly in 1918 when Roosevelt thought him extremely rude. Churchill was desperate to ingratiate himself with the American President, but Roosevelt was prevented from helping Britain directly by the Neutrality Act and, in any case, saw through Churchill's flowery phrases and had no intention of being led up some imperialist garden path by this cunning politician. Despite his public warmth before the cameras, FDR never fully trusted Churchill and always carefully distanced himself from his plans. Some of Roosevelt's advisers felt much the same. Joseph Kennedy, American ambassador to London, openly predicted Britain's defeat, while Sumner Welles found Churchill's continual bombast distasteful and described him to Roosevelt as a "drunk and a windbag."[4]

Churchill also had to contend with a strong anti-war cabal[5] behind his back that included a number of very high-ranking people who believed that, as Poland had fallen to the Germans, there was no point in continuing the war and that peace should be made with Hitler, thus giving him a free hand to attack Russia, since the British upper classes disliked communism as much as did the Nazis. The leaders of this group were Lord Halifax and R. A. Butler, who put their ideas to Kennedy in London (who forwarded them to Roosevelt) and also sent secret messages via Sweden to the Germans, but never received any firm proposals back from Hitler. Churchill was furious when he found out about this and told Halifax and Butler that if they did not stop all such discussions he would have them imprisoned as traitors. The whole affair was most embarrassing for Churchill, because Roosevelt was receiving two totally divergent views from London at a time when Churchill had only just become Prime Minister.

From the moment Churchill took office, he had but one aim, and that was to bring America into the war against Germany at any price. Churchill made no secret of this to his close advisers, for he knew that without America's direct involvement Britain could not defeat the Nazis. For this he needed Roosevelt's friendship and in the first year of the war continually bombarded the President with a stream of messages, sometimes cajoling and other times almost threatening in order to get his way.

But Roosevelt was unmoved, and when eventually he agreed to send Britain fifty aging destroyers to help bolster the Atlantic convoys (bypassing Congress to do so), he extracted as his price eight American bases to be established on British sovereign territory, causing Churchill to complain: "How am I going to explain all this to the British people?[6] They will say Americans are taking our property." In the end the deal soured because the destroyers were so old as to be almost unseaworthy.[7]

Churchill quickly realized that although Roosevelt had for many years neglected foreign policy, this did not mean that he would dance to Churchill's tune to save the British Empire. To "drag America into the war" it would be necessary to shock the country in a manner that would totally overwhelm the isolationists. Immediately after Pearl Harbor he said to Alan Brooke, "Oh, that's the way we talked to her [America] while we were wooing her. Now that she's in the harem [war], we talk to her differently."[8]

The war in Europe had scarcely touched the Far East except to increase the importance of countries like Malaya as a primary source of supply for Britain's essential raw materials. During 1939, it was decided that FECB was too vulnerable in Hong Kong and should move down to Singapore, while retaining the powerful intercept station on Stonecutters Island, augmented by another one at Singapore. The transfer took some time, and Nave stayed on in Hong Kong until August 1939 before going to Singapore. As the last days of peace trickled away, Nave took time off from his increasingly arduous duties and on 2 September 1939 was married in Singapore Cathedral to Helena Gray, who had been a nursing sister at Queen Mary's Hospital in Hong Kong.

Then he was back to work at FECB, which had set up its new offices in very cramped conditions in the giant naval base on the northeast corner of Singapore Island. The administrative head of FECB in 1939 was Captain F. J. Wylie, who was officially known as Chief of Intelligence Staff (COIS). But as this was a secret title, he was publicly known as Captain on Staff (COS) HMS *Sultan,* in order to conceal his duties. (Messages from FECB used this prefix.) FECB was also more affectionately known as the Loony Bin,[9] and someone pinned up a notice reading, "You do not have to be mad to do this work, but it helps."

In addition to Nave[10] and Wylie were Paymaster Captain Purvis Shaw (who had originally set up FECB in Hong Kong), Lieutenant Commander W. W. Mortimer, RNR, Lieutenant Commander Colgrave, and Paymaster

Lieutenant Commanders "Bouncer" Burnett (who had brought out the JN-25 solution from Bletchley Park), Barham, Merry, and Foreman. There were also two civilian clerks named Bennett and Habbitch, and a number of temporary women assistants (TWA's) working the Hollerith tabulating machines who were the wives of Burnett, Barham, Merry, Colgrave, Mortimer, Bennett, and Habbitch. At this stage, it was still a very small affair, with all the staff living in a group of bungalows on the naval base.

ONCE THE messages arrived at Bletchley Park from FECB, they went straight to the naval section in Huts 8 and 4[11] under the control of Frank L. Birch,[12] who had joined GCCS on 6 September 1939. Like so many codebreakers, Birch was a colorful and somewhat eccentric character who had worked in Room 40 during World War I (see Chapter 1) and been a Fellow of King's College, Cambridge, from 1915 to 1934. He then left Cambridge to become an actor and theatrical director and was said to spend every Christmas vacation playing the leading woman's role, the Dame, in provincial pantomime.

Unlike the GCCS sections handling Army and Air Force codebreaking in Huts 6 and 3 and the Purple diplomatic intercepts, the naval section in Huts 8 and 4 remained a separate unit within Bletchley Park. Analysis of information from decoded Army and Air Force Enigma signals was sent directly by Bletchley Park via special liaison units (SLU's) to selected field commanders at operational units both in Britain and around the world, while Purple decrypts went to the Foreign Office.

But all decoded naval signals from Hut 4 went only to the Operational Intelligence Centre (OIC) at the Admiralty in London. The OIC had been established in June 1937, with Paymaster Lieutenant Commander Norman Denning as its head, and together with the Director of Naval Intelligence (DNI), Rear Admiral (later Admiral) J. H. Godfrey, they alone decided how the material from Frank Birch's Hut 4 should be used and distributed and whether any of the information would be shared with the other two services. So the raw JN-25 material was seen by very few people working in Huts 8 and 4, and a select few at the OIC who knew the source of the information. Bletchley Park worked in watertight compartments, with codebreaking information available only on a "need to know" basis, so that someone working on Army signals in Hut 3 would have no idea of what was being done next door in Hut 4. In view of all these restrictions on handling JN-25, it is hardly surprising that so few firsthand accounts exist today.

One person who saw the raw decrypts of all important Japanese naval signals—particularly JN-25—was Churchill, no matter where he might be, and the decision to pass on this information in either its raw or paraphrased form to the Americans was a matter that he alone decided. The whole question of how much codebreaking information Churchill permitted either GCCS or FECB to share with the Americans or the Dutch remains an extremely sensitive issue. During 1941, there were numerous secret meetings in Singapore and later in Washington between representatives from Britain, America, Holland, Australia, and New Zealand. One of these, known as the ADB Conversations,[13] took place in April, and the list of delegates is shown in Appendix 4. The meeting resulted in a joint basic war plan—called ABC-1—which stated that the defeat of Germany was the primary strategic objective. But the Americans would not accept any obligation to enter the war in the Far East or specify any circumstances under which they might do so. In the end, the American delegation refused to ratify the ADB resolutions.

The minutes of the meeting also show that, at the time, Royal Navy liaison officers were serving on the USS *West Virginia, Boise,* and *Sterrett,*[14] while the U.S. Navy and Army had observers in Singapore, as did the Dutch, who in turn had an observer stationed in Manila. In 1941, the U.S. Army's liaison officer at FECB was Colonel F. C. Brink,[15] the U.S. Navy's was Captain John M. Creighton,[16] while Lieutenant Lietwiler (who had worked on JN-25 with Mrs. Driscoll) and Commander Rudy Fabian, both codebreakers at OP-20-G, also visited FECB at various times.

But the fact that American liaison officers and observers were stationed in Singapore did not automatically mean that they were able to see everything that was being done by the codebreakers. In fact, all accounts suggest they had no access to the codebreaking sections at all. Throughout 1941 the British government continued to warn that "At the present stage when the United States are not at war their officials should be treated frankly. . . . [but] . . . future operations will not be disclosed . . . [and] . . . information from most secret sources should not be passed to the United States observers but . . . through FECB."[17]

As a result the Americans in Singapore were certainly unaware until after Pearl Harbor that the British had broken JN-25. Equally, when Burnett visited Station Cast at Cavite, he said nothing about British codebreaking achievements, as one American observer recalls:

> There was a visitor from GCCS Singapore, a RN Lieutenant Commander whose first name was Malcolm. I do not know what his peace offering was or even if he had one, but I do remember he was greatly impressed with what we were doing in the way of cryptanalysis at the time. We received little if anything from the British in Singapore. . . .

I am reasonably certain we would have seen anything produced by
the British out of JN-25 up to the [out]break of hostilities. There was
not a free exchange of material between the US, the British, and the
Dutch. . . . [we] read nothing out of JN-25 up to the outbreak of hostilities.[18]

Burnett returned to Singapore distinctly unimpressed by the work
being done at Cavite and told Nave that they were only breaking the
Appointments Code, which was a low-grade system containing no information of any operational value and had been read by FECB for a long
time, and that they were also carrying out direction-finding work on the
movements of Japanese ships. As far as JN-25 was concerned, Burnett
claimed that they appeared to show no interest in it, which is certainly
quite contrary to subsequent American accounts, which claim that Cavite was working on JN-25 and had achieved some limited success. It
seems both sides were not being totally open with each other.

Mortimer recalls [19] that all the intelligence information he sent back to
London was clearly marked for repetition to CINCPAC, as authorized by
the Director of Naval Intelligence (DNI) at the Admiralty. Only after the
war Mortimer discovered that CINCPAC had never received any of this
information,[20] which explains why he was not allowed to give evidence
to the congressional Pearl Harbor inquiry in 1945. It would have needed
someone very senior to veto the DNI's order to share this intelligence
with the Americans.

The phony war continued, and on 2 April 1940, Chamberlain, review-
ing the progress of the war, assured Parliament that Allied strategy was
strangling the German economy [21] and the trade agreements made between Britain and Norway, Sweden, Iceland, Belgium, Holland, and Den-
mark, would ensure they no longer supplied Germany with essential raw
materials for the Nazi war machine. Indeed, as he put it so naively,
"Hitler had missed the bus." But this optimism was rudely shattered on
10 May, when German armored columns rolled through Holland, Belgium, and France, shattering everything in their path. In less than a
month the remnants of the British Army, having abandoned their guns
and equipment, were forced into an ignominious evacuation from the
Dunkirk beaches.

In Washington, Roosevelt did his best to help Churchill, who daily
cabled him with urgent demands for weaponry and for the U.S. Navy to
send a strong force of warships to Singapore to deter the Japanese from
any pre-emptive action. But Roosevelt had his eye on the forthcoming
November elections, when, in order to get re-elected for an unprece-

dented third term, he needed to distance himself from the European war. Already his rival for the White House, Republican Wendell Willkie, was accusing him of dragging America into Churchill's war.

However, the fall of Paris on 14 June was enough to shock Congress into approving vast budgetary increases[22] for naval expenditure, providing eleven new battleships, eleven new *Essex*-class aircraft carriers, fifty new cruisers, and a hundred new destroyers. But they took time to build, and it would be several years before the U.S. Navy could hope to enjoy supremacy throughout the Pacific.

In Tokyo, the Japanese watched and waited. The success of Hitler's thrust through Europe had demonstrated how a sudden surprise attack could defeat a far more powerful enemy, and the defeat of the Royal Navy during the Norwegian campaign revealed that perhaps it was not as invincible as it seemed. The Germans turned to Admiral Mitsumasa Yonai's government, offering a treaty that would enable them to exploit the weakness of the British and the Dutch in the Far East and give them access to the much-needed supplies of oil upon which the entire future military strategy of Japan depended. The basis for the proposed Tripartite Pact was that Germany would invade Britain, and later Russia; Italy would defeat the British in the Mediterranean; and Japan would attack Singapore.

Admiral Yamamoto had been moved from his post as Vice Minister of the Navy to the most prestigious post of all, C-in-C of the Imperial Japanese Combined Fleet. But neither Yonai nor Yamamoto had any wish to go to war with either Britain or America. Yamamoto was unhappy about an attack on Singapore, because it would mean splitting his fleet against the Royal Navy and the U.S. Navy. The very least he would need was a promise from the Germans that they could first capture the Suez Canal and thus prevent British naval reinforcements from reaching Singapore quickly.

On 27 September 1940, Japan signed the Tripartite Pact in Berlin. Now the war in Europe was directly linked to the Far East, because the three nations agreed to go to war against any nation, not then a participant in the European war or the long-running Sino-Japanese conflict, which attacked one of the signatories. Although the pact gave Roosevelt the excuse he needed to support Britain openly and by so doing increase the chance of conflict with Germany, he still had to tread cautiously. With opinion polls sagging on 30 October, Roosevelt took his election campaign into the heartland of Boston isolationists and told his audience, "I have said this before, but I shall say it again and again and again: Your boys are not going to be sent to any foreign wars."[23] Less than a week later, Roosevelt trounced Willkie and swept back into the White House with a majority of five million votes. In London, Churchill breathed a sigh of relief.

Even before the election, Roosevelt had embarked on a series of measures that deliberately tightened the economic stranglehold on Japan. On 26 January 1940, the America-Japanese treaty lapsed, and during the rest of the year a number of executive orders banned the shipment of aviation gasoline, scrap metal, and machine tools to Japan. On 9 October, America ceased subsidizing wheat shipped to the Far East. These measures continued into 1941. On 29 May 1941, the President ordered a ban on all further exports of raw materials from the Philippines to Japan, and on 25 July, as a result of Japan's seizure of French Indo-China (following the French armistice with Germany), America, Britain, and Holland together froze all Japanese assets and ceased trading with her.

Churchill naturally encouraged the President in all these moves, as he saw them bringing America closer to war, and certainly Roosevelt embarked on this strategy with the full knowledge that either Japan would have to abandon her grandiose expansion plans throughout the Far East or go to war to break out of his deliberate policy of economic encirclement.

The defense of the Far East had always been predicated on the assumption that an adequate British fleet would arrive at Singapore within seventy days of war with Japan. At the end of July 1940, while the Battle of Britain raged overhead, Churchill asked his Chiefs of Staff, Air Marshal Sir Cyril Newall, Admiral Sir Dudley Pound, and General Sir John Dill, to report on the future defense possibilities of Singapore, Hong Kong, Malaya, and the Dutch East Indies.

In March 1937,[24] the Chiefs of Staff had calculated that the longest period the defenders of Singapore could hold out, plus the time required for a fleet to sail from Britain around the Cape of Good Hope to Singapore, was seventy days. This optimistically assumed that Britain would not be at war with Germany and thus could spare ten battleships and two battle cruisers, which with their attendant escorts plus the Royal Navy's China Station ships would be more than a match for Japan's fleet of only nine battleships.

During the prewar years, the governments of Australia and New Zealand had never had much faith in this plan and had continually pressed for a Far East battle fleet to be permanently stationed at Singapore as a deterrent to any Japanese aggression. But despite a huge exchange of reports and letters, the Admiralty refused to be drawn into any firm commitment. By November 1938, the earlier plan had been considerably diluted, and the Australian High Commissioner was told that seven capital ships would be sent to Singapore in the event of war with Japan.

In London, there had been a division of opinion between the Foreign Office, which wanted a strong British naval presence in the Far East, and the Admiralty, which refused to commit itself to such an arrangement when it seemed likely the primary task would be protecting the nation's supply routes in home waters against the German Navy. On 10 February 1939, the Japanese took over without a struggle the island of Hainan, owned by China, 300 miles south of Hong Kong, and in June seized the Spratly Islands, 775 miles northeast of Singapore. Both the Admiralty and the Australians had seen this as establishing a steppingstone for future expansion down toward the oil fields of the Dutch East Indies, which were quite plainly Japan's primary strategic objective.

In the summer of 1939, the Australians had held several high-level meetings in London to try and establish whether the Admiralty could still guarantee a fleet at Singapore within seventy days, only to find that the figure had increased to ninety days. When war in Europe broke out in September 1939, it soon became clear that the majority of the Royal Navy's capital ships would be required in home waters to defend the convoy routes. While at first it could be assumed they would be augmented by the French fleet, after the fall of France in June 1940 this possibility vanished. In the meantime, both Australia and New Zealand were sending more troops to fight in North Africa, leaving their own countries increasingly exposed to the threat of attack from Japan, which had now established bases in French Indo-China. They therefore again pressed Churchill for a firm commitment to the defense of Singapore and the Far East. Accordingly, Churchill asked his Chiefs of Staff for a new assessment.

The Chiefs of Staff asked the governor of Singapore, Sir Shenton Thomas, who happened to be in London on leave, for his views. He put forward a number of proposals of his own for improving the defense of Singapore and Malaya. The final report of the Chiefs of Staff was considered by the War Cabinet on 8 August 1940.

Consisting of eighty-seven detailed paragraphs, it made very gloomy reading. It flatly stated that Britain was not in a position to resort to war if Japan attacked either French Indo-China or Siam, and the only course of action was to try and buy time with a deliberate policy of appeasement. The report also made it quite clear that no reinforcements could be spared from the European theater of war, that the Royal Navy could not produce a Far East fleet, and that Hong Kong, Malaya, Singapore, and the Dutch East Indies were all indefensible in the face of a Japanese attack.

Churchill considered the report so pessimistic[25] that he decided not to have his War Cabinet discuss it or to send copies to the Australian and New Zealand governments. He did agree that, in great secrecy, a copy should be sent to Air Chief Marshal Sir Robert Brooke-Popham, C-in-C Far East, at his headquarters in Singapore, but that it should not be seen by the governor or anyone else. Accordingly, the Foreign Office were asked to arrange for a copy to be sent by special courier to Brooke-Popham. Although Shenton Thomas could have taken the report back with him by flying boat, it was instead sent by sea mail from Liverpool in late September.

In the meantime, another seemingly unconnected piece of the jigsaw puzzle had fallen into place with the arrival in the South Atlantic of the first German surface raider. Originally the 7,862-ton *Goldenfels,* the vessel had been taken over by the German Navy on 19 December 1939 and renamed *Atlantis,*[26] or *Ship 16* (also known to the Royal Navy as Raider C), and was commanded by Captain Bernhard Rogge with his first officer Lieutenant Ulrich Mohr.

After delays due to bad weather and heavy icing around the port of Kiel, the *Atlantis* finally sailed disguised as a Norwegian freighter and then changed her identity to that of the Russian fleet auxiliary cruiser *Kim,* flying the hammer and sickle. By late April 1940, the *Atlantis,* now disguised as the Japanese steamer *Kasii Maru,* had reached the South Atlantic and on 3 May sank her first victim, the 6,199-ton British ship *Scientist.* A week later, on 10 May, it laid ninety-two mines twenty-six miles off Cape Aghulas on the South African coast east of Capetown in the main shipping lane. *Atlantis* then sailed on into the Indian Ocean and on 11 July stopped and boarded the 7,506-ton *City of Baghdad.* Among the documents found on board was a copy of the current British Allied Merchant Shipping code (BAMS) and sets of Admiralty sailing instructions to Allied merchant vessels with their call signs. The *Atlantis*'s radio operator, Lieutenant Adolf Wenzel, and his assistant, Heinrich Wesemann (the latter having spent two years with the German Navy's codebreaking department), then began reconstructing the BAMS code.

Unfortunately, despite the advances in machine cryptography (see Appendix 8), even in late 1940, over a year into the war, the Royal Navy and the British merchant navy were still using simple tabular book codes unchanged from World War I. The system was in two parts, with a dictionary of phrases, each with a five-digit group of numbers to which was added or subtracted a five-digit superencipherment group from a set of additive tables that were changed at regular intervals. Although the superencipherment table taken from the *City of Baghdad* was not the current one, there were enough older tables to enable Wesemann to partially reconstruct the system. He then signaled the German Navy's codebreaking section at B-Dienst in Berlin, which had been reading all British naval codes[27] without difficulty since the beginning of the war and was able to quickly radio back to Wesemann in the Indian Ocean the missing parts of the code.

As a result, Rogge was now able to read messages[28] passing to and from other British merchant ships in the area, identify them from their call signs, and anticipate their future movements. He took great pleasure in telling his prisoners which ship they would intercept the next day.[29] On 10 September, using this technique, Rogge intercepted and captured the *Benarty,* from which he recovered further cryptographic material. Wenzel and Wesemann also became adept at canceling the distress calls sent out by ships they intercepted, which caused endless confusion with the British naval authorities and greatly delayed the hunt for the raider by the Royal Navy.

By this time, Rogge had sailed more than 23,000 miles and accumulated 327 prisoners, whom he was forced to hold in very cramped conditions, placing a severe strain, beyond the problem of feeding them, on the operating efficiency of his ship. So Rogge was anxious to secure a prize vessel in which to send his prisoners to Japan. The following month, November, he seized two Norwegian tankers, the 6,748-ton *Teddy* on 8 November and the *Ole Jacob* on 9 November, laden with 10,000 tons of aviation gasoline. Rogge sank the *Teddy,* which was carrying fuel oil, but kept the *Ole Jacob* as a prize to transport some of his prisoners to Japan,[30] where he intended to barter the aviation fuel for diesel oil for his own ship.

Before this happened, however, Rogge was able to intercept another vessel. On the morning of 11 November 1940, Rogge placed the *Atlantis* off the Nicobar Islands and waited for the 7,528-ton Blue Funnel steamer *Automedon.* At about 7 A.M., the two ships sighted each other, but as the *Atlantis* was disguised as a Dutch vessel[31] with some of the crew on deck dressed as women hanging out washing, Rogge was able to close with the *Automedon* without arousing suspicion. By 8:20 A.M., the two vessels were on a parallel course some 350 yards apart, when *Atlantis* suddenly increased speed, identified herself, fired a shot across the *Automedon*'s bows, and ordered her to stop. The *Automedon* immediately started to transmit a "Raider sighted" distress call, intercepted by *Atlantis,* which ran up a string of flags in the international code ordering *Automedon* to stop using her radio. However, before these could be decoded, *Atlantis* opened fire again, aiming at the bridge to silence the radio. But because of *Automedon*'s radio room was sited in the aft portion of the ship, and as it continued to transmit, the *Atlantis* fired a total of twenty-eight rounds from her 5.9-inch guns at the *Automedon* until the emergency generator was destroyed and the radio finally silenced.

Because of the ferocity of the attack, Captain McEwen, two officers, and a steward on the bridge were killed. Also on the bridge at the time of the attack was Captain M. F. L. Evans, a merchant navy master who on this voyage was acting as a special Admiralty courier in charge of the *Automedon*'s secret mail. Evans was under strict instructions that at the first sign of any danger he was to throw overboard certain items of highly secret mail which were packed in heavily weighted canvas bags. But the first shell to hit the bridge knocked Evans unconscious. By the time he recovered, the German boarding party led by Mohr was already in control and had blown open the master's safe and the ship's strongroom.

Mohr, who had carried out many similar raids on captured ships and read and spoke English fluently, thus was able to seize important and confidential documents without delay before sinking the vessel. In the case of the *Automedon,* his haul was an incredible treasure trove of secrets,[32] far beyond his wildest expectations. First of all there were all the usual ship's confidential papers, including another copy of the BAMS code and current superencipherment tables. Then there was $6 million worth of new Straits currency fresh from the printers in England. Next, the entire secret mail for Far Eastern Command, Singapore, which included sets of new Royal Navy fleet codes and new sets of BAMS codes valid from 1 January 1941. Some of the other sixty sealed packages contained secret mail from MI6 to their stations in Singapore, Hong Kong, Shanghai, and Tokyo, which included summaries of the latest intelligence reports of Japanese military and political activities.

But in one green Foreign Office canvas bag, heavily weighted, sealed, and marked "Safe Hand—British Master Only," was an envelope addressed to the C-in-C Far East, Singapore. And when Mohr opened this, he found inside the copy of the secret Chiefs of Staff report approved by the War Cabinet on 5 August and destined for Brooke-Popham.

Immediately recognizing the importance of this and the other documents, Rogge decided to suspend his raiding operations and get to Japan as fast as possible. Having sunk the *Automedon,* he transferred the prisoners and mail to the *Ole Jacob,* which sailed without delay for Japan, arriving at Kobe on 4 December. The prisoners were taken off at night to avoid their being seen by British MI6 agents (who kept the movements of German vessels in Japanese ports under constant surveillance), and were transferred to the German liner *Scharnhorst.*

The mail from the *Automedon* reached the German Embassy in Tokyo on 5 December, where Admiral Wenneker photographed the most important items, including the Chiefs of Staff report, before sending the originals off to Berlin in the custody of a German naval officer, Paul Kamenz, who crossed to Vladivostok and then traveled on across Russia, via Moscow, by train.

On 7 December, Wenneker sent a long four-part cipher telegram[33] to naval headquarters in Berlin summarizing the main parts of the Chiefs of Staff report. For this he used an Enigma cryptograph, but because the message went by Postal Telegraph across the Soviet Union, it could not be intercepted by British codebreakers at GCCS located at Bletchley Park. Wenneker's summary was immediately shown to Hitler, who scrawled in the margin, "This is of the utmost importance," and ordered that a copy be given to Captain Yokoi, the Japanese naval attaché in Berlin.

This was done on 12 December, whereupon Yokoi sent his own shortened version back to Tokyo. Yokoi's message was enciphered on his cryptograph known to the Japanese as 97-Shiki In-ji-ki san Gata (and to the Americans as Coral). Although his message went by direct beam radio and was therefore intercepted,[34] its contents could not be read because U.S. Navy codebreakers did not break the Coral machine until the spring of 1943.

On the same day (12 December), Berlin authorized Wenneker to give copies of the *Automedon* documents to the Japanese, and that evening Wenneker personally handed over a copy of the Chiefs of Staff report to Vice Admiral Kondo the Vice Chairman of the Japanese Naval General Staff. After studying them, Kondo's first reaction was that the documents were far too good to be genuine and were obviously part of some deliberate false trail being laid by British intelligence to mislead both the Germans and Japanese.

However, when Wenneker explained the manner in which the documents had been captured and the loss of life involved, Kondo finally accepted the authenticity of this incredible windfall. Because the Chiefs of Staff report was considered so secret and valuable, knowledge of its existence was restricted to a very few senior members of the Naval General Staff and any reports based upon it were paraphrased in terms that precluded the reader from knowing the source of the information. For this reason there is no reference in any of the official Japanese war histories to this document or the effect it had on subsequent military and naval plans.

What is known, however, is that in early 1941 Yamamoto suddenly changed his mind. He agreed that, although an attack on Pearl Harbor was strategically illogical and extremely hazardous, the British Chiefs of Staff report showed that the Japanese need no longer worry about British intervention, since they were too weak to do so and had already accepted the inevitable loss of Singapore. On the diplomatic front, the report told the Japanese that it was safe for them to encroach upon territories such as Indo-China, since the British had nothing to offer but diplomatic protests. There is no doubt, therefore, that possession of the Chiefs of Staff report in 1940 fundamentally affected Japanese war planning throughout 1941, providing them with an intimate insight of Churchill's most secret decisions.

The *Automedon* documents came at an opportune moment, because on the same day as they were seized (11 November 1940), the Royal Navy had carried out its carrier-borne air attack, Operation Judgment, against the Italian Navy at Taranto.

Taranto was the main base of the Italian fleet, which had not shown much inclination to do battle with the Royal Navy but nevertheless posed a considerable threat to British convoys passing through the Mediterranean for Malta and Egypt. Admiral Andrew Cunningham, C-in-C of the British Mediterranean Fleet, had originally planned the attack for 20 October, but weather conditions had forced postponement until the next full moon on 11 November.

To make this first torpedo-bomber strike in history from carriers, twenty-one elderly Swordfish biplanes[35] (twelve carrying torpedoes, the remainder bombs and flares) were launched from the carrier HMS *Illustrious,* 170 miles away over the horizon. Because the Swordfish were so slow, the attack was made at night so as to avoid the more modern Italian fighters.

The Swordfish swept in at only thirty-five feet above the waves, dodging the anti-aircraft fire and barrage balloon cables, and using just eleven torpedoes, sank three battleships—*Littorio, Conte di Cavour,* and *Caio Duilio*—damaged two destroyers, sank two supply vessels, and destroyed the Taranto oil depot, all with the loss of only one aircraft. The success of the attack was highlighted by the excellence of the photographs taken of the devastation by Glenn Martin reconnaissance aircraft[36] that had just arrived in Malta from America. Although the shallowness of the harbor meant that eventually all three battleships were salvaged without much difficulty, for a crucial year three Italian capital ships were out of action.

Churchill was delighted with the results and at last had something cheerful to tell Parliament—"We've got some sugar for the birds this time"[37]—on 13 November after a long string of defeats. So encouraged was Churchill that on 22 November he wrote the First Lord of the Admiralty and the First Sea Lord: "Should Japan enter the war on one side and the United States on ours, ample naval forces will be available to contain Japan by long-range controls in the Pacific. The Japanese navy is not likely to venture far from its home bases so long as a superior battlefleet is maintained at Singapore and Honolulu."[38]

As Churchill and his senior naval advisers knew perfectly well that no superior British battlefleet would be available to defend Singapore, his comments were obviously meant to impress Roosevelt and were included in his report *Notes on Action at Taranto,* which Churchill sent the President, hoping it would encourage the Americans to station units of the U.S. Pacific Fleet at Singapore.

But Churchill was not alone in being impressed by Taranto. The Germans were also particularly impressed and sent Baron von Gronau, who had been German air attaché at their embassy in Tokyo, and Colonel John Jebsen from Canaris's intelligence staff down to Taranato to find out exactly how the harbor defenses had been penetrated. Gronau gave a full report[39] to the Japanese Embassy in Berlin, which sent it by code over the landline to Tokyo. It was soon clear from Gronau's report that Taranto was a miniature version of what could be done to Pearl Harbor. But Yamamoto was still adamant that he would not risk splitting his forces in an attack against large modern fleets in both Singapore and Pearl Harbor.

Now, only a month later, he had discovered that there would be no fleet at Singapore and the fortress, which was indefensible, had already been abandoned.

It is therefore a legitimate conclusion that the capture of the Chiefs of Staff report from the *Automedon* was the catalyst that sent the Japanese on the path to Pearl Harbor and precipitated the disastrous attack on America's Pacific Fleet. By any standard, the incident remains one of the worst intelligence disasters in history.

After the fall of Singapore in 1942, the Japanese Emperor presented a samurai sword of honor to Rogge in recognition of his achievement. Only two other Germans received such an award—Hermann Goering and Erwin Rommel. On several occasions, Kondo told Wenneker how this one particular document had enabled the Japanese to open hostilities against the United States so successfully. Wenneker's diary recalls: "Kondo repeatedly expressed to me how valuable the information contained in the [British] War Cabinet memorandum was for the [Japanese] navy. Such a significant weakening of the British Empire could not have been identified from outward appearances."[40]

DESPITE THE heavy shelling, the *Automedon*'s distress call[41] had been intercepted by two ships, the *Matara* and the *Helenus,* which passed it on to Singapore and London. But because it was incomplete, it did not include a position, and therefore the Royal Navy had little to go on but assumed the vessel had been sunk by Raider C (as they called *Atlantis*), which they knew had been successfully prowling these waters.

However, on 30 December 1940, Naval Intelligence in Singapore sent a secret telegram[42] to the Admiralty in London advising that one of the Norwegian prisoners taken from the *Ole Jacob* had been interviewed by MI6 agents in Tokyo and had reported that all the mail on board the *Automedon* had been seized by the Germans before it was sunk. From this date onward, London cannot have been in any doubt that the Chiefs of Staff report had also fallen into enemy hands and that a copy would certainly have been passed on to the Japanese.

But Churchill decided that this information was so sensitive that no one was to know about it. As a result, British War Cabinet records contain no mention of the loss,[43] nor were the governments of Australia and New Zealand told that the innermost deliberations of the War Cabinet were now in enemy hands. Furthermore, neither Shenton Thomas nor Brooke-Popham (for whom the report had been intended) was warned.[44]

In his postwar memoirs,[45] Churchill went into considerable detail about the manner in which Malaya and Singapore fell so easily to a much smaller invading force and was highly critical[46] of the lack of proper leadership and defenses for both the island and the mainland. Indeed, in January 1942, General Archibald Wavell, whom Churchill had recalled from India to take charge of the defense[47] of the southeast theater of war, received a telegram from Churchill expressing surprise that Singapore was so badly defended that surrender was inevitable. This was, of course, Churchill the politician carefully distancing himself from an impending disaster so that others, like Brooke-Popham and Shenton Thomas, would take the blame.

By also failing to tell the Australians the truth about Singapore and Malaya and the *Automedon* disaster, Churchill allowed them to continue pouring more reinforcements into the island believing it was an essential part of his Far East strategy. The Australian government in Canberra was poorly served with information from London, as their representative was not permitted to attend War Cabinet meetings and was only told about Churchill's plans via the Dominions Office. This infuriated some Australian politicians, who argued that as their soldiers were dying in the North African desert alongside Churchill's, they should be privy to his plans.

For some time, members of Australian Prime Minister Robert Menzies's cabinet had been unhappy about his style of leadership and felt he was too easily influenced by Churchill's oratory and flattery. There was increased criticism voiced when Menzies spent far too long away from Australia's problems during 1941 being feted by Churchill in London. Eventually, Sir Earle Page,[48] a previous Australian Prime Minister, was allowed to attend Churchill's War Cabinet meetings, but it was not until after the Pearl Harbor attack that he accidentally learned about the *Automedon* affair and the loss of the Chiefs of Staff report and advised Canberra of the truth.

The Australian Premier, by then John Curtin, who had replaced Menzies, immediately challenged Churchill[49] about sending further reinforcements of Australian troops to an island which he now suspected Churchill had long abandoned. Caught in the web of his own deception, Churchill was forced to allow Curtin to bring his troops back to Australia from the Middle East and as a result had to divert replacement British troops to Singapore who disembarked almost immediately into Japanese prisoner-of-war camps. Even so, many thousands of Australians were captured at Singapore, more than a third of whom later died as Japanese prisoners.

In the immediate postwar years there were one or two accounts of the exploits of German surface raiders[50] in the Far East and, though these made fleeting reference to the capture of secret documents from the *Automedon,* the precise identity of these was not given, because at that time the relevant Cabinet papers had not been released in the Public Record Office. In the official history,[51] *The War at Sea,* details are also given of the *Automedon*'s capture, but again the account does not identify the material involved, nor was there any mention of how the German radio operators had broken the BAMS codes. The official history of the war in the Far East also makes no mention of the incident but instead concentrates on finding scapegoats for the Singapore disaster.

Public knowledge of the loss of these Cabinet papers came to light quite accidentally, as is so often the case with skeletons that are lingering in some dusty cupboard. In 1980, the U.S. National Security Agency suddenly declassified[52] over 130,000 pages of wartime Magic decrypts. This was done in a haphazard fashion so that researchers were confronted with marching rows[53] of anonymous gray cardboard boxes on the thirteenth floor[54] of the National Archives in Washington. As these were in no particular order, it was a matter of luck that anyone came across anything of interest. In the course of researching his book *The Pacific War,*[55] John Costello found the copy of Yokoi's Coral decrypt of 12 December 1940. By itself it was an amazing document. At a time when Britain was fighting for her survival, the Japanese naval attaché in Berlin was telling Tokyo that he had just been given a copy of the British War Cabinet minutes.

Seen in the harsh light of the 1980s, when the number of Soviet spies in the Foreign Office both during and after the war had become part of history, this new revelation seemed yet another example of treachery in high places. Inquiries to Prime Minister Margaret Thatcher[56] in 1983 produced no response, despite the fact that the Prime Minister is in charge of all intelligence matters and had more than once expressed concern about the manner in which confidential government papers had found their way into unfriendly hands. The inquiry was eventually deflected to the Foreign Office, which professed surprise and ignorance of the whole affair,[57] claiming that an incident so far in the past would be very difficult to trace in its files.

After seven months had passed, the Foreign Office finally stated[58] that although it would "not be proper" for the public to know how these documents came to be lost, they hinted that they had been leaked to the Russians by the spy Donald Maclean[59] and, in turn, the Russians had given them to the Germans (then their allies) and thence to the Japanese.

In fact, the Foreign Office knew this was untrue, for in an archive at the Public Record Office, an old Foreign Office index of files that have never been publicly released shows that at least three separate files[60] once existed concerning the loss of diplomatic material on the *Automedon*. When asked if these three could now be made available, the Foreign Office replied that they had all been destroyed, as the contents were "not considered worthy of preservation."[61]

And so, by a curious chain of unconnected circumstances, one of the nails in the horse's shoe came loose far away in a totally unexpected manner, and thereby provided one of those pieces of the intelligence jigsaw puzzle that encouraged the Japanese along the path to Pearl Harbor and embroiled the whole of the Pacific in a bloody conflict, culminating in the dawn of the atomic age.

CHAPTER 6

The Uneasy Relationship

THE YEAR 1941 started off on a somber note. Europe lay defeated under the iron rule of the Germans. Although for the moment Ultra decrypts showed that the invasion of Britain had been postponed, Britain still stood entirely alone, with very few trained and properly equipped forces to defend either herself or the rest of the free world.

Already financially exhausted by the cost of the war, Churchill turned to Roosevelt for further help.[1] Now safely back in the White House following his inauguration on 20 January, Roosevelt put into action the Lend-Lease legislation that he had first proposed in his famous Fireside Chat of 29 December 1940, when he made the analogy of comparing this with the loan of a garden hose to enable a neighbor to put out a fire endangering his house: "I have been thinking very hard about what we should do for England, and it seems to me the thing to do is to get away from the dollar sign. . . . We will say to England, we will give you the guns and ships you need, provided that when the war is over that you will return us in kind the guns and ships that we have loaned you."[2]

Roosevelt was a great communicator and had that necessary American ability to obscure controversial policies with banalities. Even so, Roosevelt had a hard struggle to force the Lend-Lease legislation through Congress in the face of continuing opposition from the isolationists, who were greatly helped by the gloomy forecasts being relayed back to Washington from London by Joseph Kennedy. In the end, the bill passed in the House by 260 votes to 165 in February 1941, and a month later in the Senate by 60 to 31. Initially Lend-Lease was to cost $7 billion, but by 1945 it had totaled $27 billion.[3]

But Lend-Lease was not the only two-way trade going on across the Atlantic. On 8 July 1940, following the fall of Paris and the collapse of the British and French armies, Churchill instructed Lord Lothian, the British ambassador in Washington, to present to Roosevelt a highly secret letter[4] which stated, "'His Majesty's government would greatly appreciate it if the United States government, having been given the full details of any British equipment or devices, would reciprocate by disclosing certain secret information of a technical nature which our technical experts are anxious to have urgently."

Roosevelt approved the request and sent it to the U.S. Army and Navy for action. In August 1940, a technical mission headed by Sir Henry Tizard set out for America, taking with them details of the latest Marconi-Adcock direction-finding system, proximity fuses for use in anti-aircraft shells and bomb aiming devices, and the radar cavity resonator or Magnetron. Tizard was the scientist primarily responsible for the development of radar in Britain and, as chairman of the Aeronautical Research Committee, was personally responsible for the early development of airborne radar.[5]

Tizard's mission had its first meeting in Washington on 2 September 1940 in the offices of Major General Joseph O. Mauborgne, the U.S. Army's Chief Signal Officer. But the subject of Purple did not arise, because neither Churchill nor Tizard knew anything about the American codebreakers' achievements. Tizard was also forbidden by Churchill to tell the Americans anything about GCCS's first successes at breaking Enigma.

While Tizard and his group were in Washington, General George V. Strong, chief of the U.S. Army's planning staff, accompanied by Major General Emmons of the U.S. Army Air Corps, made a quick visit to London and told the British War Office about their first break into Purple. Whether he did this unofficially or had been authorized by General George Marshall to tell the British is unclear, but certainly approval could not have come from Roosevelt, because in September 1940 the President knew nothing about Purple. Churchill was very excited by the news, because GCCS was still unable to read these Japanese diplomatic messages and therefore proposed that the exchange of technology should be widened to include "A full exchange of cryptographic systems, cryptanalytical techniques, direction-finding radio interception, and other technical communication matters pertaining to the diplomatic, military, naval, and air services of Germany, Japan, and Italy."

On their return, Strong and Emmons delivered a secret report (G4 #4368 of 25 September 1940) to General Marshall, recommending that the Purple machine be included in the deal. Subsequently, Admiral Robert L. Ghormley, USN, Assistant Chief of Naval Operations (who was stationed in London as an unofficial liaison officer), agreed that the exchange should also include the U.S. Navy's Japanese codebreaking secrets.

Marshall took the view that as the U.S. Army had broken Purple, it was entitled to share out the machines as it wished. But when news of the deal reached Admiral Walter S. Anderson, director of U.S. Naval Intelligence, and Admiral Leigh Noyes, director of U.S. Navy Communications, they were furious that Marshall had made such an arrangement without first consulting them and that he had given the British far too much at the expense of American security when Britain was not America's ally. The U.S. Navy also argued that, apart from playing a major part in building Purple, Britain had no solutions to other Japanese cryptographic systems to offer in return, and therefore Marshall should demand that GCCS at least give them an Enigma cryptograph in exchange for the Purple machines. This would allow the U.S. Navy to break the signals from German U-boats operating off America's eastern seaboard.

After a good deal of haggling, Marshall got his way, mainly because he claimed that, having promised Britain a Purple machine—in fact he had promised them two—he could not go back on his word. He firmly believed that if America was totally open about its codebreaking secrets with Britain, they would reciprocate in a similar manner.

It had been intended that William Friedman would lead the team to Britain, but the effort of breaking Purple had caused him to have a nervous breakdown. Instead, the team consisted of two naval representatives from OP-20-G, Lieutenant Robert H. Weeks and Ensign Prescott H. Currier, and two from SIS, Abraham Sinkov and Leon Rosen. At the time,[6] there was a law forbidding American civilians to travel on a vessel of a belligerent, so the pair were commissioned in the Army. Sinkov at the age of thirty-four was given the rank of major, and Rosen became a captain, and both were made assistant military attachés and issued diplomatic passports.

In January 1941, the quartet traveled by train to Baltimore and boarded the 35,000-ton British battleship HMS *King George V,* which had just arrived with the new British ambassador, Lord Halifax. Their precious cargo of Purple machines was swung on board and locked away below, with the only keys being held by them. Since no one on board knew what the group of Americans was doing and they could not discuss their mission, Sinkov recalls they were treated with considerable reserve by the officers during the long voyage, which finally ended at Scapa Flow.

Here they were met by Brigadier John Tiltman from GCCS, who arranged for their journey south. The four Americans were taken to Shenley Park, near Bletchley, the palatial house of Lord Cadman,[7] the chairman of the Anglo-Iranian Oil Company (today known as British Petroleum), where they were greeted by Lady Cadman. Having shown them over the house and introduced her staff, she explained she had to leave for Wales, where her husband had been taken ill. Sinkov recalls: "We never saw her again, nor did we ever meet Lord Cadman. We had a cook, butler, servants, extensive grounds with their own farm and poultry. It was very elegant living at a time when Britain was suffering acute restrictions."

Having established themselves in these comfortable surroundings, the four were then taken to GCCS, where they handed over their treasure trove of codebreaking secrets. This included:

JAPANESE DIPLOMATIC

Two Purple machines with current keys, plus the three-letter keying code, and techniques of solution.

Two Red machines with current keys and techniques of solution.

Two sets of Consular codes (J-17), and current keys with techniques of solution.

Two sets of minor diplomatic codes.

JAPANESE NAVAL

Two sets of JN-25 fleet codes with current keys (additive tables) and techniques of solution produced by OP-20-G since the initial breakthrough in October 1940.

Two sets of merchant ship codes with current keys.

Two sets of naval attache ciphers, but not the Coral cryptograph.

Two radio naval call-sign signal lists.

GCCS were delighted to have the two Purple cryptographs so that they could start reading the long, detailed messages being sent by the Japanese ambassador in Berlin, Baron Hiroshi Oshima,[8] to Tokyo. Although these now went by direct-beam radio instead of Cable & Wireless, they could still be monitored by GCCS. One of the Purple machines was sent out to FECB, where it was used to read the Japanese diplomatic traffic between Batavia and Tokyo, which was being intercepted by the Dutch at Kamer 14 and also between Tokyo and Washington, which could be easily monitored at the Stonecutters intercept station.

The Americans stayed more than six weeks at Bletchley Park, and Sinkov spent much of his time with the Italian section exchanging information. But when it came to the secrets of Enigma, GCCS was most unhelpful. They refused to give the Americans a captured Enigma cryptograph, as had been promised, because the Foreign Office had vetoed this on the grounds that it was against British policy to share its codebreaking secrets with a neutral. Not surprisingly, the Americans were furious at this blatant double-cross, since they had handed over the Purple machines in good faith to help Britain in its hour of need, even though their laws about sharing cryptographic secrets with other nations were equally strict.

The U.S. Navy had good cause to be upset, because they had earmarked the two Purple machines to go to Station Hypo at Pearl Harbor and were even angrier when a third Purple machine was also shipped to GCCS later in 1941 instead of going to Hypo.

As to the extent of GCCS's work against Japanese codes, Weeks and Currier were only told that GCCS was reading the naval attaché, J-17, and PA-K2 consular codes but professed ignorance of the Red machine and JN-25. GCCS therefore pretended to be extremely grateful and amazed at these gifts, thus giving the impression that it was all quite new to them. So the Americans returned to Washington and reported: "[GCCS] had not requested the Jap Fleet Code [JN-25], did not expect it, didn't even know the US had solved it, *and had no use for it in London* [emphasis added]. However to save the [American] Mission embarrassment they had sent the copies out to Singapore together with all other material pertaining to Japanese naval and military communications."[9]

This news upset Admirals Noyes and Anderson, because they had wanted to send the JN-25 codebooks[10] out to Stations Hypo and Cavite and had only agreed to let them go to GCCS because of the promise of an Enigma. It was two years before the Americans realized the extent of Churchill's duplicity and his concealment of codebreaking matters with them. On 23 April 1943, Adolph A. Berle Jr. of the State Department wrote a secret letter to John G. Winant, the American ambassador in London, concerning a planned visit by codebreaking expert Colonel Alfred McCormack to GCCS, warning: "A feeling has grown up in certain circles that while there is a full interchange on our side, certain information has not been forthcoming from the British side."[11]

The outcome of the whole affair was that Churchill got what he needed most, the two Purple machines, but gave nothing in exchange. The visit by the Americans to GCCS and the gift of the two Purple machines has to this day not been acknowledged by the British government, and no reference to them has been allowed to appear in the official histories. In his own memoirs Churchill made only one brief mention of Magic:

From the end of 1940 the Americans had pierced the vital Japanese
ciphers, and were decoding large numbers of their *military* [emphasis
added] and diplomatic telegrams. In the secret American circles
these were referred to as "Magics." The "Magics" were repeated to
us, but there was an inevitable delay—sometimes of two or three
days—before we got them. We did not know therefore at any given
moment all that the President or Mr [Cordell] Hull knew. I make no
complaint of this.[12]

One can now see this is nonsense designed to conceal the fact that
after January 1941 Churchill was getting from GCCS and FECB decrypts
of Purple messages between Tokyo and Washington and Berlin as fast
as, and possibly faster than, Roosevelt. What is particularly interesting
about this passage from his memoirs is that Churchill states that he was
also getting "military telegrams" from this same source. As we know,
the Japanese never used Purple for military traffic. So this remark confirms that Churchill was also getting military intelligence from GCCS and
FECB as the result of reading JN-25.

GCCS did not call their Japanese diplomatic intercepts Purple (as did
the Americans) but rather BJ (British-Japanese), colloquially known as
Black Jumbos. All files relating to them are withheld from Britain's Public Record Office (PRO) and remain under the control of GCHQ so that
it will not appear that GCCS was reading any Japanese diplomatic messages before the war. However, a few BJ's[13] have slipped past the censors and are reproduced in Appendix 3.

What is revealing about these BJ's is their serial numbers and dates.
The first on 9 April 1941 carries the serial #089585, whereas the next
two on 3 May are serials #090501 and #090502. This suggests that in
less than a month GCCS intercepted 916 messages on the Berlin-Tokyo
circuit. Between 3 May and 10 May the serials indicate 272 messages
and to the end of May a further 827 messages. As these totals do not
accord with the numbers of Purple messages being intercepted by the
Americans, which only totaled around 230, either the serials were not
consecutive or they must have included other diplomatic intercepts.
Nevertheless, it gives an idea of the volume of traffic GCCS was able to
read with the Purple machines provided by the Americans.

Wherever Churchill was, he had BJ material sent to him by GCCS,
along with other Ultra material from Enigma decrypts. "Where are my
eggs?" he would demand, for he described his codebreakers at GCCS as
"the geese who laid the golden eggs but never cackled." Churchill
makes only very fleeting references to his "special intelligence" in his

memoirs, but there is a brief note[14] in his papers for 5 August 1941 which reads:

(3) As regards papers to be sent, [to Churchill at the Atlantic meeting] the following would be responsible for the selection:

Boniface	"C"
BJ	Major Morton
Agents' reports	Major Morton
Foreign Office telegrams	Foreign Office
Service telegrams	Minister of Defence

Boniface was a codeword originally used to conceal the source of Ultra material by pretending there was a spy of this name providing the information. Unfortunately, when senior military commanders received information bearing this prefix, they downgraded its value, because they refused to believe that any single agent could have access to such a wide range of high-grade intelligence. As a result, the codeword was changed to Ultra,[15] but Churchill continued using Boniface. "C" was— and still is—the codename for the head of MI6, then Sir Stewart Menzies, who also controlled GCCS.

Major Desmond Morton[16] was Churchill's personal assistant and had been a close friend since 1916. On 5 August 1940 Churchill ordered, "I do not wish such [Ultra] reports as are received to be sifted and digested by the various intelligence authorities. For the present Major Morton will inspect them for me and submit what he considers of major importance. He is to be shown everything and submit authentic documents to me in their original form." As a result of this arrangement, Churchill saw every day selected raw decrypts from all sources of codebreaking—German, Italian, and Japanese—and was able to make his own judgments. The British Chiefs of Staff disliked Churchill having direct access to raw Ultra and BJ's, because it meant he knew more than they did about enemy plans. They would have preferred he received summaries after they had analyzed the raw material. But Churchill would have none of this.

The availability of a Purple and a Red machine at FECB soon started producing dividends, and a few of these messages[17] are reproduced in Appendix 3. The one for 28 October 1941 (page 116) is particularly interesting. Its origin indicator 'C.O.S. Singapore" is of course FECB. "Consular Special Intelligence" could mean a message in either Red or Purple but probably the former. The comment at the bottom is particularly significant: "No repetition no action should be taken which could

<u>NOTE</u>

This was discussed at a meeting between
Sir Edward Bridges, "C", Colonel Cornwall Jones,
Mr. Bevir and myself this morning and the following
arrangements were agreed:-

1. Colonel Cornwall Jones would settle the
arrangements regarding the aircraft with the C.A.S. and
would inform us of the time at which papers for despatch
should be ready.   He would also arrange with the Air
Ministry about the method of packing.

2. General Ismay would make any necessary
communication to Lord Beaverbrook.

3. As regards papers to be sent, the following
would be responsible for the selection:-

Boniface	"C"
✓ B.J.	⎱ ~~Foreign Office~~
✓ Agents' reports	⎰ Major Morton
✓ Foreign Office telegrams	Foreign Office to make suggestions
✓ Service telegrams	Office of the Minister of Defence

compromise irreplaceable source. Pass to D.M.I. [Director Military Intelligence] and compositely [paraphrased] Canberra."

The message dated 12 September 1941 originated in Batavia, so it is fair to assume this was the product of Kamer 14's codebreaking and was passed on to the ANLO (Australian Naval Liaison Officer) working there. Again it could have been either Purple or Red, since the Japanese used both at their consulate in Batavia.

What is also particularly significant about the visit of the Americans to Bletchley Park is that if the U.S. Navy was able to give GCCS reconstructed JN-25 codebooks, even though incomplete,[18] in January 1941, with current additive tables, and to show them how to continue breaking the system, then OP-20-G had made remarkably quick progress breaking the code from their first decrypt only three months earlier, in September 1940. Furthermore, OP-20-G had obviously been reading some JN-25 intercepts during the previous months, and so one would expect to find these today in the archives along with the Purple diplomatic decrypts for the same period. But they are not there.

In America, the veneer of neutrality was wearing thin. Now with a majority in both houses of Congress, Roosevelt began wiping out the many years of underfunding America's armed forces. By the end of 1940, Congress had voted an immediate increase of the Army to one million men with an eventual goal of four million. There were to be 50,000 aircraft for the U.S. Army Air Corps, 170,000 men for the Navy, and 34,000 for the U.S. Marines. The Navy Air Force was to have 15,000 aircraft and 10,000 pilots. The new naval shipbuilding program included seventeen battleships, fourteen heavy cruisers, forty light cruisers, nearly two hundred destroyers, and over seventy submarines. To fund this, Roosevelt submitted to Congress in January 1941 the nation's largest peacetime military budget, totaling a staggering $10.8 billion. And quite apart from Lend-Lease, America took another step toward the European war on 10 April 1941, when it acquired defense rights in Greenland; and in July American forces occupied Iceland with Denmark's permission to frustrate any German takeover.

The Purple cryptograph at Bletchley Park was soon producing results.

◀ This is the only reference in any of Churchill's papers to BJ's (Black Jumbos), the British-Japan diplomatic intercepts the Prime Minister received from the Purple machines given to GCCS in January 1941. Boniface was Churchill's codename for Ultra intercepts. "C" was and remains to this day the codename for the head of MI6, then Sir Stewart Menzies. This note is dated 5 August 1941, shortly before Churchill left for his meeting with Roosevelt off Newfoundland. (PREM 3/485/6, Public Record Office, Kew.)

[N.Z.N.F.—87.
(Revised Aug. 1939.)
Chapter V303.]

Method of
Transmission:

RECORDS / ACTION COPY.

1368

W/T

2384

Priority:

Secret or Confidential:

SECRET

Cypher or Code used, or P/L:

TO:
D.N.I. .... N.O.I. WELLINGTON (R)
D.N.I. ....

FROM:
C.O.S. SINGAPORE

Message: Consular special intelligence report
.... Both October.

TOKYO telling Minister Melbourne and Consul Sydney
.... General Staff have asked him to collect
.... information on Australia and New Zealand. Any
.... obtained should be sent Investigation Bureau Foreign
.... General Staff want maps of all kinds, geograph-
.... and statistic, guide books and directories.
Comments. Text indicates Japanese residents will be
..... obtain material. No repetition no action should be
.... could compromise irreplaceable source. Pass to
..... immediately Canberra.

0818x/27

Remarks:		Initials of Typist.	Initials of Cypherer or Coder.	Time of Receipt or Despatch.	Date.
		P.F.H.	L.L.	0755	28/10/41

Related to ....

NAVY OFFICE MINUTE.

File: N.D. ....

DECLASSIFIED

175-7-41]

Within a month of its operation listening to the Berlin-Tokyo circuit, Churchill was able to tell Roosevelt on 15 February 1941, "Many drifting straws [19] seem to indicate Japanese indications to make war on us, or something that would force us to make war on them, in the next few weeks or months."

Roosevelt had received equally disturbing information from his own ambassador in Tokyo, Joseph Grew, who on 27 January had cabled, "My Peruvian colleague told a member of my staff that he had heard from many sources including a Japanese source that the Japanese military forces planned, in the event of trouble with the United States, to attempt a surprise mass attack on Pearl Harbor using all their military facilities. He added that although the project seemed fantastic the fact that he had heard it from many sources prompted him to pass on the information." [20]

The information had come from Dr. Ricardo Schreiber, the Peruvian ambassador in Tokyo, who had told Grew's first secretary, Edward S. Crocker, about the tale at a party. Grew's cable was sent to ONI for evaluation, and McCollum, who headed the Far East desk and was cleared to see Magic, wrote on 1 February, "The Division of naval intelligence places no credence on these rumors. Furthermore based on known data regarding the present disposition and employment of Japanese naval and army forces, no move against Pearl Harbor appears imminent or planned for the foreseeable future." [21]

This was a typical response from the military to any civilian observer, no matter how well placed, for daring to suggest that he might know more than the armed services.

Encouraged by the way the war was going in Europe and North Africa, Yamamoto in April 1941 decided to put his ideas onto paper and ordered work to begin on Operation Z [22]—a carrier-borne aircraft attack on Pearl Harbor. It was dangerous, illogical, and easy to fault. Yet its illogicality was its best hope of success, because the Americans would not expect such an attack.

In fact this was untrue. Rear Admiral Patrick L. N. Bellinger, head of the Hawaiian naval air patrol, and Major General Frederick L. Martin,

---

◀ As the Japanese diplomatic missions in Melbourne and Sydney did not have a Purple machine, this was almost certainly sent in the Red machine code, and the prefix "Special Intelligence" denotes it came from codebreaking. Note also the final warning about this being an "irreplaceable source." The term "compositely" means that when sending the message to Canberra, where it will be seen by many people, the wording should be changed so as to give no hint that it came from breaking Japanese diplomatic codes. *(New Zealand National Archives.)*

head of the Hawaiian Army Air Corps, recalled a carrier-borne air strike against Pearl Harbor during a fleet exercise that had been successfully demonstrated by Admiral Ernest J. King from the American carrier USS *Saratoga* in 1938, and wrote a strikingly prescient joint report on 31 March 1941:

> In the past[23] Japan has never preceded hostile actions by a declaration of war. Japanese submarines and a fast raiding force may arrive in Hawaiian waters with no prior warning from the US intelligence service. It appears that the most likely and dangerous form of attack would be an air attack. At present such an attack would most likely be launched from one or more carriers which would probably approach inside of 300 miles in a dawn air attack and there is a high probability that it could be delivered as a complete surprise. A successful raid against the ships and naval installations in Pearl Harbor might prevent effective action by [U.S. Navy] forces in the west Pacific for a long period.

It was almost as if they were looking over Yamamoto's shoulder. The Chief of Naval Operations in Washington read the report and sent a reminder to all commands that past experience showed that the Japanese and the Germans liked to launch their attacks on a Saturday or Sunday or a national holiday.

Certainly the Japanese had no difficulty[24] in getting intelligence about the Pearl Harbor base, as there were 160,000 Japanese-Americans living in Hawaii, and in addition there was a large Japanese fishing fleet that was based in Hawaii and regularly sailed through the areas used for naval exercises. The Japanese also had a large and active consular staff in Hawaii that included specially trained intelligence officers like Takeo Yoshikawa and the German spy Otto Kuehn, whose movements and telephone calls should have been monitored by the FBI.

Yamamoto was not the only naval officer to appreciate the lessons taught by the attack on Taranto. Secretary of War Henry Stimson ordered that more interceptor aircraft, radar equipment, and anti-aircraft guns be installed to protect Pearl Harbor against an aerial attack. But Pearl Harbor was only one of a number of places the Japanese could attack. The Philippines, Malaya, and the Dutch East Indies were all potential targets. What the Americans needed was some specific piece of operational information that would clearly show that Japan would attack Hawaii.

The value of the Purple decrypts[25] would have been better analyzed if they had been seen by senior military commanders, but because of an unfortunate leak in April 1941 the distribution had been severely restricted. One explanation for the leak was that Sumner Welles, Under Secretary of State, had revealed to Constantin Oumansky, the Russian ambassador in Washington, part of the contents of an intercepted message between Hiroshi Oshima in Berlin and Tokyo. Oshima had reported that Hitler intended invading Russia in June. Oumansky did nothing with Welles's information other than confront Hans Thomsen, the German envoy in Washington with the accusation. Naturally Thomsen claimed it was American disinformation but immediately warned Berlin that it appeared the Americans were reading Oshima's messages to Tokyo.

Another explanation[26] suggests that the Germans intercepted a message sent from the British Embassy in Washington to the Foreign Office in London on 30 April 1941, which was accidentally transmitted in a low-grade code instead of the high-grade Typex system. It quoted verbatim from a Magic decrypt that had been passed to the British ambassador reporting an agreement Japan had reached with Berlin. Of the two accounts, this sounds the more likely, because simple errors of this kind have accounted for the majority of codebreaking successes over the years.

The first the Americans knew about it was when they decoded a message from Tokyo to Washington on 5 May 1941 warning: "According to a fairly reliable source of information it appears almost certain the United States government is reading your code messages. Please let me know if you have any suspicion of the above."

The Japanese ambassador, Kichisaburo Nomura, carried out an investigation and eventually on 20 May signaled Tokyo, fortunately in Purple, that he believed the Americans had been reading one of their low-grade codes but that Purple was secure. Evidently Tokyo accepted this and continued to use Purple as before.

But it certainly frightened the Americans, who clamped down on the future distribution of Magic decrypts. Two of those taken off[27] the distribution list were Admiral Husband E. Kimmel, C-in-C Pacific Fleet, and Lieutenant General Walker C. Short, Commanding General U.S. Army, in Hawaii. This foolish move meant the two commanders were entirely dependent on Washington for all their intelligence.

In the confusion, Roosevelt also got taken off the Magic list because Colonel Rufus S. Bratton of Military Intelligence found a Magic decrypt crumpled up in the wastebasket of General Edwin "Pa" Watson, Roosevelt's military secretary. The Army decided that since Magic was diplomatic material, the State Department should furnish the President with only suitably paraphrased summaries that protected its source. OP-20-G also stopped sending Roosevelt raw decrypts but allowed his aide, Captain John R. Beardell, to brief him orally. It evidently took some while before Roosevelt realized he had been cut off from raw intelligence, and his access was not restored until 12 November 1941. If nothing else, the episode showed the arrogance of senior naval officers who felt they had the right to deprive their Commander-in-Chief of such vital intelligence.

On the morning of 22 June 1941, Hitler's dramatic invasion of Russia diverted attention from the Far East as over a hundred divisions of his army and panzer units smashed their way with ease through Stalin's 7-million-strong army that had been caught hopelessly unprepared. Within ten days, the city of Minsk, halfway to Moscow, had fallen, and the Germans were rolling back the Russians along a front 1,800 miles long. From FECB's viewpoint in Singapore, once the political differences between Japan and Germany had been sorted out, the invasion served to free Japan from the fear of a Russian attack on her western flank, so that she could pursue her grandiose ambitions throughout the Pacific.

For Churchill it also brought relief, although the overnight recognition of Russia as an ally required a swift somersault in public relations that he was never able to accept fully. Nevertheless Churchill promised Russia "whatever help we can. We have offered any technical or economic assistance in our power. We are resolved to destroy Hitler and every vestige of the Nazi regime. From this nothing will turn us." He then added enigmatically, "I gave clear and precise warnings to Stalin of what was coming. I can only hope these warnings did not fall unheeded."

By this, Churchill implied that he did all he could to warn Stalin of Hitler's impending attack, short of actually telling him how the information had been obtained. Churchill refused to tell Stalin anything about the success of GCCS and the Ultra material because he considered Soviet security so poor that the Germans would soon find out. Nevertheless William Cavendish-Bentinck (later Duke of Portland), as chairman of the Joint Intelligence Committee (JIC), warned the Russian ambassador in London, Ivan Maisky, that Germany was planning to attack Russia on 22 or 29 June 1941, although he did not tell Maisky his source. Maisky chose not to believe him.

Following the German attack, intelligence based on Ultra was regularly passed to the Russians via the MI6 representative in Moscow, Cecil Barclay, who disguised its source. But Stalin paid little or no attention to any of this information. In fact, the Russians knew all about GCCS's successes with Enigma, the Ultra material, Purple, and probably JN-25, because their spies [28] Anthony Blunt, who had access to Ultra, and John Cairncross, who worked at Bletchley Park, had told them.

Japan was not slow to take advantage of the situation in Europe and with the help of their German allies persuaded the French Vichy regime to allow them to move thousands of troops into French Indo-China. On

25 July 1941 Major General Sumita took control of the capital, Saigon, and set up his headquarters. Meanwhile 8,000 more Japanese troops began disembarking in Cambodia and occupied the city of Phnom Penh. Using the information they had gleaned from the *Automedon's* documents, the Japanese knew the British were unable to do more than make ritualistic diplomatic protests.

On 13 August, Churchill and Roosevelt met in the fog-shrouded remoteness of Placentia Bay off Newfoundland. Five days later, amid much stage-managed publicity and newsreel hyperbole, they signed the Atlantic Charter. This act satisfied Churchill's love of the dramatic and helped drag America toward war by authorizing U.S. Navy anti-submarine patrols far out into the Atlantic, thus encouraging direct confrontation with the Germans.

Unlike Churchill, who had by necessity become a virtual dictator in Britain and could do almost as he pleased, Roosevelt remained a cautious pragmatic politician who liked to speak to his people in a simple, homely manner, well aware that three-quarters of them did not want to go to war. On his return to Washington, Roosevelt told his cabinet of his admiration of Churchill as a trader, commenting, "But of course Grandpa's pretty good at trading too,"[29] causing one Cabinet member to caution that perhaps Churchill was letting Roosevelt win the first round.

But despite this lighthearted banter, there is evidence[30] that in private secret talks Roosevelt exceeded his executive powers and promised Churchill that America would go to war if Japan attacked British territory in the Far East, which was a course the President had no power to follow without the authority of Congress. Certainly Admiral Harold E. Stark, one of the Joint Chiefs of Staff (JCS), had no doubts that this guarantee had been given, as he told the JCS later on 3 November, "In the case of a Japanese attack against the Philippines or British or Dutch possessions, the United States should resist the attack. In case of a Japanese attack against Siberia, Thailand or China . . . the United States should not declare war."[31] No one other than Roosevelt and the JCS apparently knew anything about this attitude at the time.

Just six days later, on 9 November, Churchill wrote to General Jan Smuts in South Africa, "I do not think it would be any use for me to make a personal appeal to Roosevelt. . . . At the Atlantic Meeting I told his circle that I would rather have an American declaration of war now and no supplies for six months than double the supplies and no declaration. He [Roosevelt] went so far as to say to me: 'I may never declare war; I may make war. If I were to ask Congress to declare war they might argue about it for three months.' "[32]

Did Roosevelt really say this to Churchill? There is no official record of the President making such a startling statement. Or was it what Churchill wanted to believe? On 12 November, Churchill told his War Cabinet, "Nobody but Congress could *declare* [original emphasis] war. It was however in the president's power to make war without declaring it."[33]

Six months later, on 27 January 1942, Churchill faced a censure motion in Parliament concerning his handling of the war, particularly in the Far East. In a very long speech lasting over two hours, he asked for a vote of confidence, warning members, "We have had a great deal of bad news lately from the Far East, and I think it highly probable, for reasons which I shall presently explain, that we shall have a great deal more. Wrapped up in this bad news will be many tales of blunders and shortcomings, both in foresight and action."[34]

Churchill continued: "We therefore have lain[35] . . . for nearly two years under the threat of an attack by Japan with which we had no means of coping. . . . I have explained[36] how very delicately we walked, and how painful it was at times, how very careful I was every time that we should not be exposed single-handed to this [Japanese] onslaught. . . . On the other hand,[37] the probability, since the Atlantic Conference, at which I discussed these matters with Mr. Roosevelt, that the United States, *even if not herself attacked, would come into a war in the Far East* [emphasis added], and thus make final victory sure . . . that expectation has not been falsified by events. . . . As time went on, one had greater assurance that . . . we should not fight alone."

Although this surprising admission passed unnoticed in the British Parliament, Harry Hopkins sent the President a memorandum on 21 February 1942 warning Roosevelt that the isolationists who were now after his blood for having betrayed America at Pearl Harbor would see this statement as an admission of his illegal collusion with Churchill. Hopkins's note read, "This is the extract from Churchill's speech that I think some day soon [Senator Burton K.] Wheeler and some of his crowd may pick up."[38]

During the 1945 Pearl Harbor inquiry, the charge was frequently made that Roosevelt had entered into an unconstitutional secret agreement with Britain. But as no record of Roosevelt's private talks with Churchill existed and the JCS records were not made available to the inquiry, the truth of the allegation was never proved. As things turned out, Roosevelt was not called upon to honor his promise.

After his meeting with Roosevelt, Churchill said to his son that America had to be brought into the war "boldly and honourably"[39] but in fact Churchill was already deeply involved[40] in numerous dirty tricks to plant false evidence upon the President and the American people. For this he used his MI6 agency in New York, the British Security Coordination (BSC), run by William Stephenson. BSC forged numerous documents apparently showing German plans to attack and take over various regimes in South America, and these were allowed to fall conveniently into the hands of the President and sympathetic sections of the American press, who were thus able to provide the President with useful questions at his press conferences.

It is most unlikely that Roosevelt really believed in these supposed Nazi threats to Latin America, but they made good headline material and helped confuse the isolationists. Churchill even sent the Hungarian-born filmmaker Alexander Korda[41] to America to make anti-German films, which he hoped would influence American public opinion.

Throughout the darkening autumn days of 1941 the game of diplomatic bluff and counterbluff intensified. Roosevelt still refused to impose a total oil embargo on Japan and instead gave the economic noose[42] around her neck an occasional jerk by freezing Japanese assets in America and restricting other forms of trade. But this was not enough for Churchill. German panzers were at the gates of Moscow, Britain's convoy lifeline across the Atlantic was being decimated by Doenitz'a wolf packs,[43] while in North Africa all Wavell's gains[44] had been wiped out and Rommel stood[45] astride the Egyptian border, apparently ready to seize Cairo and the Suez Canal in a vast pincer movement that would link up with the German thrust into southern Russia. How could Churchill drag America into the war?

The solution was provided for him on the morning of 6 September 1941, when Prime Minister Prince Fumimaro Konoye led his frock-coated cabinet into the hallowed conference chamber of Tokyo's royal palace. Before Emperor Hirohito, Konoye and his military commanders formally outlined their plan for a simultaneous attack on America, Britain, and the Dutch. Their stated purpose was: "To expel the influence of these three countries from East Asia, to establish a sphere for the self-defense and self-preservation of the Japanese empire, and to build a new order in greater east Asia."[46]

In keeping with his divine position, Hirohito questioned the commanders through the Privy Council President, Yoshimi Hara. They were forced to admit that they could not guarantee a quick victory. Suddenly, to everyone's surprise, Hirohito broke with royal protocol and in a very obtuse manner spoke directly[47] to the assembled leaders, cautioning them against war and recommending further efforts at a diplomatic solution with America. In considerable confusion Konoye and his cabinet withdrew, and it was subsequently agreed to postpone any further warlike moves until October 15.

But despite this royal setback, the war machine was irrevocably on the move. As FECB and GCCS watched the Purple messages passing between Washington, Berlin, and Tokyo, it was plain that the game of diplomatic bluff was fast running out of time, because neither America nor Japan was going to make any worthwhile concessions. There were further sinister portents when FECB began analyzing JN-25 intercepts that not only showed increased Japanese naval activity off the Indo-China coast in the form of large-scale exercises but also what appeared to be the creation of a new task force combining Japan's latest and largest aircraft carriers. The intercepts also gave the first sketchy details of a new Japanese battleship called *Yamato*,[48] which had in fact been secretly launched on 8 August 1940. Fortunately, as Japan's Navy intensified its activities in foreign waters, so the volume of JN-25 traffic increased.

This gave FECB the opportunity to update its knowledge of Japanese signal procedures, call signs, and all the inevitable radio gossip that accompanies large-scale maneuvers. Put together, it provided FECB with a unique insight into the Japanese Navy's operations that was to serve it well in the dark days ahead as the final plans for the attack on Pearl Harbor were laid.

The rapidly worsening situation in the Far East belatedly awoke the Australian government to the fact that they had no proper Sigint organization of their own, despite the fact that they had always appreciated the threat of Japanese military expansion in the Far East with Australia as a potential target. It was only in December 1939 that the Defence Committee had suggested[49] to Prime Minister Sir Robert Menzies that Australia should create a Special Intelligence Organisation (SIO), which would include a cryptographic division capable of breaking enemy codes. This suggestion resulted in a considerable flow of paperwork passing back and forth between the chiefs of staff of all three services over the next few months.

The RAN argued that the only worthwhile enemy traffic would be from the Atlantic area and that very little could be monitored in Australia and went on to point out that breaking an enemy code required a large organization that would take a long time to build up and be very expensive to maintain. Even in 1939, the RAN evidently did not consider Japanese naval signals of importance and were plainly unaware that one of their own officers had been breaking them since 1925 in London and later in Singapore.

The Australian Army thought the idea was a good one, adding that codebreaking was very skilled work and needed much practice but that it might be possible to intercept some Japanese military signals from their operations in China. But the Air Force felt that the three services would not be justified in setting up a cryptographic organization.

On 11 April 1940, Menzies wrote[50] London a very cautious letter pointing out all the difficulties in setting up a cryptographic organization and asking for the British government's views. With the Battle of Britain raging overhead and German invasion forces expected on the beaches any moment, Whitehall had other things on its mind. On 26 July, having heard nothing, Menzies gently jogged their memory, asking for a reply "at an early date."

This spurred Downing Street into action, and on 15 October Lord Cranborne, the Secretary of State for Dominion Affairs, replied to Menzies, saying it would be inadvisable to try to establish an agency like GCCS but that a small naval interception unit might be useful working with FECB in Singapore. Cranborne also added that GCCS would be willing to organize some training courses in cryptography to which Australia could send likely recruits.

Eric Nave, Malcolm Burnett, and F. J. Wylie, in charge of administration at FECB, held a conference[51] in Melbourne on 4 January 1941 at which Nave presented a report outlining what he thought the SIO could achieve. To start with, it was a very small organization, with only four full-time and six part-time Sigint operators at HMAS *Harman,* the intercept station near Canberra, and four part-time operators each at the Coonawarra station near Darwin and Park Orchards station at Melbourne.

Nave pointed out that this would inevitably limit the amount of Japanese traffic that could be intercepted, and rather than duplicate the work already being done so successfully at FECB, it would be better to concentrate the SIO's resources on the Japanese consular, shipping, and, later, aircraft codes.

The discussion covered a wide range of subjects, including how best to obtain full cooperation between the three services, which caused Commander R. B. M. Long, director of Australian Naval Intelligence, to comment: "Whether [cooperation] would be upset by the other two services I really cannot say. . . . the [Australian] army have a horror of any form of combined activity and even something of a disinclination to combine operational intelligence."

"Bouncer" Burnett, now promoted to captain, pointed out that at least the Australians could copy what had been done at FECB, to which Long commented, "Yes, but the adaption of that organisation to Australian conditions has not yet been puzzled out."

The meeting then considered liaison between the Australians and the Dutch codebreakers in Batavia at Kamer 14. Wylie was asked if anything of great interest had come from the Dutch, to which he replied, "Nothing at all. Intelligence outside the Netherlands East Indies interests the Dutch very little."

This was certainly an odd remark, because Kamer 14 had been very active in breaking not only Japanese consular codes including Purple traffic between Batavia and Tokyo (which they sent to FECB for decryption), but also some JN-25 signals as well. It is hard to see why Wylie was so dismissive[52] about the Dutch contribution, except that codebreakers are very jealous and often denigrate the abilities of others. When the meeting discussed actual codebreaking by SIO, Wylie said there was no real objection to the Australians doing this, provided it was controlled from FECB. But there was certainly no enthusiasm on his part.

As the RAN had no codebreakers of their own, they asked the Admiralty if Nave could stay on in Australia at the end of some sick leave to help get things started at SIO.[53] Although FECB wanted him back, they reluctantly agreed, so Nave found himself in the bizarre situation of being loaned by the Royal Navy back to the RAN,[54] where he had first started his career twenty-five years earlier. It is ironic to think that, had the RAN been more astute, they could have enjoyed the fruits of Nave's expertise over the previous fifteen years and established their own codebreaking agency instead of having to rely on what bits of information London decided to give them.

As the pace of war quickened, the news came flooding in, most of it depressing and some quite devastating. On May 24, the whole of Britain was shocked by the news that HMS *Hood* had been sunk and HMS *Prince of Wales* badly damaged by the German battleship *Bismarck* after a brief encounter in the North Atlantic. There then followed a nail-biting wait until *Bismarck* was finally trapped and sunk three days later. Although there was a feeling of grim satisfaction that the loss of *Hood* had been avenged, the faulty use of Sigint and other startling errors by the Royal Navy nearly allowed *Bismarck* to escape.

It was only a fortuitious error in German cipher security that saved the day. After sinking *Hood*,[55] *Bismarck* shook off the pursuing ships at night and made for the French port of Brest, because Captain Lutyens had made the incredible error of failing to fill *Bismarck*'s tanks before leaving Norwegian waters and was short of fuel. On 25 May, not realizing that the Royal Navy had lost him, Lutyens, using his four-rotor naval Enigma, sent off a long 30-minute signal to Berlin, which was intercepted by GCCS and also enabled direction-finding stations in Britain, Iceland, and Gibraltar to plot his position.

The position was radioed to Admiral Sir Francis Tovey on board the flagship HMS *King George V,* whose navigator, Captain Frank Lloyd, mistakenly plotted it onto a standard Mercator projection chart instead of a gnomonic chart essential for plotting DF bearings. As a result, it showed the *Bismarck*'s position to the north of them instead of the correct position to the south. Tovey turned *King George V* around and started retracing his course to the north, assuming that *Bismarck* was attempting to return to Norwegian waters, where Lutyens would have air cover from the German Air Force (GAF).

The Admiralty's OIC saw Tovey's change of course but were reluctant to interfere, because before the start of the operation Tovey had insisted that he be supplied only with actual bearings by OIC and left to draw his own conclusions from them. Eventually OIC plucked up enough courage to tell Tovey he was going in the wrong direction, and after further delays, *King George V* turned around again and went back onto the correct southerly course.

Meantime Lutyens's long message had arrived at Bletchley Park, but at that time there was a long delay breaking naval Enigma messages. Far away in sunny Athens, General Hans Jeschonnek, Chief of the GAF, knew that a member of his staff had a son serving as a midshipman on the *Bismarck* and asked his headquarters in Berlin for news of the ship. The GAF contacted the Navy, who sent them a copy of Lutyens's long message, which GAF headquarters simply repeated verbatim to Jeschonnek in Athens using a GAF three-rotor Enigma key, which was also intercepted by GCCS.

Because everyone at Bletchley Park was concentrating on messages from the Atlantic area to try and locate *Bismarck,* the GAF message to Athens was put to one side until someone chanced to notice that the cipher text length precisely matched that of Lutyens's unbroken signal. As the GAF keys had long been broken, it was relatively simple to break the Athens message, whereupon GCCS was able to tell OIC that *Bismarck* was heading for Brest.

On the evening of 24 May, *Bismarck* was sighted near Greenland by the U.S. Coast Guard cutter *Modoc,* ostensibly on weather-reporting duties. As the result of this sighting, a long-range PBY Catalina aircraft on loan from the U.S. Navy to the RAF, piloted by Ensign Leonard Smith, USN, sighted *Bismarck* at 8:30 A.M. the following day and radioed her position to the Admiralty. By now a large force of warships had gathered, blocking *Bismarck*'s escape, and the aircraft from the carrier *Ark Royal* succeeded in scoring two torpedo hits, one of which jammed her rudder. Early on the morning of 27 May, the battleships HMS *King George V* and HMS *Rodney* engaged *Bismarck,* and after a long battle the German battleship was sunk at 10:30 A.M.

FECB's intercepts had meanwhile prompted Churchill to revive his idea of sending out to the Far East a small, fast deterrent force of battleships and an aircraft carrier. The plan had originally been envisaged after Churchill's meeting with Roosevelt at the Atlantic Conference in August, when it was agreed that the Americans would send their new B-17 bombers to the Philippines, while Britain would provide the seapower. So by November 1941 there would be a strong combined air and naval force in the area of sufficient size to deter any Japanese plans of aggression. Unfortunately, the Admiralty rejected the idea, both because they had insufficient ships to deal with existing theaters of war and because the new *King George V*–class battleships had crews consisting of men aged less than twenty-one who had never been to sea before.

Now in October, with the worsening news in the Far East and a military-backed hard-line government in Japan, Churchill and Eden, pressed by Prime Minister Menzies of Australia, insisted that a naval force must be sent, and the Admiralty reluctantly compromised by suggesting that four old battleships should form the basis of a Far East fleet that, hopefully, could link up with the U.S. Navy. But renewed pressure from Australia to send modern warships so as to match the Japanese caused Churchill to override his admirals, and in the end, on 20 October 1941, the new battleship HMS *Prince of Wales,* the aging battle cruiser HMS *Repulse,* and the new aircraft carrier HMS *Indomitable* were ordered to Singapore. Unfortunately, *Indomitable* ran aground on a Caribbean reef; and although HMS *Hermes* was available in South African waters, it was not substituted, so the two capital ships arrived in Singapore without air cover. Churchill told Roosevelt, "There is nothing like having something that can catch and kill anything, and the firmer your attitude and ours, the less chance of their [the Japanese] taking the plunge."[56]

But in reality it was no more than a bluff to keep the Australians happy and to try and entice the Americans into sending naval units to Singapore. Others did not share Churchill's view, and when the ships put into Capetown on their way to Singapore, the South African Prime Minister, Jan Smuts, cabled Churchill with the prescient comment: "If the Japanese are really nippy there is an opening here for a first class disaster."[57]

On 10 November 1941, at London's Guildhall, Churchill, pointing out that he had voted for the Anglo-Japanese alliance forty years ago and had always been a "sentimental well-wisher" to the Japanese, then raised the political temperature by saying, "Viewing the vast, sombre scene as dispassionately as possible, it would seem a very hazardous adventure for the Japanese people to plunge quite needlessly into a world struggle in which they may well find themselves opposed in the Pacific by states whose populations comprise nearly three-quarters of the human race. If steel is the basic foundation for modern war, it would be rather dangerous for a power like Japan, whose steel production is only about seven million tons a year, to provoke quite gratuitously a struggle with the United States, whose steel production is now about ninety millions; and this would take no account of the powerful contribution which the British Empire can make. I hope therefore that peace of the Pacific will be preserved in accordance with the known wishes of Japan's wisest statesmen."[58]

CHAPTER 7

The Infamous Dawn

MEANWHILE IN WASHINGTON, increasingly sinister decrypts were being analyzed as Japanese interest in Pearl Harbor intensified. On 24 September 1941, Tokyo sent message #83 in the J-19 code to their consul, Nagao Kita, in Honolulu. It read:

> Henceforth we would like to have you make reports concerning vessels along the following lines insofar as possible:[1]
> 1. The waters of Pearl Harbor are to be divided into five sub-areas. . . .
> Area A. Waters between Ford Island and the Arsenal.
> Area B. Waters adjacent to the Island south and west of Ford Island. . . .
> Area C. East Loch.
> Area D. Middle Loch.
> Area E. West Loch and the communicating water routes.
> 2. With regard to warships and aircraft carriers, we would like to have you report on those at anchor, (these are not so important) tied up at wharves, buoys and in dock. (Designate types and classes briefly. If possible, we would like to have you make mention of the fact when there are two or more vessels along side the same wharf.)

The message was intercepted by the Army's monitoring station MS-5 at Oahu, which, apart from eavesdropping on the Tokyo-Berlin and Tokyo-Moscow radio circuits, also kept watch on all messages passing between Tokyo and the Japanese Consulate in Honolulu that were sent by radio over the Mackay Radio & Telegraph's or RCA's direct-beam circuits. But a crucial gap in the coverage existed because the Army could not intercept Japanese cables passing over Postal Telegraph circuits, since the cable companies were still forbidden by law from handing over copies.

But far more important was the fact that neither the Army nor Navy codebreakers in Hawaii were cleared to handle Magic material.[2] Their orders were to pick out the most important intercepts and send them back to Washington by radio. But since they had no way of knowing the messages' contents, this was impossible for them to do. As a result they sent back everything they intercepted.

Although there was no problem in breaking the J-19 consular code, Washington did not have a translation of message #83 from SIS until two weeks later, on 9 October. The delay was because there was only one Pan American Clipper flight each week between Honolulu and San Francisco, and these were frequently delayed by bad weather, as happened on this occasion. As a result, the head of Station MS-5, Major Carroll A. Powell, bundled up all his accumulated intercepts—including message #83—and sent them off by surface mail on September 28, so they arrived at San Francisco on October 3, finally reaching the SIS codebreakers in Washington on October 6. In 1945, William Friedman told the Hewitt Inquiry that the "Honolulu intercept station . . . accumulated a large amount of traffic which had to be forwarded and we didn't have the radio circuits and facilities adequate to . . . forward all of the intercepted material by radio. In any case . . . there is no use in forwarding by radio which is a relatively expensive method as compared . . . with mail."[3]

It seems amazing that at this late stage, when war was obviously drawing near, that concern over expense still dominated. However, once decoded by SIS in Washington, the purpose of the message could not have been clearer; it divided Pearl Harbor into a number of target areas for an aerial attack and thus became known as the Bomb Plot message and was one of the most important operational messages sent by the Japanese prior to the attack. At no time did the Japanese ever ask for a similar Bomb Plot for any other American military installation. But despite its obvious importance, SIS did not send a copy of the translation back to Hawaii,[4] so the commanders there never knew anything about the Bomb Plot.

Once again the lack of proper coordination between the various naval Sigint offices and SIS, in addition to the split responsibility between the Navy and Army, compares badly with GCCS and FECB, which had direct teletype links so that decrypts could be flashed back and forth between London and Singapore without delay.

On 29 September, Ensign Yoshikawa (a member of Yamamoto's intelligence staff working at the consulate) replied in message #178[5] setting up a two-letter code for each of the five Pearl Harbor areas. The repair dock became KS, the Navy dock KT, the battleship moorings alongside Ford Island FV and FG. Because this message went by Postal Telegraph from Honolulu to Tokyo, it was missed by the Army and Navy in Hawaii, but fortunately Consul Kita sent a copy to his embassy in Washington and to the consulate in San Francisco, which enabled OP-20-G to get a copy (illegally) and decode it by 10 October. But no details were sent back to Hawaii.

On 15 November Tokyo sent message #111: "As relations between Japan and the United States are most critical make your 'ship in harbor report' irregular but at a rate of twice a week. Although you are no doubt aware, please take extra care to maintain secrecy."[6]

This message was not decoded by the Navy at OP-20-G until December 3, and again its contents were not sent back to Hawaii. So the growing interest by Japan in the U.S. Navy's movements at Pearl Harbor remained unknown there. The instruction to make the reports irregular was a timely security reminder not to send identical messages at the same time with roughly the same cipher text lengths. The Bomb Plot message and the reply were circulated among the few people cleared to see Magic— Roosevelt, Hull, Marshall, Stimson, Gerow, Miles, Bratton, Stark, Noyes, Anderson, Knox, Turner, Ingersoll, McCollum, and Watts—but no one saw anything very sinister or important. Military Intelligence thought it entirely a naval matter, while ONI concluded it was a Japanese plan to monitor how quickly the American fleet could leave harbor. No one felt the naval and military commanders in Hawaii should be told, so in the end the messages were filed and forgotten.

In the early days of November, Yamamoto supervised a rehearsal of Operation Z,[7] the attack on Pearl Harbor, at the naval war college in Tokyo. The rehearsals were conducted on a large plotting board with somewhat skeptical umpires introducing unexpected hazards such as the discovery of the force by American warships. The southern city of Kagoshima was used as a training target for Pearl Harbor, and surprised residents watched as 350 aircraft from the six carriers of the newly formed Task Force *Kido Butai*—roared in low overhead, using the local department store building as a target. Finally satisfied on 7 November, Yamamoto issued his Operation Order No. 2 specifying December 8 Tokyo time (December 7 Hawaiian time) as a Y-Day, or the preliminary date for the attack on Pearl Harbor.

Three days later, the ships of the Task Force, comprising six aircraft carriers *(Akagi, Kaga, Hiryu, Soryu, Shokaku,* and *Zuikaku),* two battleships, two heavy cruisers, one light cruiser, and nine destroyers, slipped their anchors at intervals and individually made their way in strict radio silence to the remote fogbound anchorage of Hitokappu Wan (Tankan Bay), in the far north of the Kurile Islands. By 16 November, the Task Force was assembled and waiting.

Over the years, history has become almost as fogbound as Tankan Bay, with mythology and cover-up playing their part in creating two false claims. The first of these is that as each ship in the Task Force sailed, its call sign was reassigned to a destroyer remaining behind in the Inland Sea so that there would be no sudden change in the pattern of radio traffic. This is untrue. What the Japanese did was to change the carriers' call signs as they sailed, and it took a little time before these could be identified among all the mass of general radio traffic. FECB found this much easier because they were reading the JN-25 messages.

The second piece of mythology quoted in previous accounts about Pearl Harbor is that after sailing to Tankan Bay, the Task Force maintained total radio silence, so there were no messages for the British and American Sigint teams to hear and, consequently, there was no way in which they could have learned of the Task Force's plans. This is also untrue. Although Yamamoto had planned Operation Z with meticulous care, and the commander of each ship in the Task Force had a copy of his fifty-page operational order[8] detailing the attack on Pearl Harbor, the final three instructions were missing. These were: the date the Task Force would sail from Tankan Bay; the refueling date in mid-Pacific; and the date of the actual attack. Yamamoto could not pass these three final pieces in his complex jigsaw to the Task Force until the diplomatic negotiations in Washington had run their course.

He therefore had to get his Task Force out into the Pacific to a holding point after refueling and await the outcome of the negotiations between Ambassadors Kurusu and Nomura and the State Department, in case there was a last-minute agreement—which, right up to the last moment, seemed a real possibility—in which case the Task Force would turn around and go back to Japan. Yamamoto also needed to be certain that the entire U.S. Pacific Fleet, including the carriers, was in Pearl Harbor, otherwise he would not launch the attack.

As it transpired, his intelligence from the Japanese Consulate in Hawaii was faulty, as they failed to warn him that the two carriers were not in harbor. The USS *Enterprise* had sailed for Wake Island on 28 November, and the USS *Lexington* had sailed on 5 December for Guam, in both cases ferrying aircraft.

If there had been a Postal Telegraph connection between Tokyo and Tankan Bay, the first of his orders (before the Task Force sailed) could have been sent by teletype and then signaled visually to the ships out in the bay or taken out by launch in complete secrecy. But no such link existed. Yamamoto had to send his final orders, together with other routine information, by radio from Tokyo naval headquarters in JN-25. Once these messages were transmitted, they became available to any eavesdropper, including the ever-vigilant Royal Navy's intercept stations in Hong Kong and Singapore, and also those operated by the U.S. Navy. While it is true that the Task Force did not have to reply to any of these signals, nevertheless the outgoing messages from Tokyo could not be concealed in any way.

It was these operational messages sent in the JN-25 naval code, not the diplomatic Purple messages then passing between Tokyo and Washington, that contained the vital information about the attack. Therefore, anyone who could intercept and read these JN-25 messages would automatically know about Yamamoto's plans to send a Task Force to sea.

ON 19 November 1941,[9] Japan commenced hostilities. Not against America or Britain but Australia, when the German surface raider, the 8,736-ton *Kormoran* met the Australian *Perth*-class 6,830-ton cruiser HMAS *Sydney* off the western coast of Australia and fought the most mysterious sea battle of World War II. The *Sydney* was equipped with eight six-inch and eight four-inch guns, and the *Kormoran* with six 5.9-inch guns. The two ships commenced firing at each other when only 1,200 yards apart, and soon both were badly damaged. The *Kormoran*'s crew surrendered and began to abandon ship, making their way in lifeboats over to the *Sydney*. But before they could reach her, a single torpedo struck the *Sydney*, and burning fiercely, she drifted away into the night and was never seen again.

Despite the damage to the *Kormoran*, 318 of her crew of 390 survived. But not a single member of the *Sydney*'s 645 crew survived, nor was a single body ever found. Since the *Kormoran* was not in a state to fire the last torpedo, it must have come from another vessel. By 24 November, the Australian Naval Board was satisfied (although they had no absolute proof) that a Japanese I-class submarine had been operating in conjunction with the *Kormoran* and had sunk the *Sydney*. The Admiralty were advised of this at once. The only one of the *Sydney*'s life rafts to be found was riddled with bullets, plainly suggesting that her survivors were machine-gunned in the water to ensure there were no witnesses to the incident.

ON 2 December 1941, *Prince of Wales* and *Repulse* arrived in Singapore and were given a rousing welcome as further proof of the island's impregnability. It is worth capturing the euphoria of the occasion from a contemporary account [10]

> The *Prince of Wales* and *Repulse* were greeted on their entry into Keppel Harbour as though they were the main attraction of a seaside carnival. The press played up the arrival of the capital ships as though, with the fleet there, the Royal Navy had command of the eastern seas. A peacetime atmosphere pervaded the city which was gay and brightly lit and, on the surface at any rate, confident that the advent of the Eastern Fleet would counteract and lull the insistent sabre-rattling of the Japanese warlords. The general feeling was that "They [the Japanese] might do it to the Americans but not to us. They wouldn't dare. It's bluff."

There were by now 130,000 troops in Singapore and Malaya (few of whom had any experience of jungle warfare), not a single tank, and a few squadrons [11] of F2A Brewster Buffalo aircraft [12] that had already been rejected by the U.S. Navy as useless. But according to C-in-C Brooke-Popham, "Let England have the 'Super' Spitfire and the 'Hyper' Hurricane, Buffaloes are quite good enough for Malaya." [13] It was hard to judge which was the greatest danger facing Singapore: Churchill's duplicity, the incompetence of its commanders, or the fighting skill of the Japanese.

When a nation is preparing for war, as Japan was in November 1941, it naturally wants to make sure that all its means of secret communication and its confidential files are destroyed well in advance of hostilities commencing, because once this happens, their embassies and consulates will be seized.

As a result, on 19 November 1941, the Foreign Ministry in Tokyo sent coded message #2353 [14] to the Japanese Consulate in Melbourne. It read:

> Owing to the pressure of the international situation, we must be faced with a generally bad situation. In that event, the communication between Japan and the countries opposing her would be severed immediately. Therefore, should we be on the verge of an international crisis we will broadcast twice during the Japanese news broadcast to overseas and at the end of it, the following in the form of a weather report:
> Japanese-American crisis: "East wind rain" *(Higashi no kaze ame)*.
> Japanese-Russian crisis: "North wind cloudy" *(Kita no kaze kumori)*.
> Japanese-British crisis, including the invasion of Thailand, or an

attack on Malaya, or the Netherlands East Indies: "West wind clear" *(Nishi no kaze hare)*.

Action should be taken as regards codes and documents in accordance with the above.

The same message had been sent to other Japanese diplomatic missions around the world and therefore had been intercepted without difficulty not only in Melbourne but also by FECB. It was also easily intercepted by the U.S. Navy's intercept station, Station S, at Bainbridge Island, Seattle, on the West Coast of America and sent by direct-line teletype to Washington, D.C. The Winds messages did not contain any specific details of how and where war might break out, because this was not information Yamamoto needed to share with Japanese diplomats, even those negotiating in Washington.

In Melbourne, message #2353 was sent to the Special Intelligence Organisation,[15] where Eric Nave was chief codebreaker. He immediately identified it as being in the normal consular code, called TSU[16] by the Japanese, and J-19 by the Americans. The code was well known to Nave and the Americans, both of whom had, quite separately, broken it. William Friedman, the U.S. Army's chief codebreaker, later explained that it was "A high grade code[17] involving keyed columnar transposition of code text distributed in a form established by the Japanese when they set up the system . . . we were in a position to process this traffic fairly readily in view of the fact that we had reconstructed the entire code . . . and were able to reconstruct . . . as necessary the transposition keys for superencipherment."

Nave regarded J-19 as a tiresome code to break because the key changed daily, but nevertheless he had no problems in producing the plain text. Neither did FECB or GCCS. But because the American codebreakers were fully occupied decoding other Japanese messages (such as Purple) that they considered more important, it took them nine days, until 28 November, before they had a complete translation of #2353.

Nave had a copy of the first part of what was now called the Winds message typed up and sent to Commodore J. W. Durnford,[18] second naval member of the Australian Naval Board, who in turn wrote a "Most Secret and Personal"[19] letter to Frederick Shedden.[20] Secretary of the Department of Defence, asking that it be shown to Prime Minister Robert Menzies. He immediately added, "As this information has been obtained by most secret methods[21] *it is essential* [original emphasis] that it should not be compromised in any way."

Durnford also told Shedden that extra staff would be drafted in to monitor all the Japanese overseas news broadcasts. In America, the same happened, and all the Army and Navy intercept stations, together with those of the Federal Communications Commission, were alerted to listen for the "execute" part of the Winds message. The head of the U.S. Navy's codebreakers, Commander Laurence F. Safford, issued secret dispatch[22] #282301, dated 28 November 1941, instructing the American intercept stations at Bainbridge Island, Washington; Winter Harbor, Maine; Amagansett, Long Island; Jupiter, Florida; and Cheltenham, Maryland, to listen for the second part of the forecast.

The exact total of messages sent by Yamamoto between 20 November and 7 December to his Task Force at Tankan Bay, and later while at sea en route to Pearl Harbor, is not known, because all Japanese naval records were destroyed before the end of the war. But at least twenty such messages were intercepted and exist today[23] in the National Archives, Washington, D.C., thus proving beyond any doubt that radio silence with the Task Force was broken after it had assembled and sailed. These messages were intercepted by the Americans in Hawaii and on the West Coast of America and therefore would certainly have been intercepted by the much nearer British stations in Hong Kong and Singapore. The American intercepts all bear postwar decryption dates, thus *apparently* supporting the claim that no JN-25 was read prior to the attack. What cannot now be disputed is that radio silence was not complete and that messages were sent to the Task Force from Tokyo and intercepted by the Americans.

The British position is far less clear, because, unlike America, not a single intercepted Japanese signal has been released into the public domain. But Nave is adamant that every message intercepted by the Americans would also have been intercepted by the British, and because JN-25 had been broken by him since the autumn of 1939, all these intercepted messages would have been read without difficulty or delay by FECB and GCCS.

A "Most Secret" message,[24] never before seen in public, sent in Typex (the highest security encoding system used by the British) from FECB to the Admiralty in London at 6:11 A.M. (London time), on 7 December, with a copy to the British Admiralty Delegation (BAD) in Washington, mentions receiving Japanese messages over the previous days and refers to "the majority of signals originating from the C-in-C Combined Fleet (Yamamoto)." This confirms there must have been quite a number of intercepts during these days and that FECB had no difficulty in decoding them, recognizing that they came from Yamamoto, addressed to his fleet.

Some of these messages were relatively routine and concerned the distribution of secret orders[25] to various units and lists of new call signs, but others were far more important. One of the first, decoded by FECB on 20 November, was from Yamamoto in Tokyo, using his Combined Fleet C-in-C call sign, KE RO 88, to his Task Force waiting at Tankan Bay. Here for the first time in print is the signal that effectively set in motion the war in the Pacific: "This dispatch is top secret. To be decoded only by an officer. This order effective as of the date within the text to follow: At 0000 (midnight) on 21 November, repeat 21 November, carry out second phase for opening hostilities."[26]

The prefixes at the start of this message, which were known to FECB because they could read JN-25, showed that it was addressed to the Second Fleet (YA KI 4), the Third Fleet, (E MU 6), the Fourth Fleet (O RE 1), the Combined Fleet (RI TA 3), and the Eleventh Air Fleet (SU YO 4), indicating that a large group of warships, including carriers, had assembled somewhere as part of the first phase of opening hostilities, and that the second phase was about to begin.

Although the message contained no details of a particular target, it showed that, as far as Japan was concerned, war had already begun. In fact, FECB had already deduced this,[27] because during November, Mortimer had been carefully checking the whereabouts and movements of all Japanese merchant ships around the world and preparing charts of their positions and movements. Mortimer noticed they were steadily making their way back to Japan. Plainly the Japanese had no intention of having any of their merchant ships caught in foreign ports, as had happened to the Germans in 1939.

The information obtained by FECB from these JN-25 messages was far more specific and vital than the Purple diplomatic messages, which contained no military information at all, and were still suggesting that further negotiations might be possible in the light of compromise proposals put forward by both Japan and America.

By 23 November, Mortimer's chart at FECB showed that all Japanese merchant ships would be back in home waters by the first week in December. When this information was sent to OIC in London, the view was taken that war would break out any time after 5 December.

On 25 November FECB decrypted Yamamoto's next set of instructions to his waiting Task Force in JN-25: "The Task Force will move out of Hitokappu Wan [Tankan Bay] on the morning of 26 November and advance to the standing-by position on the afternoon of 4 December and speedily complete refueling."[28]

This message was particularly important, because for the first time it showed FECB and the Admiralty that a task force had assembled in the Kuriles and was about to set off for a long sea voyage requiring refueling at sea in eight days' time. The message prefixes showed that the Task

Force included the First Fleet (a battle force), the Second Fleet (a scouting force), and a number of aircraft carriers. Where was the Task Force headed?

There were a number of possibilities. First, an attack against Malaya in the south. Second, an attack, also to the south, against the Dutch East Indies to secure the vital oil fields. Third, an attack against the Philippines. And fourth, an attack far out to the east in the Pacific.

Although the Japanese aircraft carriers had a top speed of between thirty-one and thirty-four knots, this was normally used only when aircraft were landing or taking off, and their long-range cruising speed was eighteen knots, which matched that of the other ships in the Task Force, thus allowing them to cover around 400 miles a day. The distances between the various possible targets were:

Tankan Bay–Pearl Harbor	3,150 miles
Tankan Bay–Singapore	3,394 miles
Tankan Bay–Manila	2,257 miles
Tankan Bay–Java	3,060 miles

Because it was necessary to maintain absolute secrecy while the diplomatic negotiations continued in Washington, the problem of taking such a large Task Force south would be having it sail through waters used by merchant ships and under regular surveillance by British and American air patrols. It would only require a single sighting of this huge armada for the element of surprise to be lost. If the target was Manila, then the Task Force would have to stand off out to sea to the east, leaving them highly vulnerable to detection. More importantly, there were no targets to the south requiring the use of a large group of carriers, since the naval bases in Malaya and the Philippines were within range of Japanese bombers already based in Indo-China, which did, in fact, attack them on 8 December.

So while the Task Force might be going south and linking up with landing craft for a seaborne invasion, the other obvious possibility was that it was headed due east out into the Pacific. In that case Pearl Harbor was the only target of importance that would require the use of carrier-borne aircraft to destroy the U.S. Pacific Fleet in the manner shown by the earlier Bomb Plot message. Wake Island and Guam were unlikely targets, as their military importance would not justify such a battle fleet. Thus anyone able to read JN-25—as could Churchill—knew by 25 November that a large Japanese task force was at sea, with the intention of commencing hostilities, and that one of the most likely targets was Pearl Harbor.

Details of these intercepts reached London late on 25 November at a very critical and sensitive time. Roosevelt knew that, apart from isolationist opposition, America was not ready for war. During the previous weeks, he and his advisers had struggled hard to reach some sort of compromise—or what became known as a modus vivendi—with the Japanese over the trade embargo.

The aim of the modus vivendi was to temporarily defuse the situation, allowing America to build up its defenses in the Pacific, while Japan would not lose too much international prestige. In return for Japan's withdrawing her troops from southern China, leaving only 25,000 troops in the rest of Indo-China, and advancing no farther, America would resume oil shipments—for civilian use only—on a monthly basis, together with food products, chemicals, raw cotton, and silk. The agreement would be reviewed in three months' time with the aim of achieving a permanent settlement for lasting peace in the Far East and Pacific. Even if this failed, it would have given America a vital breathing space. When Churchill was told of these proposals, he was most alarmed, because it looked as if America was veering away from direct conflict with Japan, leaving Britain on its own.

Churchill's ambassador in Tokyo, Sir Robert Craigie, supported the modus vivendi. Some years later Craigie wrote, "I consider that had it been possible to reach a compromise with Japan in December 1941 involving the withdrawal of Japanese troops from Indo-China, war with Japan would not have been inevitable." [29]

Craigie was the Foreign Office's most skilled negotiator and had spent over nine years handling international disarmament affairs with great success. He was certainly no supporter of the Japanese and always saw them as expansionists and military extremists. It was Craigie's view that had the modus vivendi been accepted, war could have been avoided, and as the tide of war turned against Germany in Europe, the extremists in Japan would have lost power. (The full text of Craigie's report is in Appendix 9.)

Churchill was outraged by Craigie's report and tried to have it suppressed. He wrote, "It is a very strange document [30] and one which should be kept scrupulously secret. A more one-sided and pro-Japanese account of what occurred I have hardly ever read. It was a blessing that Japan attacked the United States and thus brought America wholeheartedly into the war. Greater good fortune has rarely happened to the British empire than this event."

However, in his memoirs, written in 1950, Churchill adopted an attitude of bogus naiveté:

When I read the draft reply . . . called the *modus vivendi,* I thought it inadequate. This impression was shared by the Dutch and Australian governments, and above all by Chiang Kai-shek, who sent a frantic protest to Washington. I was however deeply sensitive of the limits which we must observe in commenting on United States policy . . . I understood the dangers attending the thought "The British are trying to drag us into war."[31]

At 3:20 A.M. (London time) on 26 November, Churchill sent Roosevelt a message containing the following: "Of course it is for you to handle this business and *we certainly do not want an additional war* [emphasis added]. There is only one point that disquiets us. What about Chiang Kai-shek? Is he not having a very thin diet?"[32]

Churchill's sudden interest in China was surprising and not particularly convincing. He had certainly shown little interest in Chiang Kai-shek before. Nor does his remark that he did not want Japan to commence hostilities with America ring true, when he had always made it plain that this was what he wanted most. He had frequently repeated his intention to drag America into the war at all costs because he knew it was the only way to ensure Britain's survival.

But this message was not the only one that passed between Churchill and Roosevelt that day. Sometime later on 26 November, Churchill's private secretary Anthony Bevir sent by hand to the American Embassy a second message[33] to be transmitted to Roosevelt, accompanied by a note: "I enclose a telegram from the Former Naval Person to the President for dispatch as soon as possible. I am so sorry to trouble you at this hour."

Of all Churchill's voluminous correspondence with Roosevelt during World War II, this is one message that cannot be read, since the file[34] containing it is withheld from the Public Record Office in London for the next seventy years. According to Britain's Foreign Secretary, to release it would harm national security.

That some such message was received by the Americans on 26 November was later confirmed by the Army inquiry, which sat from July to October 1944, and the naval inquiry, which sat during the same period. At the Army inquiry it was stated: "On 26 November there was received specific evidence of the Japanese intention to wage offensive war against Great Britain and the United States."[35] But no details of what this "specific evidence" consisted of were placed before the inquiry.

At the naval inquiry, Admiral Kimmel was allowed to question Admiral Stark and asked, "Do you recall whether on or about 26 November you received information from the office of naval intelligence that gave specific evidence of Japan's intention to wage offensive war against Britain and America."[36]

Stark refused to answer, claiming: "It would involve the disclosure of information detrimental to the public interest."[37]

Aside from his excuse being remarkably similar to that used by today's British Foreign Office for refusing anyone access to Churchill's file for that period, it is also extraordinary that the naval board agreed that Stark need not reveal his sources when the whole purpose of the inquiry was to establish how much was known about Japanese plans prior to the attack. A year later, at the extensive 1945 congressional inquiry, both Stark and General Marshall had got their acts together and pleaded poor memory[38] as to what messages had been received on 26 November from any source. And the committee was unable to discover what intelligence had been made available by the British, because those like Wisden and Mortimer, who had worked at FECB, were refused permission by the British government to attend.

The contents of this message must have been remarkably startling to cause Roosevelt such a sudden change of attitude. When Ambassadors Nomura and Kurusu called at the State Department later on 26 November to hear the response to their proposals, they were astonished to be brusquely rebuffed and told the modus vivendi was no longer on the table. In its place, Hull countered with a Ten Point Plan which called for a mutual non-aggression treaty and the evacuation of all Japanese troops from China and Indo-China. Naturally the two ambassadors rejected it on the spot. Knowing nothing about the sailing of the Task Force, Nomura told Tokyo, "In view of our negotiations all along we were both dumbfounded and said we could not even cooperate to the extent of reporting this back to Tokyo. We argued furiously but Hull remained solid as a rock."[39]

What new information had Roosevelt suddenly acquired? Clearly it had nothing to do with China, and therefore could not have been the first message sent by Churchill on 26 November. That serves only as a historical smokescreen. According to Henry Stimson's diary (which was reconstructed after the event): "I talked to the President over the telephone[40] [on the morning of 26 November]. I asked him whether he had received the paper which I had sent him over last night about the Japanese having started a new expedition from Shanghai down towards Indo-China. He fairly blew up—jumped up into the air, so to speak, and said he hadn't seen it and that changed the whole situation. . . . [The President] was shocked and at once took it as further evidence of bad faith on the part of the Japanese."

The "paper" Stimson was referring to was a Magic intelligence report received in Washington on the afternoon of 25 November, which Stimson's diary records as reporting, "A Japanese expedition had started with five divisions of troops arriving at Shanghai, where they had embarked on ships—30, 40, or 50 ships—and have been sighted south of Formosa."[41]

However, Stimson's version is confusing and does not accord with another passage in his diary, which states that the convoy preparations had been anticipated for at least a month. Furthermore, the original of the Magic message shows the ships were not at sea but: "A more or less normal movement of ten to thirty troopships in the Yangtse River below Shanghai."[42]

If Stimson thought this Magic message so important, it is surprising he had not discussed it with Roosevelt as soon as it arrived the previous afternoon. This suggests that Stimson may have confused this message with some other piece of information that arrived later and was responsible for alarming the President so greatly and causing him to break off further negotiations with the Japanese. This must have been quite separate from the innocuous message sent by Churchill at 3:20 A.M. on 26 November from London.

One such message that might have achieved this also reached Washington on 26 November from Britain's MI6. It read:

> Secret source[43] (usually reliable) reports that (A) Japanese will attack Kra Isthmus [in south Thailand] from sea on Dec[ember] 1, without any declaration of break, with a view to getting between Bangkok and Singapore. (B) Attacking forces will proceed direct from Hainan and Formosa. Main landing point to be in Songkhala area. Valuation for above in [sic] No. 3. [only about 55 to 60 percent accuracy] American military and naval intelligence informed.

Churchill may also have told Roosevelt that the Australians believed the *Sydney* had been sunk by a Japanese submarine. Although this would certainly have confirmed the treacherous nature of the Japanese, it would not have caused Roosevelt to react so strongly, as it had not involved an American warship.

The only other piece of new and vital intelligence that Churchill possessed, and could have given Roosevelt, was the FECB decrypt of 25 November, showing that a Japanese task force, complete with aircraft carriers, was about to sail from the Kuriles for an eight-day voyage before refueling at sea. That would be news of such a cataclysmic dimension that it would shock Roosevelt out of any euphoria that war could be avoided and thus make the modus vivendi and any further discussions useless.

But how could Churchill give this information to the President? To cause Roosevelt to act on it, Churchill would have had to disclose sufficient information about its source to authenticate the report. This would mean telling Roosevelt that GCCS and FECB could read JN-25. Churchill must have believed Roosevelt was not receiving JN-25 decrypts, since it had never been mentioned in their regular exchanges as had the Magic diplomatic decrypts. Equally, OP-20-G believed the British were neither reading nor even interested in JN-25, as this was what they had been told during their visit to GCCS in January 1941. If Churchill now suddenly admitted to Roosevelt that he had deceived him[44] over JN-25 all along, it would open up a whole can of worms and irrevocably sour their relationship just at the moment when Churchill needed America's support.

Furthermore, once Roosevelt received this information from Churchill, apart from breaking off negotiations with the Japanese, he would immediately do two other things. First, he would warn Kimmel and Short in Hawaii so that they could set a trap for the Japanese, and second, tell OP-20-G that FECB had broken JN-25 and were getting vital information from their decrypts that he was not seeing. Since we know the President did neither of these things, it is legitimate to conclude that Churchill did not pass on this information from FECB, because he believed it to be in Britain's interest that the Japanese attack Pearl Harbor in such a dramatic manner that it would brush aside any further thoughts of isolationism.

It seems that the only "specific evidence" of Japanese aggression that reached Roosevelt by the morning of 26 November was the news from Australia that a Japanese submarine had probably sunk the *Sydney*, the (incorrect) report of a large convoy on the move south near Formosa, and the MI6 report that the Japanese would invade Siam (Thailand) on 1 December without warning.

This interpretation of events is borne out by a warning sent out by the U.S. Navy in Washington the same day:

> This dispatch is to be considered a war warning.[45] Negotiations with
> . . . Japan have ceased and an aggressive move by Japan is expected
> within the next few days. The number and equipment of Japanese
> troops . . . indicate an amphibious expedition against either the Phil-
> ippines, Thai or Kra peninsula, or possibly Borneo. A similar warning
> is being sent by War Department. SPENAVO [Special Naval Observer
> in London] inform British.

There is no mention at all of Pearl Harbor, nor is there any suggestion that the U.S. Navy had suddenly become aware of vital new information derived from breaking Japanese naval codes. Furthermore, this warning could not have been connected with the Task Force's sailing from Tankan Bay, because the message decoded by FECB showed that it had to sail for eight days before refueling, which would have been unnecessary if its destination had been the Malay peninsula.

One also needs to bear in mind that Stimson only spoke to Roosevelt over the telephone, rather than personally showing him the specific message. Therefore, when Stimson claimed the President "fairly blew up," it is possible that Roosevelt, not having access to raw decrypts (like Churchill), may have been confused as to which message the pair were discussing.

There remains one final piece of mythology that has helped obscure the truth about Pearl Harbor: the date of the second change of the JN-25 additive table in 1941. The first had occurred, as expected, on 1 June, and as far as FECB was concerned they were back in business again, reading the code within the usual few weeks.

The next change was expected on 1 December, and many accounts of the attack, including those published by official government agencies, claim that because the change took place then, it prevented American codebreakers from reading any JN-25 messages sent during the remaining days before the attack. Apart from the fact that American codebreakers are not "officially" supposed to have been able to read *any* JN-25 messages in the two years prior to Pearl Harbor, this excuse is invalid for the simple reason that the table change did not take place on 1 December.

On 2 December, naval headquarters in Tokyo sent a message to all their units including the Task Force now seven days out into the Pacific:

> Starting 4 December 1941 additive system #8 of Naval Code D [JN-25] will be used, and additive system #7 will be discontinued. From Office of Naval Communication. As there are some communication units who have not yet received additive list #8 in communicating with them additive list #7 will be used.[46]

Messages like this are a codebreaker's dream. No one could have believed that the Japanese would have been so helpful, and it clearly demonstrated the disadvantages of using a cumbersome book code compared to a cryptograph. The enormous buildup of naval units in preparation for war had stretched the resources of the signals department so greatly that they had been unable to distribute all the new tables in time for the routine change on 1 December. Not only was the introduction of the new additive table to be delayed by a few extra vital days, but it meant the same message would have to be sent simultaneously using the old and new tables and, because the text lengths would be identical, provide a perfect crib. Had the Japanese Navy been using any form of cryptograph, key changes could have been made throughout the entire fleet at a predetermined time. This fundamental error in code security (which had occurred earlier with the Red and Purple machines) explains why FECB and GCCS were able to recover the new system so quickly after Pearl Harbor. Ships' call signs were changed on 1 December in accordance with a JN-25 message intercepted on 25 November giving the details, which, of course, FECB could read.

Later that same say (2 December), FECB intercepted another message from Yamamoto to his Task Force that read: "Climb Niitakayama 1208, repeat 1208."[47] It hardly needed a codebreaking genius to deduce that this was the date of the opening attack. Mount Niitakayama (also known as Mount Morrison), is a 13,113-foot peak in Formosa, the highest mountain in what was then part of the Japanese empire, and climbing it was regarded as a great feat, so it was typically bombastic of a nation about to go to war to use such an expression. This was the only occasion that the date of the attack—the eighth day of the twelfth month—was sent by radio, because previously it had only been mentioned as Y-Day in the operational orders given to the Task Force before it sailed.

Although Pearl Harbor was never mentioned by name, all the clues were there. FECB knew that the Task Force had sailed from the Kuriles on 26 November, refueled at sea eight days later, and that an attack would take place on 8 December (Tokyo time). The Philippines and Malaya still remained potential targets, but as each day passed without a sighting of the Task Force anywhere south of Japan (although on 2 December American patrol aircraft from the Philippines had sighted twelve Japanese submarines off Indo-China), they became far less likely.

Mortimer recalls that at FECB the conclusion was that the only other target that fitted the length of voyage, midocean refueling, and the inclusion of aircraft carriers was Pearl Harbor, and that an attack on a Sunday (7 December, local time across the international date line), would offer the greatest element of surprise.[48] As with all the earlier JN-25 decrypts, this information was routinely sent back to London with a request to repeat it to the Americans. Since FECB were told nothing to the contrary, they naturally assumed this was done. Had the JN-25 additive table been changed as planned on 1 December, FECB would have been unable to read Yamamoto's final message containing the date of the attack for at least a week or more.

Apart from FECB, the Dutch codebreakers at Kamer 14 on Java had by this time made considerable progress against Japanese codes, some of which information they appear to have been sharing daily with FECB, with whom they had a direct radio link,[49] as well as a liaison officer[50] in FECB's offices. Japan's diplomatic traffic between Batavia and Tokyo was sent to Singapore for decoding on the Purple machine they had there, while Kamer 14 also exchanged details of their work on JN-25.

The Dutch C-in-C, General Hein ter Poorten, concluded from their reading of JN-25: "During the first days of December '41 our intelligence reports showed Japanese naval concentrations near the Kuriles. Former [previous?] informations had me already convinced that Japan was about to start a Pacific war and this would be done with a surprise attack similar to its attack in 1904 at the opening of hostilities against Russia."[51]

On 27 November, Kamer 14 decrypted a JN-25 message from Tokyo to the Task Force ordering it to sail;[52] this was the 25 November message intercepted by FECB, which had taken Kamer 14 rather longer to decrypt. The Dutch formed the impression that the Japanese fleet was sailing in a southerly direction and sent the decrypt with their analysis to their naval attaché in Washington as well as Singapore. After examining all the details of the message, the attaché concluded the Task Force's direction was easterly rather than southerly and that it could be headed for Pearl Harbor. He passed on the decrypt with his own evaluation to OP-20-G but heard nothing more.

NEWS BROADCASTS from Tokyo[53] that carried the "execute" weather forecasts were designed to be heard around the world—in Britain, Western Europe, Australia, and South America—and were repeated several times during the day of December 4. They had been easily picked up in Melbourne, and FECB had no problem hearing them at their powerful intercept station on Stonecutters Island in Hong Kong,[54] which could eavesdrop on everything sent by radio from Japan.

But besides Melbourne and Singapore, others also heard the broadcasts. On that day, the duty radio operator[55] at the Japanese Embassy in Washington, D.C., Chief Petty Officer Kenici Ogemoto, rushed into the office of Captain Yuzuru Sanematsu, the naval attaché, shouting, "The wind blew." Sanematsu ran into the radio room just in time to hear the news reader repeat the weather forecast, *Higashi no kaze ame.* There was great excitement, and immediately preparations were set in hand to destroy the cryptographs while codebooks and other secret documents were piled in heaps in the garden ready to be burned.

The "execute" broadcast had been made several times that day and had been received at the Japanese Embassy in midafternoon on 4 December. The earlier message had not been intercepted, because the duty radio operator, Ogemoto, did not start work until after 9 A.M.

Another person who heard that same "execute" message was Ralph Briggs,[56] then a senior radio operator with the U.S. Navy at their powerful intercept station at Cheltenham, known as Station M, in Maryland, some twenty-five miles southeast of Washington, D.C.

Briggs was born in 1914 and as a young boy had been fascinated with both the Navy and radio communications. As a teenager he was a keen radio ham (with the call sign W9NCM, Nan Charlie Mike), and in 1934 at the age of twenty Briggs joined the U.S. Navy Reserve. Two years later he transferred to the regular U.S. Navy. Because of his knowledge of radio, in 1937 Briggs was interviewed by his fleet intelligence officer, Lieutenant John Harper, who asked him if he would be interested in working with the Naval Intelligence Group that was intercepting Japanese radio traffic. Briggs was delighted and was ordered to report to Washington. Here Briggs joined Class 20[57] of the "On-the-Roof Gang," so called because they were literally located in a steel-reinforced blockhouse on the roof of Wing 6 of the old Navy Building on Constitution Avenue in Washington, D.C.

By August 1941, Briggs was a chief petty officer and had been posted to the Naval Communications Station at Cheltenham. He was one of the few members of the staff there who could actually read Japanese *kana*. The intercept section was divided into two groups. There was the Enigma group working on German intercepts and high-frequency direction-finding, and his group handling Japanese signals.

The head of Briggs's section was Chief Petty Officer Radioman Daryl Wigle, who was one of the original members of the On-the-Roof Gang. All Cheltenham's intercepts were sent to OP-20-G, headed by Laurence Safford. A carbon copy of each intercept was kept at Cheltenham, and after thirty days, if there had been no query back from OP-20-G, it was destroyed.

On 1 December 1941, Safford drove out to the Cheltenham station and "made a personal check of the Winds message watch and, as I recall, found that Chief Radioman Wigle was monitoring the Tokyo news broadcasts 24 hours a day and had assigned qualified *kana* operators to this duty."[58]

In the evening that same day, Briggs came on duty and before starting work checked the watch supervisor's log. "On this particular date the station chief, Daryl Wigle, had listed the three sets of Japanese forecasts. He didn't put down the meaning. Just the Japanese characters," Briggs recalled forty-six years later. "I immediately recognized them as words connected with the weather. And underneath, Wigle had stuck a note saying we were to be on the lookout for any messages containing these groups." Briggs went to see Wigle, who was still on duty. "Hey, Daryl, what's the scoop on this? These are regular weather words, aren't they?"

Wigle told Briggs that all operators were to be on the lookout for these words contained in any sort of broadcast, or any combination of them. Briggs asked, "But they're just weather forecasts, what do they mean?" Then finally Wigle opened the drawer of his desk and took out a card prepared by Safford which had the full meaning on it. "So then I knew. But as none of the other operators understood *kana,* they hadn't asked what the Japanese characters meant, so they didn't realize what the phrases meant."

And so it was that, early on Thursday morning, around 8 A.M. local time on the East Coast of America, Briggs intercepted the "execute" portion of the Winds message *Higashi no kaze ame*—East wind rain. It was hidden in the middle of a weather forecast approximately 200 words long.

Briggs at once recognized the *kana* characters and immediately took the intercept and typed it up. In the process he made an original plus two carbon copies. He then went to the teleprinter in the Enigma department (because his own section's teleprinter was not yet connected) to send the intercept directly to OP-20-G in Washington. However, as Briggs recalls, "I had a little argument with a guy named Dave Howley, who was sitting on the Enigma circuit, and he didn't want to break the network circuit and let me get in on the system so that I could get into Washington. I explained that my message was very important, top priority. So I said if you've any argument call Daryl Wigle. So then he gave in and let me get on the circuit and I typed up the message myself. I then called Wigle, who was in his quarters, and told him the 'execute' message was in. He said get it on the teletype to Washington, and I said I'd already done that. O.K., says Wigle, that's good, I'll be up shortly."

Briggs's teletype produced an original and a copy at the Cheltenham end of the teleprinter circuit and another pair of copies at the Washington end. So at this stage there were seven copies of the "execute" message in existence.

Briggs's intercept was received at OP-20-G sometime between 8:30 A.M. and 9 A.M. and was passed to Lieutenant Commander Alwyn D. Kramer, USN, who was head of the translation section. Safford was on his way into the office while all this was happening, and by the time he arrived Kramer had translated the message and rushed up to him with it and the original teletype in his hand and said, "This is it." Safford read the original intercept and saw that Kramer had underlined the three code groups and added his own interpretation: "War with England (including Netherlands East Indies); war with the United States; peace with Russia."

Safford immediately sent the original of the Briggs intercept by hand to Rear Admiral Leigh Noyes, USN, Director of Naval Communications, and shortly afterward Safford received confirmation that Noyes had received the message. Safford then made seven more copies of the tele-printer message (making a total of fourteen in all), and sent these over to his opposite number at the War Department, Colonel Otis K. Sadtler, head of U.S. Army Signals Intelligence. An hour or so later, Safford had typed up some smooth translations of the intercept, and these went to the Navy Department and the White House for distribution to those on the Magic intercept list. Safford's final task was to send a "Well done" message [59] to Cheltenham, which Briggs and others on his watch saw.

But despite all the information and warnings that had been snatched out of the ether, there was still an incredible air of lethargy.

CHAPTER 8

Churchill's War

CHURCHILL'S OWN ACCOUNT of what happened in the immediate days before Pearl Harbor is remarkably uninformative and inaccurate compared to his detailed description of previous events and his regular exchanges with Roosevelt. His last mention of receiving a Purple decrypt[1] is on 2 December, when he claims the Americans sent him one (Telegram #985) from the Tokyo–Berlin circuit that Roosevelt and Hull had already seen, which told Oshima to warn Hitler and Foreign Minister Ribbentrop: "Say very secretly to them that there is extreme danger that war may suddenly break out between the Anglo-Saxon nations and Japan through some clash of arms, and that the time of the breaking out of this war may come quicker than anyone dreams."[2]

Churchill's claim is untrue. Telegram #985 was first intercepted and decrypted by GCCS on 1 December, using the Purple machine given them by the Americans, and GCCS sent the plain text to Washington at 3:30 P.M. that same day. Thus Churchill knew the contents before Roosevelt.

There is then a curious unexplained blank in Churchill's memoirs covering the next six days. He makes no mention of receiving any more Magics, the Winds "execute" message received by FECB and GCCS on 4 December, or the various instructions from Tokyo to their diplomatic missions ordering the destruction of codebooks and cipher machines. Nor does Churchill make any reference to the long thirteen-part Purple message the Japanese sent on 6 December to Washington, answering Hull's Ten Point Plan of 26 November, which was intercepted by the Americans between noon and 3 P.M. in Washington, and by GCCS between 5 P.M. and 8 P.M. in London. The American codebreakers got a complete translation of the thirteen parts to Roosevelt at the White

House by 9:15 P.M. on the evening of the sixth ("This means war" was the President's response), so assuming GCCS and FECB were equally efficient, Churchill would have had his copy around 2 A.M. on the Sunday morning of 7 December.

The fourteenth part of the message, containing Japan's final ultimatum, read: "The Japanese government regrets to have to notify hereby the American government that in view of the attitude of the American government it cannot but consider that it is impossible to reach an agreement through further negotiations."[3]

This reached OP-20-G in Washington at 3 A.M. on the morning of Sunday, 7 December, and GCCS by 8 A.M. With the final part was another message[4] containing instructions to submit the entire fourteen-part reply to the State Department at exactly 1 P.M. Washington time or 6 P.M. in London. There were some further Purple messages from Tokyo to Washington, one of which thanked Nomura and Kurusu for their efforts, and a final one ordering the destruction of the last Purple machine.

OP-20-G had to send the second message (about the time of delivery) to the Army's codebreakers, because only they had Japanese translators on duty. So once again the split responsibility delayed matters, and it was not until 9 A.M. that both messages were ready in plain text. But GCCS had neither a shortage of translators nor this ridiculous split responsibility, so Churchill would have had the same information during Sunday morning, although he makes no mention of this in his memoirs. Thus by the middle of the afternoon on 7 December (still early morning in Washington), Churchill knew that the deadline of 1 P.M., when set against the "Climb Niitakayama" decrypt of 2 December, must mean a dawn attack somewhere out in the Pacific, with the most likely target being Pearl Harbor. The jigsaw was virtually complete. All Churchill had to do was to wait and America would soon be in the war.

When Roosevelt's special envoy,[5] Averell Harriman, and the American ambassador in London, John Winant, arrived at Chequers on Sunday, 7 December 1941, Churchill told Winant that if America was attacked by Japan, Britain would immediately declare war on Japan. Would America do the same if British possessions were attacked? Unaware of any secret agreement between Roosevelt and Churchill, Winant politely parried the question by pointing out that in America only Congress could declare war.

THE FIRST bombs had started to fall on Pearl Harbor just before 8 A.M. or 6 P.M. in Britain. At 2:15 P.M. in Washington (7:15 P.M. in Britain) Roosevelt telephoned Lord Halifax[6] at the British Embassy and told him "that the Japanese were bombing Hawaii, and asked me to pass it on as quickly as I could to London. Most of the fleet was at sea . . . none of their newer ships [were] in harbour." Obviously Roosevelt was basing his information on the first sketchy reports that had arrived from Pearl Harbor, because, in fact, only the two aircraft carriers were at sea.

Shortly before 9 P.M. at Chequers, Churchill led Harriman and Winant into dinner. Only the three of them were present at this somber meal.[7] By this time, Churchill already knew of the attack on Pearl Harbor from Halifax but said nothing. At 9 P.M. he asked his butler, Saunders, to bring in a small portable radio Harry Hopkins had given him so that they could listen to the BBC's main evening news. As with all tube radios, it took a few minutes to warm up, by which time the main evening news was already in progress and Churchill missed the first paragraph reporting the attack.

The broadcast had begun: "Here is the news and this is Alvar Lidell reading it. President Roosevelt has just announced Japanese air attacks on American bases in the Hawaiian Islands. The Japanese envoys are now at the State Department."[8]

At this point the radio had warmed up.

> In Libya, the tanks have joined battle south of Tobruk, and Richard Dimbleby has sent a despatch on the fighting; our mobile columns have reported successes in pressure on the enemy throughout the battle area, and our air support has been strongly maintained along the African coast, with other attacks on Axis shipping and the Naples base.
>
> Today's earlier news from Russia was again of even stronger resistance to the German thrust at Moscow and of more harassing of the enemy's retreat in the south.
>
> The Royal Air Force have continued their daylight attacks on the enemy's Western Front.
>
> Tonight's postscript will be Vernon Bartlett.

At this point Churchill switched off the set, thus missing the next part, which went on: "The news has just been given that Japanese aircraft have raided Pearl Harbor . . . the announcement of the attack was made in a brief statement by President Roosevelt."

It was a terrible anticlimax for Churchill, who, having stage-managed the dinner party, now assumed news of the attack had not yet reached the BBC. While he gloomily pondered on what to do, Saunders reappeared and told the three that the staff had heard all the broadcast and that the Japanese had attacked the Americans.

Although Churchill obviously did not know then that 4,575 Americans had been killed or wounded at Pearl Harbor, and even more terrible losses were to come as a result of his betrayal of Singapore, at no time did he ever show any remorse for his deliberate deception of the Americans, Australians, and even his own people. For Churchill it was a time of rejoicing.

> No American will think it wrong of me if I proclaim that to have the United States on our side was to be the greatest joy. . . .[9] England would live; Britain would live; the Commonwealth of Nations and the Empire would live. How long the war would last or in what fashion it would end no man could tell, nor did I at this moment care. Once again in our long island history we would emerge . . . safe and victorious. We should not be wiped out. . . . Being saturated and satiated with emotion and sensation, I went to bed and slept the sleep of the saved and thankful.

But in Singapore at FECB there was no jubilation.[10] The next day the shocked and bewildered staff gathered around Tommy Wisden, who asked incredulously, "With all the information we gave them. How could the Americans have been caught unprepared?" Everyone at FECB went back through their records to ensure that every scrap of information, including JN-25, had been sent to London for repetition to CINCPAC. None had been missed.

It was to be many years before the truth began to trickle out and it finally became plain that, had Britain shared with the Americans its full knowledge of the work of FECB and GCCS against Japanese naval codes throughout 1941, the attack on Pearl Harbor would never have occurred, and Yamamoto's Task Force might have been decimated in a well-laid trap. The denial of this information was no accident but the deliberate policy of Churchill himself to achieve his aim of dragging America into the war.

CHAPTER 9

Drawing the Blinds

... shall ne'er go by,
From this day to the ending of the world,
But we in it shall be remembered—
We few, we happy few, we band of brothers;
For he that today sheds his blood for me
Shall be my brother.

—ARIZONA MEMORIAL DEDICATION

EVERY YEAR MORE than two million people[1] visit the *Arizona* Memorial at
the Pearl Harbor naval base in Hawaii. They first gather at the impres-
sively dignified memorial center set in a peaceful landscaped garden
overlooking the harbor with a large museum[2] containing many relics
and pictures of the battleship. Visitors are then shown a twenty-minute
film of the history of the USS *Arizona* and the attack on Pearl Harbor on
7 December 1941.

Presumably to assuage modern consciences and the economics of
Japanese tourism and business interests in Hawaii, the film has been
carefully sanitized so as to play down the treacherous nature of the
attack that morning, which was made while diplomatic negotiations
were still in progress. President Roosevelt's "infamy" speech to Congress has been excised and is shown only mute, thus robbing it of its
dramatic impact. Even the final surrender of the Japanese on board the
USS *Missouri* in 1945 has been delicately edited so that there is only a
fleeting glimpse of the defeated enemy. Revisionist history is commonplace in communist countries, but it is bizarre to find it so grotesquely
displayed at one of America's great national shrines.

But though the emphasis and morality of history can be tailored to suit political expediency, the true majesty of the *Arizona* Memorial cannot be tampered with. Each boatload of visitors is shuttled out across Pearl Harbor toward Ford Island in trim U.S. Navy launches, often conned by young women sailors whose parents were not alive in 1941. As they approach Alfred Pries's starkly functional structure[3] that spans the wreck, each launch pauses to let the visitors get their first glimpse of the USS *Arizona.*

As the launch lies idle in the still waters, the chatter dies away. Each visitor—no matter what his age—senses he is about to enter a world where time has stood still and belongs to another generation. Quietly visitors file up the steps into the memorial. First into the bell room with the USS *Arizona*'s bell[4] hanging silent before them. Then out along the main catwalk, where they see the remains of this great battleship lying beneath the clear waters. Just a few pieces reach up out of the water toward the blue skies as a reminder of the death that came so treacherously that Sunday morning fifty years ago. And from these rusty relics still proudly flies the Stars and Stripes, reminding visitors that the USS *Arizona* remains in commission[5] with the U.S. Navy.

Finally, at the far end, visitors to the Hall of Remembrance look in silent awe at the names of the 1,177 officers and men of the USS *Arizona* who lie entombed below. The names are carved into the marble wall that flickers with sunlight reflected off the waters that ebb and flow around their final resting place. Like many before them, and since, these brave men risked their lives in the service of their country, knowing full well the perils of the sea, and now lie at peace secure within its protection for all time. Some visitors to the *Arizona* Memorial find it a numbing experience. Young and old stand there in silence gazing into the waters around the wreck, with the thin iridescent slick of fuel oil that still leaks from the tanks ruptured by Japanese bombs and torpedoes half a century ago.

Certainly there are plenty of other memorials and shrines to American war dead elsewhere around the world. They nestle in leafy woodlands in England, in the sleepy cowfields of rural France, the plains of Belgium, near the industrial heartland of Germany, in sandy deserts, and remote rocky islands. But none generates such strong emotions as does the *Arizona* Memorial. Why should this be so?

Because it is part of the story of the attack on Pearl Harbor, which even with the passage of fifty years is still close to the minds and hearts of Americans. The Pearl Harbor attack was a shattering defeat for American military and political leadership. By itself this is sufficiently topical to keep the story alive today in the context of a surprise attack from another enemy. "Remember Pearl Harbor" is a cry frequently heard when military budgets are being debated, and it is one that politicians ignore at their peril.

But there is much more to it than that. The story of Pearl Harbor remains an enigma to this day, containing all the elements of one of the world's greatest mystery stories. Over the intervening years the American people have been given highly selective accounts of what happened, with the truth obscured by a combination of official secrecy, false testimony, coercion to tell lies, a deliberate attempt to hide the facts within a web of bogus mythology, and poor research.

Despite eight official investigations, a score of books, and hundreds of historical studies totaling many millions of words, vital questions have remained unanswered because of a lack of accurate firsthand or archival material.

According to the official version, the idea of an attack on Pearl Harbor seemed so illogical when compared to an attack on targets nearer Japan that, due to cognitive dissonance (refusing to accept what you do not wish to believe), no senior officer at OP-20-G or the Army War Plans Division was willing to consider it seriously or even discuss it with the commanders in Hawaii. As a result, important messages, like the Bomb Plot signal, were ignored because they did not fit in with a preconceived idea of what the Japanese might do.

In other words, the information was in Washington, but no one recognized it. As the historian Roberta Wohlstetter put it in her 1962 history, *Pearl Harbor: Warning and Decision:* "The relevant signals so clearly audible after the event [were] partially obscured before the event by surrounding noise." The military view that an attack on Pearl Harbor was unlikely was shared by the local media. On 6 September 1941, journalist Clarke Beach wrote in the *Honolulu Star-Bulletin:* "A Japanese attack on Hawaii is regarded as the most unlikely thing in the world, with one chance in a million of being successful. Besides having more powerful defenses than any other [American] post, it is protected by distance. The Japanese fleet would have no bases from which to operate . . . [and] . . . American patrols would spot it long before it arrived."

During the 1950s, however, a number of revisionist historians began to publish books propagating the theory that Roosevelt had deliberately concealed warnings of the attack because he needed an excuse to bring America into the war to help Britain defeat Hitler.

The revisionist theory argues that Roosevelt and his closest colleagues knew, from intelligence derived from the Magic decrypts of the Purple messages passing between Washington and Tokyo and the consular messages between Hawaii and Tokyo, that Japan planned to attack America if the negotiations in Washington failed. They also knew from the Bomb Plot message, available in Washington on 9 October, that the Japanese were planning an aerial attack on Pearl Harbor. And Roosevelt was aware from the decrypts of the Japanese consular messages from Hawaii of their close and continuous interest in the movements of the U.S. Pacific Fleet.

On 2 December, Roosevelt read the message from Tokyo to Berlin instructing Oshima to tell Hitler that war with America "may come quicker than anyone dreams." Finally, there was the pilot message sent to Washington from Tokyo on 6 December warning the Japanese Embassy that a final message, terminating further diplomatic negotiations, was about to arrive and was to be presented to the State Department at precisely 1 P.M. on 7 December 1941.

None of this information was made available to the commanders in Pearl Harbor. Despite the increasing urgency of intelligence being decrypted as late as 6 and 7 of December, no effort was made to send any form of warning to either Admiral Kimmel or Admiral Short. It has often been argued that a Purple machine at Pearl Harbor would have enabled Kimmel and Short to have warning of the Japanese attack, but this is not so. True, it would have drawn attention to the 7:30 A.M. deadline, but without the JN-25 operational details, this would not necessarily have had much impact. After all, General MacArthur in the Philippines had seven hours' warning after the Pearl Harbor attack yet was still caught unprepared, with all his aircraft on the ground. Far more crucial would have been to allow the Hawaiian commanders to see JN-25 and J-19 consular decrypts, some of which, unknown to them, were being intercepted in Honolulu but were sent to either OP-20-G or SIS for decoding. These would have shown them the intense interest being shown by the Japanese in the Pearl Harbor defenses—in particular the message of 24 September, which divided Pearl Harbor into a number of target areas for an aerial attack, and became known as the Bomb Plot message.

One of the leading proponents of the revisionist theory, Rear Admiral Robert A. Theobald, USN (Ret.), argued in his book *The Final Secret of Pearl Harbor,* that

> Everything that happened in Washington on 6 and 7 December supports the belief that Roosevelt had directed that no [warning] message be sent to the Hawaiian commanders before noon on Sunday, Washington time. Stark arrived in his office at 9:25 A.M. on Sunday [7 December] and . . . accepted . . . the [Japanese] declaration of war message [the Magic 14th part decrypt] [but] against the advice of assistants refused to inform Kimmel. At 10:05 A.M. Stark knew that the message was to be delivered at 1 P.M. Washington time [7:30 A.M. Hawaiian time], but again, despite the urging of his aides, refused to

send word to Kimmel. . . . Stark's statement to the press in August 1945 that all he did during pre–Pearl Harbor days was on the order of higher authority . . . can only mean President Roosevelt. . . . thus by holding a weak fleet in Hawaii as an invitation to a surprise attack and, by denying the commander of that fleet the information which might cause him to render that attack impossible, Roosevelt brought war to the United States on 7 December 1941.

But this attack on Roosevelt cannot be sustained, because the decision to limit the distribution of Magic material to only Stimson, Gerow, Miles, Bratton, Knox, Turner, Ingersoll, McCollum, Watts, and—belatedly—Roosevelt and Hull was taken by Stark and Marshall. In fact, the President was unaware he was being denied Magic material by his subordinates. Thus the decision to deny the Hawaiian commanders Magic material, and the refusal to permit their codebreakers to work on intercepted messages, had nothing to do with the President.

It would be convenient to claim that Roosevelt ordered that the two aircraft carriers should sail from Pearl Harbor, thus denying Yamamoto his prize should this be his target. Unfortunately, that also cannot be sustained, because the *Enterprise* left on 28 November on a perfectly routine mission. In any case, for the President to give such an order without explaining his reasons to the Navy commanders could not have passed unnoticed.

The revisionist scenario has never been accepted for three reasons. First, no evidence has ever been produced to show that Roosevelt would betray his office as President in this manner. Second, the information contained in the consular and diplomatic decrypts that Roosevelt saw gave no indication that Pearl Harbor might be the target; nor did it give any precise indication of the date of the attack. And third, even if he was aware that Pearl Harbor was the target, would a President who knew his Navy was unready for war put most of his Pacific Fleet at risk as part of a plan to get America into the war? To believe this we must believe FDR was a knave and a fool, which, manifestly, he was not.

And did Roosevelt want to help Churchill to the extent of bringing America into the war prematurely? All evidence shows quite the contrary and that FDR desperately wanted more time to enable America to rearm before commencing hostilities.

Aside from the question of FDR's morality, both the "official" and "revisionist" scenarios are outdated and invalid because their authors were unaware that the British (and most probably the Americans) were reading JN-25 during the period leading up to the attack. This is hardly surprising, because, as we have shown, the existence of JN-25 has only been officially acknowledged by the American government in 1990 to the authors of this book, while Nave's own account of how all Japanese codes including JN-25 were broken by FECB and GCCS remains the only British source. The whole question of Japanese codebreaking continues to be completely embargoed by the British government.

The question of who knew what about Japanese plans during November 1941, when Yamamoto's Task Force sailed, is the crucial factor in determining where responsibility lay. As we know the messages from Yamamoto to his battle fleet were intercepted, it follows that those who could read JN-25 possessed the final pieces of the jigsaw. If, however, they were only reading the Purple diplomatic messages, then they were blind, because these never contained any operational orders.

This fact was never appreciated during any of the eight official inquiries, because even the existence of JN-25 had been deliberately suppressed by the U.S. Navy, let alone whether it had been broken. The question of whether Britain could read JN-25 never emerged at any of the inquiries because, despite official requests, no British codebreaker from either GCCS or FECB was allowed to attend and give evidence. And Churchill's memoirs and the more recent official histories all carefully ignore the subject, just as they do the gift of the two Purple machines   · from America in January 1941.

After the Winds message had been decoded, the staff at Cheltenham was convinced that war was imminent but that America was well prepared. Briggs was on weekend leave in Ohio that Sunday,[6] 7 December, when the first news of the attack on Pearl Harbor came through. The initial reports were very sketchy[7] and Briggs was certain that in view of all the warnings that had been received the Japanese had walked into a well-laid trap. But by the time Briggs got back to Cheltenham after the weekend, the truth of the losses had begun to emerge and Briggs wondered what had gone wrong.

Briggs remembers: "When I first came off of that weekend I had a chance to talk with Wigle, and I said 'What happened?' And he said, 'I don't know, all I can say is nobody's talking,' and that was the end of our conversation. No one knew anything. So I let it rest, as by then with war declared we were very busy. But in the next month, as we began to hear the real facts about our losses, that's when I started looking back through our records for that 'execute' intercept and to see what I'd done with it."

But Briggs could find nothing in the files at Cheltenham. All the copies had vanished. When Briggs asked Wigle what had happened to all those copies, Wigle said "they had been called for, they needed additional backup, or words to that effect." But who asked for these copies? That remains a mystery. It certainly would not have been either Safford or

Lt. Eric Nave, RAN, acting as interpreter during the visit of the Japanese Navy to Australia in January 1924. The photograph was taken on board the Japanese flagship *Asama.* Seated, from left to right: Engineer Lt. Cdr. Take Oka, Eric Nave, Engineer Captain Kishimoto, Commander Nakamura, Chief of Staff. Standing, from left to right: Flag Lt. Shiraishi and Cdr. Miyoshi, staff officer. *(Eric Nave)*

Eric Nave (right) in 1924 with Vice-Admiral Saito (left) and Charles McPherson MacRobertson, a local Australian businessman who had made a large donation to the Japanese Earthquake Disaster Fund. *(Eric Nave)*

Alastair Denniston. First head of Britain's codebreaking organization, the Government Code & Cipher School. *(Robert Denniston)*

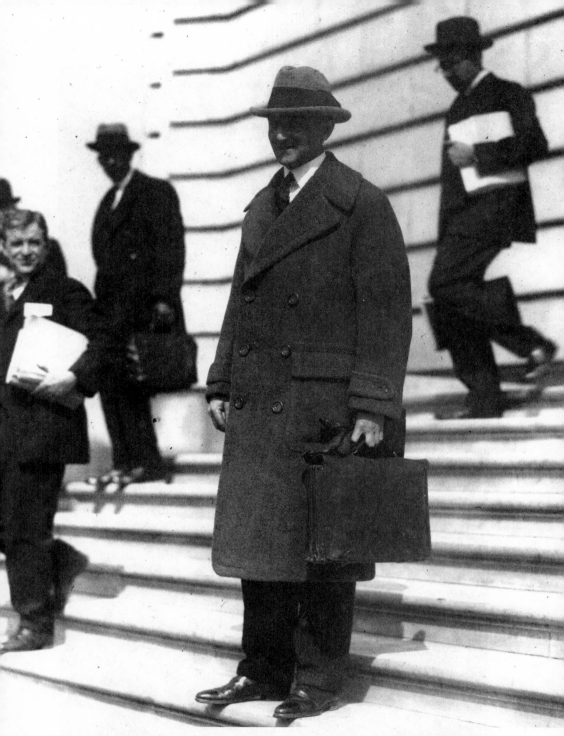

William Friedman (center) in 1924. He and his wife, Elizebeth (not shown), were the world's most famous husband-and-wife team in the history of code-breaking. *(UPI/Bettmann)*

The Underwood Code Machine designed in November 1924 by John T. Underwood and Charles A. Joerissen for Cdr. Safford at OP-20-G, where it was called RIP-5. The keys show the *romanized* Japanese *kana* characters used to send messages in Morse Code. When depressed, the typehead printed the equivalent Japanese character in brush-stroke form, thus enabling a non-Japanese-speaking radio operator to intercept Japanese messages. *(U.S. Navy Security Group Command HQ)*

The German four-rotor
Enigma cryptograph.
(Louis Kruh)

Typex Mark II
cryptograph, copies
from the German
Enigma by the Royal
Air Force in 1938. It
cost 107.40 pounds
($204.00). *(James
Rusbridger)*

Strowger telephone selector stepping switch from original (Japanese) Purple machine. *(National Security Agency)*

Part of the American copy of the Japanese Purple machine. *(National Security Agency)*

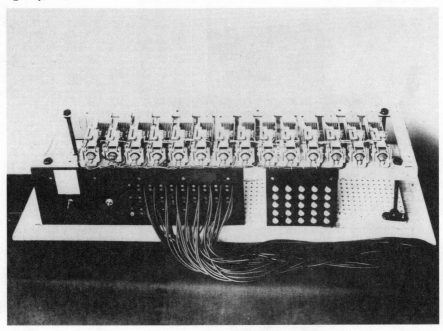

**TYPING UNIT
FRONT**

*The Japanese Coral
cryptograph, similar in design
to Purple, used only by naval
attaches. It was not broken by
the Americans until 1943.
(National Security Agency)*

Adm. Isoroku Yamamoto receiving a medal in 1938 on his appointment as Commander-in-Chief of the Imperial Japanese Navy. Yamamoto studied at Harvard after World War I, and was also naval attache in Washington, which convinced him Japan could not win a war against America because of the latter's vast economic strength. Although a great believer in Naval air power, Yamamoto's mistake was to attack Pearl Harbor with the American aircraft carriers absent, forcing him to engage in sea battles with the U.S. Navy which, in the end, they won. *UPI/Bettmann Newsphotos)*

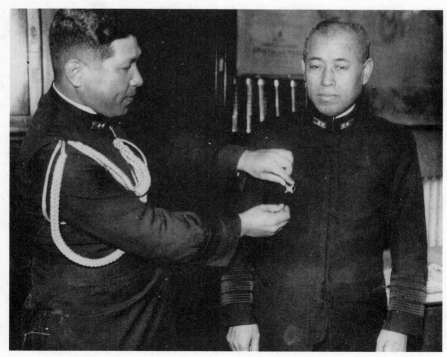

Aerial view of Bletchley Park, 40 miles north of London, the wartime headquarters of the Government Code & Cipher School. The original mansion is lower right, while behind are the huts where the codebreakers worked. *(Aerofilms, London)*

Station "Hypo," the U.S. Navy's codebreaking center at the Pearl Harbor naval base. *(U.S. Navy)*

The 7,528-ton Blue Funnel steamer *Automedon,* which was captured by the German raider *Atlantis* on November 11, 1940. In its strong room, the Germans found a hoard of secret intelligence documents, including the Chiefs of Staff report which concluded that it would be impossible to defend Singapore if the Japanese attacked, because no Far East fleet was available. *(Ocean Group plc)*

Two of Roosevelt's closest advisers, Secretary of War Henry L. Stimson (left) and Army Chief of Staff General George C. Marshall, leaving the White House in October 1941. Marshall was one of those who prevented Roosevelt from receiving raw decrypts of both Japanese naval and diplomatic codebreaking. *(AP/ Wide World Photos)*

Secretary of State Cordell Hull with the Japanese ambassador (left) Kichisaburo Nomura, and Japan's special envoy (right) Saburo Kurusu at the White House in November 1941. Later, the two diplomats were ordered to present Japan's final message just before the bombers struck Pearl Harbor. Because of administrative delays at the Japanese embassy, the pair reached the State Department after the attack had begun, thus compounding Japan's treachery. This proves beyond doubt that the diplomatic (or Purple) messages never contained any details of the actual attack. *(AP/Wide World Photos)*

Ralph T. Briggs, who, in December 1941, was a senior radio operator at the U.S. Navy's intercept station at Cheltenham, Maryland. On December 4, Briggs intercepted the second part, or "execute" portion, of the Winds message warning Japanese embassies that hostilities were about to start. *(Ralph T. Briggs)*

Lt. Cdr. W. W. Mortimer RNR, who worked at the Far East Combined Bureau in Singapore in 1941. *(W. W. Mortimer)*

Pearl Harbor, December 7, 1941. *(NPS: USAR Collection)*

The USS *Arizona. (NPS: USAR collection)*

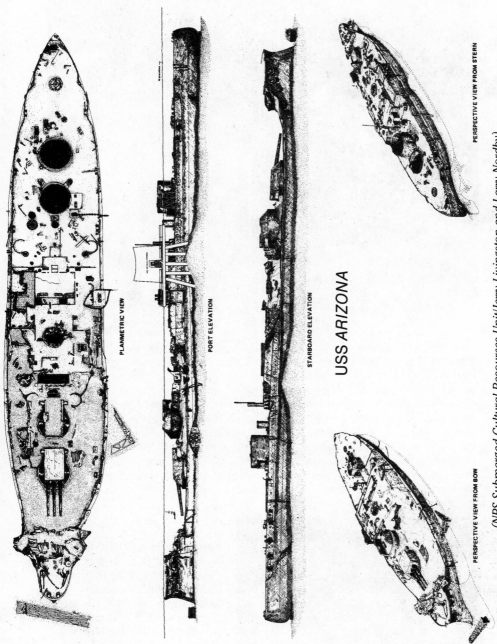

PLANMETRIC VIEW

PORT ELEVATION

STARBOARD ELEVATION

USS ARIZONA

PERSPECTIVE VIEW FROM STERN

PERSPECTIVE VIEW FROM BOW

(NPS Submerged Cultural Resources Unit/Jerry Livingston and Larry Nordby)

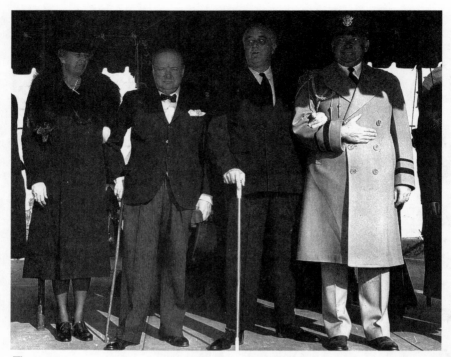

The two great wartime leaders Winston Churchill and Franklin D. Roosevelt together at the White House on Christmas day, 1941, eighteen days after Pearl Harbor. Linked by a common desire to defeat Nazi Germany, the two statesmen were very different. Churchill was impetuous, bombastic, stubborn, subject to changes of mood and bad temper; yet, he was always ready to flatter and, if necessary, deceive Roosevelt because he knew he must get America into the war at all costs. In contrast, Roosevelt was enigmatic, very experienced in domestic politics but lacking in knowledge of foreign affairs. A charming and highly popular leader who, unlike Churchill, was voted into office four times, Roosevelt was not experienced in technical matters, such as codebreaking, and left too much detail to others. *(UPI/Bettmann Newsphotos)*

Capt. Laurence Safford with Adm. Alwyn D. Kramer at the Pearl Harbor Inquiry in February 1946. In 1941, Safford and Kramer had been the two senior members of OP-20-G and had received this second part of the Winds message on December 4. At the 1945–46 Inquiry, this evidence was not believed, nor were the pair allowed to give any details of JN-25. *(AP/Wide World Photos)*

Appearing before the joint Pearl Harbor investigating committee on February 2, 1946, Capt. Safford charged that in 1945 a Navy officer had tried to persuade him to "change my testimony" concerning the receipt in Washington of the Winds warning from Tokyo in 1941. Members of the committee (backs to camera) right, shown left to right: Rep. John W. Murphy (PA), Rep. J. B. Clarke (NC), Sen. Alben W. Barkley (KY), Chairman; Sen. W. F. George (GA), Sen. Homer Ferguson (MI). *(UPI/Bettmann)*

Maj. Gen. Walter C. Short, military commander in Hawaii who, with his naval counterpart, Adm. Husband E. Kimmel, was denied access to Purple and JN-25 decrypts in the weeks before the attack, and as a result, became a convenient scapegoat at the Pearl Harbor hearings. *(UPI/Bettmann Newsphotos)*

Adm. Richmond K. Turner, head of the U.S. Navy's War Plans Division, giving evidence before the Pearl Harbor Inquiry. All evidence suggests it was Turner who stopped JN-25 decrypts, and other vital intelligence, from reaching the Hawaiian commanders. After the attack, it seemed Turner ordered the destruction of all JN-25 material so that the role of U.S. Navy codebreakers could not be investigated. *(UPI/Bettmann)*

Kramer. They already had the copy of the "execute" off the teleprinter and the carbon copies that had come by messenger. So there was nothing more for them to learn by asking for all the other copies at Cheltenham. Therefore, whoever asked for these copies was not interested in their contents but wanted to remove them altogether from the files. And so began the great Winds "execute" mystery that was to puzzle historians for the next forty-five years.

As far as Briggs was concerned, that was the end of the Winds story. He left Cheltenham and was posted elsewhere, including the naval intercept station at Skaggs Island in California. At the end of the war, in September 1945, Briggs was posted back to Washington to work at OP-20-G, where his first assignment was with the newly formed Armed Forces Security Agency. By this time there had been seven investigations into the attack on Pearl Harbor, but the Winds messages were never mentioned at any of them, and therefore neither Briggs nor anyone else from Cheltenham was called to give evidence.

ON 27 December 1941, after the attack on Pearl Harbor, the staff at FECB (except for Mortimer, who stayed behind to act as liaison officer until late January 1942), its Hollerith machines, and all its codebreaking records were safely evacuated[8] from Singapore to Colombo, in Ceylon, where the unit became known as Captain on Staff HMS *Lanki,* and nothing was left behind to give the Japanese the slightest clue that their codes were being broken. By early 1942, a large contingent of civilians from Bletchley Park, together with a team of Womens Royal Navy staff, arrived at FECB in Colombo from Britain to expand the activities, although the first group were all lost when their ship was torpedoed.

In Singapore, FECB had had a fixed radioteletype link[9] with Bletchley Park for eighteen hours a day, and a continuous radioteletype link with the naval base in Colombo, which had a separate direct link to London. There were also secret radio links with the U.S. Navy at Corregidor (Station Cast), and the Dutch in Batavia at Kamer 14. Every scrap of information, from codebreaking, direction-finding, traffic analysis, and any other form of intelligence collected by FECB, was immediately sent back to the naval section of GCCS at Bletchley Park.

GCHQ refused to provide the authors with any information about how codebreaking intelligence at FECB was handled, but a copy of the instructions[10] was found in the archives in New Zealand. This showed that messages based on codebreaking information from FECB would be prefixed "Zymotic" and also marked "Most Secret" and a warning included in any summary that the information came from Special Intelligence. A similar codeword, "Zeal,"[11] was used with codebreaking intelligence coming from Australia.

Other instructions included:

> (7) All groups and rough working are to be kept separate from other messages and are to be *burnt* [original emphasis] when no longer required for reference. This should normally be immediately and in any case not longer than a week.
>
> (8) Log copies are to be burnt when no longer required . . . normally no longer than a month from receipt.
>
> (9) Knowledge of these messages is to be restricted to as few officers as possible. The Captain on Staff or his Deputy will decide as to whom their copies are to be shown.
>
> (10) If it is necessary to pass on information contained in these messages they will be reworded so as the contents cannot be traced back to Special Intelligence.
>
> (11) In the case of (10) names of enemy ships should be avoided and positions should be expressed in a different form to that given in the [original] Ultra or Zymotic message.
>
> (12) No mention of any information is to be made in any war diaries, reports of proceedings, no matter how limited the circulation.

It is not hard to see from the foregoing why so little information about British codebreaking against the Japanese prior to December 1941 has found its way into logbooks and other official diaries of the period.

AFTER THE war there was an eighth investigation: a full congressional inquiry that was to run from 15 November 1945 to 31 May 1946. When this got under way, both Safford and Kramer were closely questioned about the Winds messages and in particular the "execute" portion. It was put to them very strongly that their memories were at fault and that they had seen no "execute" message. None of the other people who had seen the "execute" message on December 4 were called to testify before the inquiry. This included Briggs, Wigle, the rest of the staff at Cheltenham, Admiral Turner (director of War Plans), Colonel Sadtler, and Admiral Noyes. Some of the senior staff at Cheltenham, and OP-20-G had been told to prepare statements, but none of these were ever put before the committee. It soon became clear that enormous pressure had been brought on anyone who had seen the "execute" message to change his story and now say that he had not seen it, or that it was not a correct "execute" message but had been mistakenly written down.

Even Daryl Wigle (now a lieutenant), who had been Briggs's station chief at Cheltenham at the time, changed his story in a statement dated 11 December 1945 saying:

> I do not recall any Japanese language recordings being made. Cheltenham was never given any directive to record Japanese voice transmissions. There were no personnel at Cheltenham capable of understanding or speaking Japanese. To the best of my knowledge Cheltenham was not, during the period immediately preceding Pearl Harbor Day, i.e., from 28 November to 7 December 1941, given any additional Japanese, Morse, or voice assignments.[12]

Wigle died in 1974 without ever elaborating on these claims, which are plainly at variance with the conversations Briggs clearly remembers, the instructions Safford had given and saw being carried out by Wigle on 4 December, and the official version of events, which states that radio intercept stations had been specifically told to look out for the second part of the Winds message. As it turned out, Wigle never gave evidence at the inquiry, so his statement was never challenged.

Considering the passage of time and all that had taken place during the war, it was hardly surprising that some people had genuinely forgotten the exact circumstances of the Winds message incident. For example, Sadtler recalled[13] he had received the "execute" message from Safford on 5 December rather than 4 December. Nevertheless, as Briggs remembers, "There were two factions at work. One faction was trying to eliminate any further discussion and revelation about the Winds message and our capabilities of reading Japanese signals. The second group was trying to admit as much as they could in an effort to tell the truth."

In the course of looking through his files for evidence to substantiate his story for the 1945 inquiry, Safford discovered Briggs's name and, finding he was stationed in Washington, asked Briggs to come over to his office in Building 18 at the Navy Department. As a result, Briggs had three or four meetings with Safford, during which he went through all the details of the Winds message saga and his interception of the "execute" portion on 4 December.

This was the first time Safford and Briggs had ever met. "I got over there[14] and found this very soft-spoken, very pleasant man and we sat down and one of the first things he shot me with was the fact he knew my call sign. 'You were RT?' I said, that's right, that was my sign. 'Do you know you were the one who intercepted that Winds code execute on December 4?' I stopped for a minute, trying to recollect how he came by all that. You see, I didn't know all this time that Safford was the one at the other end that had gotten the message that day. Then he said: 'I'm trying to reconstruct the events on December 4, would you help me?' "

Briggs said he would and did his best to answer all the questions put to him by Safford. But, of course, Briggs's knowledge was limited only to what had happened to the intercept at Cheltenham and that he had personally sent it on the teleprinter to OP-20-G. During their second meeting, Safford asked Briggs whether he would be willing to testify before the congressional inquiry then in progress. Briggs said he would.

Shortly after that second meeting, Briggs was called before his commanding officer, Captain Harper, who, ironically, was the same officer who in 1937 had first interviewed Briggs and suggested he join the naval intelligence section. Briggs's recollection of this meeting is crystal clear.

"He asked me to sit down. He stated that he understood I had been having some meetings with Captain Safford with reference to my being called as a witness. I replied, 'Yes.' Harper wanted to know why this had been done without his knowledge and why he had not been informed. I advised the captain that I didn't know I was supposed to report to him about this matter in view that I had gotten the call from Captain Safford direct. He, in effect, advised me that I should know that he [Harper] was the commanding officer of the station, not Captain Safford.

"I agreed to that point. I said, 'Yes, indeed, sir, but Captain Safford didn't allude to the fact that you weren't aware of my being with him.' He [Harper] dropped it at that point and went on to the point in question. He seemed very serious and perturbed. He stated, in effect, that too much had already been revealed by the hearings. That he couldn't explain exactly at this point what was behind it. That someday perhaps I would understand, but at this point he couldn't give me the information necessary to sustain what he was about to tell me. Then he delivered his coup de grace.

"He said, 'You are not to confer with Captain Safford any further. You are specifically prohibited from meeting with him in his office, and if there are any further inquiries or any requests with reference to this matter, you are to report to me at once.' I acknowledged, sat there for a while, then he said 'That is all,' so I left."

Despite this starkly clear order, Briggs felt he owed Safford an explanation and telephoned him to tell him what had happened. "Safford was stunned. He said, 'Well, he didn't say we couldn't bump into each other or anything along that line. I'll call you back later.' Some days later Safford asked me to meet him, which, despite Harper's instructions, I did. During our conversation Safford told me that after receiving my intercept off the teleprinter from Kramer he had personally sent a copy to Admiral Noyes, who had in turn told Admiral Turner, Colonel Sadtler, and Admiral Stark. He also said that he had tried to have me called as a witness at the hearing and that apparently from an authority higher than

Captain Harper I was not to appear. And that was the end of the matter as far as I was concerned."

Briggs believes that Harper was far from happy with the role he had to play. "Harper seemed ill at ease that he had to tell me this. He wasn't mad at me. I didn't feel that way at all. He was bothered, deeply bothered by it all."

The saga of the Winds message and whether the "execute" portion was received or not was to occupy the attention[15] of the Pearl Harbor investigators so greatly that it distracted their attention away from far more important matters that were never investigated. The simple truth is that had both parts of the Winds message been placed before the 1945 congressional committee, they would have provided no new evidence that the committee did not already possess.

Having decided to conceal the message, it was then necessary not only to destroy all records[16] but also to continue the deception during the 1945 inquiry and pressure all those who had seen it originally into changing their stories in case they were called to testify. Unfortunately, Safford, Kramer, and Briggs were honest men who saw no reason to tell lies. The importance of the Winds saga is therefore not what the message said but that a number of sufficiently senior officers were able and willing to cover up the truth and shred files so as to falsify the records for posterity.

The question of who authorized the destruction of all the copies of the message was closely investigated in 1945 without success. Safford discovered that at one intercept station—Winter Harbor, Maine—the officer in charge admitted that in the spring of 1943 he had been told by the Navy Department to destroy all his station logbooks from 1931 through 30 June 1942. But this was not investigated to find out who had given him such an order. Similar destruction had also happened at the Cheltenham station. In Washington, Captain R. Mason stated that at various times up to spring 1943 he had authorized the destruction of old Japanese intercepts to "avoid the impossibly huge accumulation of paper" after carefully inspecting them for important matter. But Mason was never called to explain what files he considered worthy of preserving. Such wholesale destruction of important material within only a few years of its being filed is quite contrary to normal U.S. Navy archival practice.

If this relatively harmless piece of evidence could be so professionally concealed from the American people, it legitimately raises the question of what other material was kept from them.

When did the U.S. Navy begin reading JN-25? The answer ought to be as simple as it was in the case of the earlier Red and Blue Book codes.

But it is not. For forty years, the official version was that JN-25 did not exist. JN-25 was considered so secret by the U.S. Navy that even during the seven wartime investigations it was never once mentioned. And at the eighth and final postwar congressional hearing, in 1945–46, only a few vague references to it can be found in the thirty-nine volumes of evidence. It was never discussed in detail, nor was the U.S. Navy asked to give evidence as to when it was first broken.

As the official history records: "With reference to the Navy cipher [JN-25] . . . nothing appears in the Pearl Harbor testimony about this, although much is made of [the] failure to get a Purple machine [to Hawaii]."[17]

Virtually all the books and articles about Pearl Harbor that appeared from 1946 onward covering the next thirty-five years concentrated on the Magic summaries decrypted from the Purple diplomatic intercepts. The argument is that had this material been passed to the Pearl Harbor commanders it would have alerted them to the attack. Not only is this assertion quite untrue but it has also served to confuse the real issue, which lies not with the Purple decrypts but with JN-25—the only code system used by the Japanese to transmit the final instructions for the attack.

In 1979, President Jimmy Carter authorized the NSA[18] to release a mass of Japanese intercepts. But before these were placed in the National Archives, all references to JN-25 were censored. It is even more significant that not a single JN-25 decrypt was released that had been read prior to 7 December 1941, thereby giving the impression that no Japanese naval operational signals had been decrypted before the attack. The few intercepts[19] in the archives that predate Pearl Harbor all bear 1945–46 translation dates, and some of these are reproduced in Appendix 6.

The starting point[20] for research into the American history of JN-25 is the *Naval Security Group History to World War II,* prepared by Captain J. S. Holtwick, USN (Ret.), in June 1971, an extremely long and detailed account running to a total of 700 pages. On pages 396–97, the report deals with the five main Orange (Japanese), codes in current use in 1939–40. The fourth of these is called the "Operations Code system," which is in fact JN-25, as shown in a footnote. The report states: "An additive key cipher is employed with this code, and although the method of recovery is well defined the process is a laborious one requiring from an hour to several days for each message. A machine is under construction which will aid in the . . . solution [and] . . . a few code values have been recovered but . . . at least six months will be required before complete messages can be read."

This confirms that some messages in JN-25 (doubtless those with good cribs[21] that helped reveal the contents) were being broken by early 1940—some taking several days—while the six-month period mentioned would take one to the latter part of that same year.

The report continues on page 398:

> Captain Safford in August 1970 stated from memory: "JN-25 came into effect 1 June 1939 and in late September 1940 we turned in our first translation of a message, either the week before or the week after the Army [SIS] achieved their final breakthrough in the Japanese Purple machine. *By 1 December 1941 we had the code solved to a readable extent."* [Emphasis added]. Thus no one was reading anything in the . . . diplomatic [Purple] and naval [JN-25] systems [until] the latter part of 1940. On 4 January 1941 it was reported that about 2,000 values had been recovered out of 33,000 possible in the . . . JN-25 code.

Aside from the clarity of this statement, what is remarkable is that the entire history was carefully checked by the NSA and U.S. Navy prior to its declassification under Executive Order #12356 on 20 June 1985 and anything still considered sensitive is blanked out.

The comment about OP-20-G having recovered 2,000 values (in other words they had identified 2,000 words and phrases in the dictionary as a result of penetrating the additive tables) is particularly interesting, because that same month OP-20-G evidently felt confident enough to offer two reconstructed copies of JN-25 to GCCS as part of the exchange of cryptographic technology which included the two Purple machines.

The second primary source[22] is *A Brief History of Communications Intelligence in the United States,* written by Safford between 21 and 27 March 1952 and released into the National Archives by the NSA on 6 March 1982. Page 14 deals with JN-25 but is so heavily censored as to make little sense:

> On 1 June 1939 the Japanese Navy introduced a new type of numerical code referred to by Navy COMINT personnel as [censored] the Operations Code. [The next two lines are totally censored.] Mrs. Driscoll and Mr. Currier spearheaded the attack and we were soon [censored] reconstructing the code.
>
> Recovery of the [censored] keys, [the word missing here is probably *additive*] however, involved much more labor and required many more crypto-personnel than the earlier transposition keys. Main work of solution was undertaken at Washington [OP-20-G].
>
> By December 1940 we were working on two systems of keys with

this book; the "old" keys for code recovery and the "new" keys for current information [five lines completely censored].

Despite the deletions by the NSA (which, incidentally, now claims to know nothing about the JN-25 code), it is possible to confirm that JN-25 was broken by OP-20-G soon after its introduction, matching the progress made by Nave and Burnett. The reference to needing more personnel also confirms Nave's comment that JN-25 was a tedious rather than a hard code to break.

On the following page 15, there is a reference to the Japanese Flag Officers' Cipher (what FECB called the C-in-C's Code), which was used prior to the introduction of JN-25 and then discarded. The report makes the comment that "this was the only Japanese Naval Cryptographic system which the U.S. Navy ever failed to solve." The report continues:

> On 1 December 1941 the system [JN-25] became unreadable . . . this could have been a tip-off as to coming hostilities but it also could have been a mere routine change of system. After all, the code had been in use for 2½ years. Two weeks later Corregidor [Station Cast] flashed the good news that the same old code was still in use but that new keys were being used with it. This was the third or fourth set of keys used with this same codebook.
>
> In the Japanese Navy had changed the codebook along with the cipher keys on 1 December 1941, there is no telling how badly the war in the Pacific would have gone. . . . due credit for [the battles of] Coral Sea and Midway should be given to the Navy's pre–Pearl Harbor COMINT effort.

This passage is particularly interesting for several reasons. First, Safford is mistaken that the date when the key changes were made was 1 December, when in fact the change was made on 4 December. Second, he confirms that JN-25 was broken soon after its introduction and was read throughout the two-and-a-half-year period to late 1941. And third, that the basic code remained unchanged and only the additive tables (or keys) altered. All this tallies with the same progress made at FECB and GCCS.

The still censored message from Station Cast on 15 December 1941 reads: "Com 16 to OPNAV info CINCAF. TOP SECRET—151250. Two intercepts in [censored] plain code [December] 6 and 13 followed within a few hours by enciphered versions confirmed indicator [censored] already recovered by mathematical elimination code remains unchanged (.) Will send recoveries this system if you desire begin work on current period."

It is incredible to find that, a week after the attack on Pearl Harbor, Japanese code security was so poor that they were still sending the same messages in a low-grade system as well as in JN-25. Evidently Station Cast had no difficulty recognizing this. What is even more important is that if Station Cast's codebreakers knew that JN-25 remained unchanged, then it must mean that they were reading it during the previous six-month period, from 1 June 1941 through 4 December 1941.

The third primary source[23] is Safford's own account, contained in the article "Rhapsody in Purple" in *Cryptologia,* July 1982, which states, "The first completely decrypted message/translation in JN-25 followed the first decrypted Purple message by about a week. [The first Purple message was decoded in September 1940.] Both Washington units [SIS and OP-20-G] were "in business" . . . and morale was extremely high. The numerical keys [additive tables] were changed on 1 December 1940 and again on 1 June 1941. A change . . . was anticipated for 1 December 1941."

This account is virtually the same as the statement on page 397 from the official history and again shows that from early October 1940 (which roughly matches the six-month period mentioned), JN-25 was being broken by OP-20-G. Bearing in mind that GCCS had 300 people working solely on JN-25, whereas OP-20-G had to split its far smaller staff between the monthly roster of handling Purple traffic and the naval signals, it is not surprising that they took a year longer than GCCS to break JN-25.

Safford's account again confirms that the six-monthly additive table changes posed OP-20-G no greater problem than they did Nave and Burnett. Safford then explains how three copies of the JN-25 codebook were being laboriously reconstructed by hand by Phillip Cate[24] in exactly the same way as the Red and Blue books had been done previously. The reconstructed JN-25 codebooks were essentially blank ledgers with the numerical five-figure code group in the left-hand column, with the other columns containing the Chinese character, the Japanese *kana* equivalent, and the English translation. It was intended that one copy would remain with OP-20-G, the second would go to Station Hypo in Pearl Harbor, and the third to Station Cast in Corregidor.

A fourth primary source[25] is a memorandum Safford wrote on 17 May 1945 for Lieutenant Commander John F. Sonnett, USNR, which included the following statement:

Com 16 [Station Cast in Corregidor] intercepts were considered most reliable . . . not only because of better radio interception, but because Com 16 was currently reading messages in the Japanese Fleet Cryptographic System (5-number code or JN-25) and was exchanging technical information and translations with the British at Singapore [FECB].

As regards the JN-25 system the current version (JN-25b) had been in effect since 1 December 1940 [and] remained in effect until 27–31 May 1942, and was partially readable in November 1941. A new system of keys was introduced on 4 December 1941 and reported by Com 16 [Station Cast] but the carry over of the old code made their solution quite simple and we were reading messages again by Christmas, Corregidor getting the initial break on 8 December 1941. Com 16 had the benefit of its own translations plus "tips" from [FECB] Singapore.

This statement confirms that JN-25 was being read at Station Cast and that there was some degree of cooperation with FECB; it also confirms that after the additive table change on 4 December 1941 messages were still being sent in both the old and new keys and that this helped reconstruct the new tables very quickly.

Taken together, these four accounts of U.S. Navy codebreaking show beyond doubt that between 1 June 1939 and 7 December 1941 some JN-25 messages were definitely decoded by the U.S. Navy. One would therefore expect to find in the American archives a series of JN-25 intercepts in their raw state and various decrypts covering the two-year period. Some of the earlier ones would be only partly read, with many gaps for unsolved groups, while the later ones—nearer the time of Pearl Harbor —would be fully translated. But not a single pre–Pearl Harbor JN-25 intercept or decrypt can be found in any American archive.

In their letter of 8 May 1989, the U.S. Naval Security Group stated:

We regret we are unable to provide any assistance or illumination on the problem [of JN-25]. When the systematic declassification effort began in 1978 . . . the decision was made to begin with review of all Japanese message translations from the World War II era.

Since that time the question of the whereabouts and status of early JN-25 translations has been asked repeatedly but without resolution. We have been unable to locate them . . . in any form, paper or microfilm . . . the 1941 JN-25 messages that are in [the National Archives] were all translated after the war ended.

From the historical perspective we agree it would be most fascinating to be able to follow the progress of solution of the system through the evolution of the translations. Regrettably, we are unable to do so.[26]

This is an extraordinary letter that is hard to accept at its face value. The Naval Security Group on Nebraska Avenue in Washington is the direct successor of Safford's OP-20-G and has been the continuous custodian of all the U.S. Navy's cryptographic operations—including codebreaking—since July 1922. Therefore there is absolutely no reason why the archives relating to this work should not be intact, especially as OP-20-G did not move from its offices in the Navy Department on Constitution Avenue to Nebraska Avenue until 7 February 1943.

For the U.S. Navy to comment that it would be "fascinating" to follow the progress of breaking JN-25 when they themselves were responsible for doing just that is either extremely naive—which, considering the letter is from Commander George G. Henrikson,[27] special assistant for security, is most unlikely—or it is the result of many years of official policy to deflect historical inquiries.

This letter means that every single scrap of evidence relating to JN-25 between June 1939 through late November 1941 has vanished. Considering the historical importance of this material in the context of Pearl Harbor, it is impossible to believe that this could have happened throughout all the U.S. Navy's codebreaking offices, unless there had been a deliberate policy[28] beginning in the immediate aftermath of the war to conceal or destroy all evidence relating to this code. Support for this thesis can be drawn from three facts. First, JN-25 archival material continues to be censored even after fifty years. Second, the equally important and politically sensitive Purple diplomatic decrypts of the same prewar period are freely available. If this latter material could be kept intact for posterity by the Army and Navy codebreakers, then it is quite remarkable that the U.S. Navy has managed to lose all its JN-25 documents. And third, the U.S. Navy prides itself on the impeccable condition and scope of its archives.

It is also impossible to believe that the few pre–Pearl Harbor JN-25 decrypts in the National Archives (see Appendix 6) were only decoded in late 1945 and early 1946. It is a matter of uncensored public record that by early 1942 the U.S. Navy was reading JN-25 quite freely. During the next three years there were seven separate inquiries into the attack:

1. The Roberts Commission—18 December 1941 through 23 January 1942.
2. The Hart Inquiry—5 February through 15 June 1944.
3. The Army Pearl Harbor Board—20 July through 20 October 1944.
4. The U.S. Naval Court of Inquiry—24 July through 19 October 1944.

5. The Clausen Investigation—23 November 1944 through 12 September 1945.
6. The Hewitt Inquiry—14 May through 11 July 1945.
7. The Clarke Investigation—14–16 September 1944 and 13 July through 4 August 1945.

The U.S. Navy refused to allow discussion of JN-25 at any of these inquiries. Considering the defeat they sustained at Pearl Harbor, it strains credulity to believe they would not have been sufficiently curious to know what these few intercepts contained and to have decoded them as soon as possible.[29] Reluctantly, one has to conclude that these copies in the National Archives have been deliberately falsified in order to create the impression that JN-25 was not being read in 1941.

As no such policy affected the public disclosures during the 1945–46 inquiry of how American codebreakers had read the Purple diplomatic messages, why was a decision taken to conceal the similar success against JN-25 from the American people that lasts even to this day? And who authorized it?

What makes this affair so bizzare is that from 8 December 1941 onward it was a matter of great pride that U.S. Navy codebreakers were breaking JN-25, which only seven months later was to lead to the dramatic victory at the Battle of Midway, a turning point in the war against Japan, and a year after that to the shooting down of Yamamoto's aircraft. It seems a remarkable coincidence that the official record of breaking JN-25 conveniently begins only after hostilities have commenced.

The foreign ministries of some governments (like the British Foreign Office) are embarrassed even after fifty years to admit that they read another nation's codes in peacetime. But in America, no such embarrassment exists, because the revelation that their codebreakers read Japanese diplomatic traffic prior to war being declared is not disputed. What then is the difference between the decrypts from the Purple machine and the decrypts from JN-25?

The answer is very simply that the JN-25 messages contained the final operational details of the Pearl Harbor attack, whereas the Purple intercepts did not. It is therefore a legitimate conclusion that the missing material contains information that is highly sensitive and embarrassing. That is why the U.S. Navy went to such lengths to conceal the existence of JN-25 from the postwar inquiry—just as happened with the missing Winds message—and even today fifty years later still censors any material relating to the subject. This is not some casual cover-up but a carefully premeditated policy of deceit of the greatest magnitude that can only have originated from the highest authority to deliberately frustrate the truth being told.

Some idea of the paranoia still affecting the U.S. Navy about JN-25 can best be judged from their letters in 1988 enclosing a single page from a JN-25 codebook and an additive table which are reproduced on pages 84–86.

> After consultation with other concerned authorities it has been determined that one typical page from a basic code book and an additive table book can be provided without contravention of current security guidelines pertaining to cryptologic material.
>
> Attached is a copy of one page of the JN-25 Japanese Navy Fleet General Purpose Code from the 1941 era. As a single page *this attachment is currently unclassified* [emphasis added] . . . considerable effort was required to identify the document as responsive to the period in which you expressed interest.[30]

The "concerned authority" is of course the NSA, which was responsible for the release of Japanese cryptographic material in 1978. They apparently share the U.S. Navy's fear that for the public to see an entire JN-25 codebook dating from the last war would somehow compromise America's security today. When asked about prewar JN-25, the NSA could only reply with classic obtuseness: "Your request for information on the JN-25 has been processed . . . but no records responsive to your request were located."[31]

In Britain, the situation is just as bad. In 1945, immediately after the Japanese surrender, Churchill sent personal secret instructions to FECB[32] (then in Ceylon), that all archives were to be destroyed, including those brought out from Singapore in December 1941 before the surrender in February 1942. Whether Churchill had the authority to do this seems doubtful, but certainly he made no attempt to order a similar destruction[33] of archives relating to the breaking of the German Enigma codes.

Why Churchill treated Far East codebreaking differently than that against Germany has never been explained—and even after fifty years the Foreign Office still refuses to do so—but the consensus[34] at FECB at the time was that Churchill wanted to ensure that no one else was able to write a history of the war in the Far East that challenged his version and showed his true role in the affairs of 1940–41. This would also explain why when the Americans asked[35] that Commander T. Wisden, RN, and Lieutenant Commander W. W. Mortimer, RNR (who had both worked at FECB on Japanese codes), attend the Pearl Harbor hearing to give evidence on their work, the request was flatly refused by the Admiralty. The only records from FECB Colombo that appear to have survived were Mortimer's card index of all Japanese warships and merchant ships that he had begun in 1939, which was brought back to the Admiralty in London in 1945 by Lieutenant Trygve Jesperson, RNR, but has never been placed in any public archive and so presumably remains with GCHQ to this day.

Despite the destruction of FECB's records, copies of all their work remained with GCCS. These are under the control of GCHQ today and cannot be inspected,[36] nor have they ever been made available for the official histories of British intelligence during World War II,[37] which conspicuously ignore the work of British codebreaking against Japan prior to 1941. Apart from the prewar work against Japanese naval codes, these codes also contain copies of Purple intercepts that GCCS was able to decrypt from early 1941 onward.

However, some FECB pre–Pearl Harbor JN-25 decrypts have found their way into archives outside Britain, and a typical one,[38] dated 30 December 1940, is reproduced on page 175. Reading from the top, the expression "Most Secret" indicates it has to do with codebreaking. "Captain on the Staff . . . Singapore" was the cover name for the head of FECB, then Captain K. L. Harkness, RN, whose signature appears below. The expression "Most Secret Sources" again indicates the message has been derived from reading Japanese codes. The text shows that it must have come from reading messages in JN-25, since it deals with future intentions.

Another JN-25 decrypt,[39] dated 24 January 1941 (page 176), contains the intriguing comment that Japanese documents have been "examined" in Batavia, suggesting that either FECB or their Dutch friends had been involved in a burglary. The next paragraph talks about "Special Intelligence," which is another euphemism for intelligence derived from codebreaking.

Another error in declassification has resulted in a batch of JN-25 decrypts (see Appendix 2) from FECB in Colombo, Ceylon, dated January-February 1942, being accidentally included[40] in some Australian material now in the National Archives. The additive table for this six-month period began on 4 December 1941. What is particularly significant about these decrypts is that they were read immediately and are all complete, even though they were broken only five weeks into the new tables, which confirms that FECB had easily mastered the table or key changes. Since the previous table change had occurred on 1 June 1941, long before

(File N/8/40/20, National Archives, Wellington, New Zealand.)   ▶

MOST SECRET.

CONVERSION OF TRAWLERS: MANDATED ISLANDS.

From THE CAPTAIN ON THE STAFF
OF THE COMMANDER-IN-CHIEF, CHINA,
H.M. NAVAL BASE, SINGAPORE.

Date 30th December, 1940.   *No.* 656/041.

To The Australian Commonwealth Naval Board.
The New Zealand Board.
(Copy to each).

The following report received from
Most Secret Sources is forwarded for information:-

"Plans are now under discussion by the
Japanese Navy for the development of existing
repair yards, etc., in the Mandated Islands for
the purpose of converting trawlers and other
fishing boats for naval work.

A large number of Naval personnel are to
be sent to certain of the Islands and it is
intended to convert about 200 of these small
craft by arming them and fitting them with
depth charges and one or two mines for offensive
mine-laying."

(Sgd.) W. K. L. Harkness.

Sec. C.W.S.

2 N.M. 26.2.41.

O. & I. 26/2/41   C A P T A I N

S.A.S.O.

T. & M.O. 28/2   *Particulars of fortified
Japanese mandated islands
attached*

A.N.S.   27/2

For Information

N.S.

File
NA

only be for seaplanes.

Rota.

Anchorage for 3 or 4 ships.
Improvements being made. Fuel
storage. Possibly submarine
base.

Pagan.

Anchorage fo...
ported aerod...

NAVAL MESSAGE.

RECORDS / ACTION COPY.

Secret or Confidential:	Cypher or Code used, or P/L:
SECRET	D

TO:	FROM:
ADMIRALTY D.N.I. (R) C.IN C.CHINA 503 N.Z.N.B. S.O.I.SINGAPORE S.O.I.HONG KONG.	J.C.S.SINGAPORE

Japanese documents examined at Batavia reveals that plan for Military WORK SPRATLEY Island being investigated also building 2 oil tanks of 10 thousand tons each at MALAKAL – PALAU may, 1939. Military work Mandated Island to cost some tens of million YEN.

Special Intelligence September, 1940, denotes Naval Stores being landed at MAROUS Island and construction work in progress at SAIPAN and TINIAN Saipan.

(A) In Mariana Island. POMAPE and TRUK in CAROLINES RUOT (unidentified may be in KWAJALIEN ATOLL) WOTJE, TAROA in MALESIAP and WIJI (probably IMRODJ in JALUIT ATOLL) in Marshall Islands.

0336Z/23

DECLASSIF

Remarks:	Initials of Typist.	Initials of Cypherer or Coder.	Time of Receipt or Despatch.	Date
	B.G.Y.	M.R. J.B.	0959	24/1/41

Referred to:—	NAVY OFFICE MINUTE.	File: NA...

DECLASSIFIED

[Continue on Minute Sheet.

Minute Sheet. Drafts to be on separate sheet.]

November, JN-25 messages would have posed no problem to the British codebreakers in Singapore and Bletchley Park.

The message reproduced on page 192 shows that it is from the head of FECB; the codeword "Zymotic" means it contains intelligence derived from codebreaking; the phrase "Special Intelligence" repeats this; and the fact that it refers to events that will take place in several days' time confirms it is from a JN-25 decrypt.

Despite the official policy of disinformation and censorship, both British and American codebreakers were able to read the Japanese operational orders sent in JN-25 throughout the months leading up to Pearl Harbor.

What we have done in this book is to lay out all the new facts obtained from Nave's own unique codebreaking expertise, spanning the vital period 1925 through 1945 (the only firsthand account ever recorded), together with hitherto unknown archival material that has been found around the world. This clearly shows that Churchill was able to read JN-25, as well as the Purple diplomatic messages, during 1941 right up to the day of the attack. This is a fact that has never been publicly revealed before, and we believe it entitles us to re-examine the Pearl Harbor attack from a totally new viewpoint.

On the evidence presented in the book, we show that Churchill was aware that a task force had sailed from northern Japan in late November 1941, and that one of its likely targets was Pearl Harbor. Churchill deliberately kept this vital information from Roosevelt, because he realized an attack of this nature, whether on the U.S. Pacific Fleet or the Philippines, was a means of fulfilling his publicly proclaimed desire to get America into the war at any cost.

Although Roosevelt had experience in the Navy Department during World War I, unlike Churchill he was not well acquainted with the technicalities of codebreaking and, instead of having all important raw decrypts brought to him directly, relied on summaries prepared separately by the Army and Navy. The crucial question, therefore, is whether he knew anything about JN-25.

As we have explained, it is impossible to give a precise answer to this, for two reasons. First, although the evidence assembled clearly shows that the Navy's codebreakers at OP-20-G did break JN-25 long before 7 December 1941, the extent of their penetration, and how it was interrupted by the six-monthly additive table changes, is unclear, because every scrap of pre–Pearl Harbor JN-25 material has vanished.

Second, in none of the contemporary accounts of the weeks before

◀ (File: Navy 8/10/20, New Zealand Archives, Wellington.)

the attack is there any mention of the President seeing decrypts from JN-25, although there are plenty of references to his seeing the Purple diplomatic material passing between Tokyo and Washington and Tokyo and Berlin. But neither Roosevelt nor any of his closest advisers like Hull or Stimson has ever been quoted as making any remark, for example, "What are the Navy boys saying?" or something to that effect, that might provide a clue that Roosevelt, in addition to the diplomatic traffic, was also seeing JN-25. There is also no evidence that Roosevelt saw specific decrypts from the J-19 consular code like the Bomb Plot message. Furthermore, although there are guarded references in the exchanges with Churchill to intelligence based on Purple decrypts, there is no evidence that, in addition, the President ever implied he also had access to naval material from JN-25.

But, as we have shown, official histories and memoirs can be conveniently misleading. In theory, Churchill's extensive postwar memoirs (for which he was allowed privileged access to government archives, despite then no longer being Prime Minister), give an intimate and detailed record of how he conducted affairs. However, because of postwar Anglo-American agreements that there should be no revelations about code-breaking, he goes through an elaborate charade of pretending he only received Purple material from America, makes no mention at all of Japanese naval codes even being intercepted, let alone broken, and completely ignores the period between the Task Force sailing and the attack.

On the other hand, would the U.S. Navy have deliberately denied knowledge of their ability to read the vital Japanese naval code from their commander-in-chief? It has to be considered a very real possibility. We have shown from official records that the Navy did conceal their ability to read JN-25 from the Army codebreakers at SIS, because they did not trust them. We have also shown, from well-documented evidence, that both the Navy and the Army were suspicious of Roosevelt's staff, which they thought could not be trusted with sensitive intelligence material derived from codebreaking. They concealed JN-25, and all other Japanese codes, from the commanders in Hawaii. And it is a matter of record that General Marshall and Admiral Stark deliberately—and quite illegally—denied the President and Hull any knowledge of Purple for four months after it was first broken in September 1940, and then later denied the President access to Purple from May through November 1941 because of an alleged leak (see Chapter 6).

What is important about these last two incidents is that, according to all contemporary accounts, Roosevelt did not appear to realize that he had been denied such vital intelligence, which reinforces the belief that he had little firsthand knowledge of his codebreakers' achievements.

The decision to keep Roosevelt in the dark over JN-25 could only have been taken by a very senior naval officer, and the most likely candidate is Admiral Richmond K. Turner, director of the Navy's War Plans Division, who, without any apparent authority, assumed total control of the analysis and dissemination of OP-20-G's output. Turner has been described as the Navy's Patton, and certainly his abrasive manner, distrust of the Army, and his open dislike of Roosevelt's aides all suit this description.

In the immediate aftermath of the attack, it would have been realized that the Navy had all along possessed the vital JN-25 decrypts that could have warned the President, and the commanders in Pearl Harbor, but had failed to make the information available. A very high-level decision was taken to houseclean naval records of all references to pre-Pearl JN-25, so that it would seem no such messages ever existed. Therefore, Roosevelt, Kimmel, and Short could not have been more precisely warned. Since very few people had such authority and knew of the existence of JN-25, suspicion must fall on Turner. It is quite impossible to believe that all traces of JN-25 intercepts and decrypts between 1939 and 1941 could have vanished so completely unless it had been carefully planned.

As A. A. Hoehling wrote in *The Week Before Pearl Harbor*:

> That panic gripped the second deck of the navy department immediately after the attack . . . is beyond reasonable doubt. One officer, then in intelligence . . . went to his office safe . . . to find a number of Magic despatches missing. He never retrieved them. ONI had done such a thorough housecleaning of its top-secret files that . . . not even a departmental organization charge of November-December 1941 could ever be found. These conceivably were not so much willful attempts to destroy evidence, cover tracks, and remove witnesses . . . as they were the result of headlong, blind, unreasoning fear. Obviously the navy had been guilty of dire errors of both omission and commission. Its leaders . . . passionately desired to pull the curtains, draw the blinds, and shutter the windows.

In his frenzy to cover up (which included concealing the innocuous Winds messages), Turner never imagined that one day questions would be asked about JN-25, or that any JN-25 archival material would ever be placed in the public domain. Turner has been helped by the intransigent attitude of the U.S. Navy and NSA. Ironically, only as this book was in its last stages of publication, and the NSA realized the authors possessed positive proof of both British and American JN-25 codebreaking, did they belatedly confirm for the first time that a code called JN-25 had existed in 1941.

At the postwar Pearl Harbor investigation, the Navy encouraged discussion on peripheral issues about diplomatic codebreaking, counting on the excitement of the media and the naiveté of the inquiry team to overlook the real issue. And so it has remained for fifty years.

It is an inescapable conclusion that Churchill deliberately withheld from the Americans vital intelligence derived from reading the Japanese naval code JN-25 that would have alerted Roosevelt in good time to set a trap that would not only have decimated Yamamoto's Task Force but also allowed America to declare war legitimately on Japan from a far stronger military position.

Churchill rightly believed that if he told Roosevelt what he knew about the Japanese Task Force that FDR would—as a totally honorable President—immediately warn his commanders. This, Churchill feared, would alert the Japanese that their plans were known, causing them to cancel the attack and to abandon JN-25, which would have been a cryptological disaster for both the British and Americans, and leave Britain to face the Japanese on its own in Malaya.

Roosevelt was thus deceived by Churchill, who took a ghastly gamble to bring America into the war in a manner that would sweep aside all opposition; and he was also badly served by his own divided and jealous subordinates. The combination of the two brought a reluctant ally into the war. Churchill's gamble paid off even if, in the process, Britain lost an empire.

Appendix 1

THE *KATA KANA* system for sending Japanese by international Morse code.

THE KATA KANA SYSTEM

The kana syllabary, as used by the Japanese navy before
and during World War II, compresses the Japanese language
into 73 ideographs each of which has a romanji and morse
code equivalent that can be sent over international
telegraph circuits or by radio.

Despite this simplification kana still remains extremely
complex because the meaning of each symbol is altered by
the addition of one of two suffixes after each
ideograph. These are:

   (1) Hanigori, sent as ..--. in morse, and
        denotes a soft sound on the preceeding
        character. Thus HA becomes PA and HO
        becomes PO.

   (2) Nigori, sent as .. in morse, denotes a
        semi-hard sound on the preceeding
        character. Thus HA becomes BA, TA
        becomes DA, and TO becomes DO.

As a a result   the same <u>kana</u> charaacter can be translated with two different meanings, the first   as CHI, a hard sound as in CHINA if followed by the <u>nigori</u> suffix, and the second as SHI, a soft sound if followed by the <u>hanigori</u> suffix, as in SHIP.

Kana	Romaji	Morse		Kana	Romaji	Morse		Kana	Romaji	Morse
イ	I	・-		マ	MA	-・・-		カ	KA	・-・・
ロ	RO	・-・		ケ	KE	-・--		ガ	GA	-・・・・
ハ	HA	-・・・		ゲ	GE	・-・・-		ヨ	YO	--・・
バ	BA	・・・・ ・・		フ	FU	--・・		ヌ	TA	-・
パ	PA	-・・・ ・・ --		ブ	BU	---・		ダ	DA	-
ニ	NI	-・-・		プ	PU	--・・・ --		レ	RE	---
ホ	HO	-・・		コ	KO	----		ソ	SO	---・
ボ	BO	-・・・・		ゴ	GO	-----・		ゾ	ZO	---・・
ポ	PO	-・・・・ ・ -・		エ	E	-・--		ツ	TSU	・---・
ヘ	HE	・		テ	TE	・-・--		ヅ	DZU	---・・
ベ	BE	・・		デ	DE	・-・-- ・		ネ	NE	-・-・
ペ	PE	・・ --		ア	A	-・--		ナ	NA	-・-
ト	TO	・・-・		サ	SA	-・-・		ラ	RA	・・・
ド	DO	・・---・・		ザ	ZA	-・-・・		ム	MU	-
チ	CHI	・-・・・		キ	KI	-・-・		ウ	U	・-
ヂ	JI	・・-・・		ギ	GI	-・-・・・		ヰ	WI	・-・-
リ	RI	--・		ユ	YU	-・・--		ノ	NO	--・
ヌ	NU	・・・・		メ	ME	-・・・		オ	O	・---
ル	RU	----・		ミ	MI	・・-・		グ	KU	・・・-
ヲ	WO	-・---		シ	SHI	--・-		グ	GU	・・・・・
ワ	WA	-・-		ヂ	ZI	-・-・・・		ヤ	YA	・--
ヱ	YE	-・---						セ	SE	---・
ヒ	HI	--・-						ゼ	ZE	---・・
ビ	BI	--・-・・						ズ	SU	----・
ピ	PI	--・・-- --・-						ズ	ZU	----・・
モ	MO	-・・-						ン	N	・-・-

1	ichi	•－－－－
2	ni	••－－－
3	san	•••－－
4	shi	••••－
5	go	•••••
6	roku	－••••
7	sh'chi	－－•••
8	hachi	－－－••
9	ku	－－－－•
0	rei	－－－－－
10	ju	sent as ichi rei

Long sign	＿	•－•－
Period	.	•－•－•－
Bracket	[ ]	•－•－••
Parens	( )	－•－－•－
Colon	:	－－－•••
Query	?	••－－••
Slant	/	－••－•

Appendix 2

THESE ARE COPIES of JN-25 decrypts from FECB in Colombo in early 1942. Apart from the use of expressions like "Zymotic" and special intelligence," it can be seen that these messages are based on intercepted JN-25 messages, because, in many instances, they refer to events that are going to take place in the future.

What is particularly important about these messages is that the additive table in use for this period came into operation on 4 December 1941. Since the messages contain no corrupt groups, it confirms that, despite the upheaval of moving from Singapore to Colombo in late December, FECB had no difficulty in overcoming this table change within four or five weeks.

It follows, therefore, that as the previous table change occurred on 1 June 1941, FECB would have been reading all JN-25 traffic without difficulty long before November 1941. (SRMN-006, RG-457, National Archives, Washington, D.C.)

NAVAL MESSAGE   T.O.O.2339A/12

                 IN   Received: 12.2.42

                            Time   : 2210

Addressed: B.A.D. Washington 234

From   : ADMIRALTY

      Japanese aircraft carrier SHOKAKU intends
to leave Yokosuka and pick up aircraft 9th February.

      It is intended preparations of First and
Second aircraft Squadrons were to complete 7th
February, sail and embark aircraft 8th. E.T.A.
Palao 1200/12th.

      All above from special intelligence.

                     2339A/12

S.O.

E.O

Naval Special Intelligence from Colombo dated March 1st.

An unknown force possibly which is hostile from DAVAO
is to arrive ? at 5 degrees 15 minutes South? 108 degrees
East at 0700? 3rd March.   Speed 9 knots.

Rec'd 5 May.

NAVAL MESSAGE   T.O.O. 0912Z/26

                        IN   Received: 26/2/42

                                 Time: 1824

Addressed: S.O. China Force

Repeated : ADMIRALTY for D.N.I.
            B.A.D.

From   ' : Captain on Staff, Colombo

_____   _____

        ZEAL. My 0623 26th.

        Singora Air Base also included in address

which suggests possible Air Covering Force in Malacca

Strait.

                    0912Z/26

S.O.

NAVAL MESSAGE   T.O.O. 0707Z/13

                         IN   Received: 13/2/42

                                      Time: 1657

Addressed: Admiralty (For D.N.I.)

Repeated: A.C.N.B.,
              N.Z.N.B.,
              ABDAFLOAT,
              B.A.D. Washington

From: Capt. on Staff Colombo

IMPORTANT

        Naval Special Intelligence dated 12th
February. C. in C. Combined Fleet transfers his
flag to YAMATO at 0100Z/12th. Comment. No record of
YAMATO. May be new battleship.

                              0707Z/13

S.O.

BMacP

NAVAL MESSAGE   T.O.O. 2025Z/27

                         IN   Received: 27/2/42

                                     Time: 2130

Addressed: C.C.C.F.
            Admiralty for D.N.I.
            B.A.D. Washington
            A.C.N.B.
From: Captain on Staff, Colombo

_____

ZEALOUS,

Plain language and special intelligence.

        After reporting five enemy destroyers off
Bali at 1830Z 27th, unknown reconnaissance unit was
ordered to keep watch near South Eastern end of Java
and keep C. in C. 3rd Fleet informed of situation.

                        2025Z/27

S.O.

D.M.T.

NAVAL MESSAGE   T.O.O. 0623Z/26

                              IN   Received: 26/2/42

                                             Time   : 0540

Addressed: S.O. China Force

Repeated :   Admiralty for D.N.I.
             B.A.D., Washington

From   : Captain on Staff, Colombo

IMPORTANT

AIDAC

      ZYMOTIC. Naval Special Intelligence dated 25th. 10
transports for operation T for Tommy will heave Muntok vicinity
1200 Japanese time 26th. Further convoy of 10 ships will leave
Palembang and an unknown place on 28th. Comment. Call signs
believed to belong to Fourth Destroyer Squadron and an air unit
are included in address.

      S.O. China Force pass to C.Z.M·

                                               ·≺

                              0623Z/26

S.O.

HFP

Appendix 3

THESE ARE SOME of the Japanese diplomatic exchanges between Berlin and Tokyo sent on the Purple machine and intercepted and decoded by GCCS and FECB using the Purple machines given them by the Americans in January 1941. The British did not use the expression Purple or Magic but called these intercepts BJ, British-Japanese, although they were colloquially known as Black Jumbos. (Crown copyright, reproduced with the permission of the Controller of Her Majesty's Stationary office. WO 208/882, Public Record Office, Kew.)

An appreciation of the general war situation and Germany's attitude.

He points out that the aid of Japan is of importance to Germany and, the extent of this aid may determine the moment when Germany may be willing to make peace offers to England. It is not inconceivable that Germany might offer ~~Russia~~ America a free hand in the Far East to prevent her aiding Britain. Japan's fate for thousands of years depends on the acquisition of the resources of the South and Japan's original intention in concluding the Tripartite Pact was to enable her to realise this object. Japan should form an active policy ~~for~~ to realise her objectives in the Greater East Asia sphere and consolidate bases for a Southward move at the time Germany invades Britain. At the same time advantage should be taken of Germany's successes against Russia to remove the Northern threat to Japan. It is important that, before making any move, Japan should discuss her plans with Germany and Italy so as to have a cut and dried policy recognising Japan's special position in Greater East Asia.

personal

J.120.

Rome to Tokyo. (Jap.)

BJ.096781.
2.:.1a.4c
16.10.4c

MOST SECRET

MACKENSEN's views are as follows:

1) Today is the Japan's golden opportunity to attack Russia. Such an opportunity would not occur a second time.

2) If Japan fought Russia., America would not fight, as she cannot do so on two fronts.

3). Southward movie should be postponed, but carried out later at the right opportunity.

4). Japs should tell Germany about negotiations with America.

120.

09607.
30 May

Tokyo - Berlin (Toy.)
28 May.   56

Message to Ribbentrop (personal). ~~urges~~
Matsuoka urges that the ~~Japanese~~ German
Government should do their best to avoid conflict
with Russia in view of the international situation
& the internal conditions of ~~countries surrounding~~
Germany & Japan.

∇～20.

57

B 090774.

10 May 1941

TOKYO-BERLIN. Japanese.

On his return from visiting the Imperial Mausoleum
of the Emperor MEIJI and the KASHIWARI shrine at UNEBI
Mr. MATSUOKA sends a personal message to Herr RIBBENTROP,

Commenting on President Roosevelt's recent speech
he remarks that he was near despair at Roosevelt's
recklessness but there is still one ray of hope not
extinguished which he hopes cannot be extinguished.

(From context possibly a religious hope.)

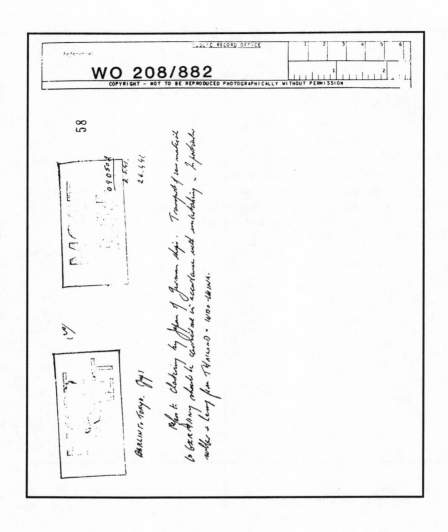

58

0905ok

2.54.

26.4.41

BERLIN to TOKYO, 941

Plan & Clothing by Japan & German troops. Transport of war material to German Army schools be carried out in accordance with undertaking. Approximate width & length from T4/15 mm D. 14/10-14/11/11.

090501.
3rd May, 1941.
26th April, 1941.

TOKYO to BERLIN (Jap).

1. Economic commisions will work in close cooperation with the General and Military Commissions.

2. Subjects to be referred to the Economic Commission.

a). The basis of the new economic order planned by GERMANY and ITALY and its harmonization with the new economic order for Eastern ASIA planned by JAPAN.

b). The question of cooperation between the Three Powers under this new order.

(1) The question of mutual cooperation within the respective economic spheres of JAPAN, GERMANY and ITALY.

(A) The exchange of raw materials, (B) exchange of technical information, (C) cooperation in connection with finance, (D) cooperation on connection with transport, (E) cooperation in connection with communications (F) an agreement about markets.

(2) The question of cooperation between the Three Powers in other economic spheres.

(A) An agreement on markets, (B) the securing of raw materials, (C) cooperation in connection with transport, (D) cooperation in connection with communications, (E) cooperation in connection with finance.

(2) The question of cooperation between the Three Powers in time of war.

(a) The question of cooperation in connection with the securing and exchange of essential commodities.

(1) The supply of commodities which each of the three countries possesses, (2) the securing of the products of other countries.

(b) The question of cooperation in connection with traffic.

(1) The question of transport via SIBERIA (2) the study of new methods of transport, (3) the transfer of shipping. (4) cooperation in connection with communications.

(c) The question of cooperation in connection with the exchange of technical information.

(d) The question of cooperation in connection with finance.

(3) The study of counter-measures against British and American economic pressure by means of cooperation between the Three Powers.

(a) Direct economic counter-measures against BRITAIN and AMERICA.

(b) Indirect counter-measures by means of political and economic action against countries other than BRITAIN and AMERICA.

BERLIN to TOKYO (Japanese)   MOST SECRET   089585.
5 April.   9 April   62

Mr. MATSUOKA saw Herr HITLER on the 4 April at
Hitler's request. The exchange of news was direct & friendly.
Mr. MATSUOKA reported on his talks with Srs. MUSSOLINI & CIANO
& the POPE.   Mr. MATSUOKA asked HITLER to arrange
for the transmission from GERMANY to JAPAN of all GERMANY's
inventions & results of her experience during this war.
    Herr HITLER agreed immediately to issue instructions

Appendix 4

THIS IS A list of delegates attending the American-British-Dutch conference in Singapore, in April 1941, and details of liaison officers serving in the Far East. (Records of Joint Army and Navy Boards, RG-225, Microfilm locator M-1421, #10-207, Reel #301, National Archives, Washington, D.C.)

AMERICAN - DUTCH - BRITISH CONVERSATIONS,

APRIL 1941.

DELEGATES.

United States of America.

Captain W. R. Purnell, U.S.N.	Chief of Staff, U. S. Asiatic Fleet.
Colonel A.C. McBride, U.S.A.	Asst. Chief of Staff U.S. Military Forces Philippines.
Captain A.M.R. Allen, U.S.N.	U.S. Naval Observer, Singapore.
Lt. Colonel F. G. Brink, U.S.A.	U.S. Military Observer Singapore.

Netherlands East Indies.

Major-General H. ter Poorten	Chief of General Staff.
Captain J.J.A. van Staveren, R.N.N.	Chief of Naval Staff.
Captain D.C. Buurman van Vreeden	General Staff.
Lt. Cdr. N. C. N. Loorman, R.N.N.	Naval Staff.
Captain L.G.L. van der Kun, R.N.N.	Naval Liaison Officer Singapore.
Major J.N.J. Tegner.	Military Liaison Officer, Singapore.

General Headquarters, Far East.

Air Chief Marshal Sir Robert Brooke-Popham, G.C.V.O., K.C.B., C.M.G., D.S.O., A.F.C. (Secretary General). Group Captain L. Darvall, M.C., Royal Air Force.	Commander in Chief, Far East.

Commander in Chief, China and Staff.

Vice-Admiral Sir Geoffrey Layton, K.C.B., D.S.O.	Commander in Chief, China.
Commodore F.E.P. Hutton, R.N.	Chief of Staff.
Paymaster Captain D.H. Doig, R.N. (Secretary to Conference)	Secretary to Commander in Chief China.

Australia.

Admiral Sir Ragnar M. Colvin, K.B.E., C.B.	First Naval Member.
Paymaster Captain J.B. Foley, O.B.E., R.A.N.	Secretary to First Naval Member.
Commander R.F. Nichols, R.N.	Naval Staff.
Group Captain F.M. Bladin, R.A.A.F.	Air Staff.
Colonel H.G. Rourke, M.C.	General Staff, Australian Imperial Force, Malaya.
Commander V.E. Kennedy, R.A.N.	Australian Naval Liaison Officer, Batavia.

(Cont'd)

AMERICAN - DUTCH - BRITISH CONVERSATIONS,
APRIL, 1941.

DELEGATES .....continued

New Zealand.

Commodore W.E. Parry, C.B., R.N.   Chief of Naval Staff.
Air Commodore H.W.L. Saunders,   Chief of Air Staff.
    M.C., D.F.C., M.M., R.A.F.
Colonel A.E. Conway, C.B.E.   New Zealand Staff
                                          Corps.

India.

Major General G.N. Molesworth.   Deputy Chief of
                                          General Staff
                                          (representing Defence
                                          Department).

East Indies Station.

Commodore A.G.B. Wilson,   Chief of Staff.
    D.S.O., M.V.C., R.N.

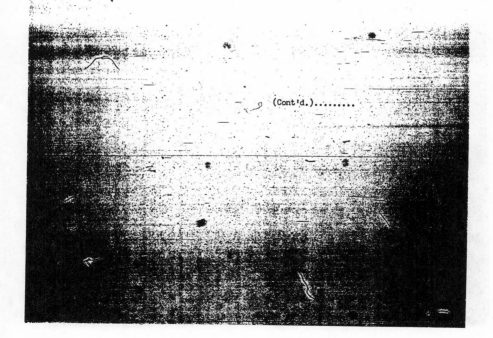

(Cont'd.).........

AMERICAN – DUTCH– BRITISH CONVERSATIONS,
APRIL 1941.

APPENDIX III.

LIST OF LIAISON OFFICERS AND OBSERVERS.

UNITED STATES PACIFIC FLEET.

British Observers U.S.S. WEST VIRGINIA Commander C.R.L.
                                         Parry, R.N.
                   U.S.S. BOISE   Lieutenant Commdr.
                                         C.C. Martell, R.N.
                   U.S.S. STERRETT   Lieutenant Commdr.
                                         Hon.D.C.Cairns,R.N.

MANILA.

Dutch Observer.   Commander H.D. Lindner,
                                R.N.N.

BATAVIA.

British Naval Liaison Officer Commander J.B. Heath, R.N.

British Air Liaison Officer   Squadron Leader Watkins, R.A.F.

Australia Naval Liaison Officer Commander V.E. Kennedy, R.A.N.

Australia Air Liaison Officer, Wing Commander Thomas, R.A.A.F.

SINGAPORE.

United States of America Naval, Captain A.M.R. Allen, U.S.N.
              Observer
United States of America   Lieutenant Colonel F.G. Brink,
         Army Observer   U.S.A.
Dutch Naval Liaison Officer   Captain L.G.L. Van der Kun.
Dutch Military Liaison
              Officer   Major J.M.J. Wegner.
New Zealand Liaison Officers   Group Captain L. Darvall,
                                M.C., R.A.F.
                                Commander E.K.H St. Aubyn.
                                D.S.C., R.N.

AUSTRALIA.

United States Naval Attache   Commander L.D. Causey, U.S.N.

United States Naval Observer   Commander M. Collins, U.S.N.
         (Darwin)
Dutch Naval Liaison Officer   Commander G.B. Salm, R.N.N.

New Zealand Liaison Officer   Group Captain T. Wilkes, R.N.Z.A.F.

NEW ZEALAND.
United States Naval Observer   Commander Olding, U.S.N.

COLOMBO.
United States Naval Observer   Commander H.M. Lammers, U.S.N.

Appendix 5

THESE ARE SOME messages regarding plans to evacuate FECB from Singapore to Colombo following the outbreak of war with Japan. Note the reference to "special intelligence" and "Zymotic" signals (those derived from codebreaking), and the "Y organization," which analyzed Japanese radio traffic but did not do any codebreaking. (File MP 1185/8, 1937/2/159, Australian Archives, Victoria.)

STP/MR.

TO ADMIRALTY 168.   N.Z.N.B.   A.C.N.B.   B.A.D.WASHINGTON.
     C.IN C. STH.ATLANTIC C.IN C. E.FLEET. 182 F.O.C. R.I.N.
     FOR ARM INDIA. C.IN C. CEYLON

FROM DEPUTY C.IN C. E.FLEET.   N. CYPHER (FLAG)
                                    { P/L.
                                    { CODE
                                    { CYPHER

METHOD OF   W/T.   DATE 27/4/42.   DATE   T.O.O. 0506z/27.
TRANSMISSION   SENT   REC/D.

SECRET.

PRESENT LOCATION OF NAVAL INTELLIGENCE STAFF EX F.E.C.B. IS
AS FOLLOWS (ii) COLOMBO HALF SPECIAL INTELLIGENCE AND 'Y' ORGANIZA-
TION AND(?) NAVAL O I C PERSONNEL ADMINISTERED BY C.IN C. CEYLON.
ZYMOTIC AND Y SIGNALS WILL CONTINUE TO BE ORIGINATED BY CAPTAIN
SUPERINTENDENT COLOMBO (iii) GENERAL MESSAGES(?) TO KILINDINI.
OTHER HALF OF SPECIAL INTELLIGENCE AND Y ORGANIZATION INCLUDING
SHAW AND FRANCIS WITH NUCLEUS SECRETARIAT AND CYPHER STAFF. AFTER
ESTABLISHMENT MAY ORIGINATE ZYMOTIC AND Y SIGNALS AS FROM CAPTAIN
SUPERINTENDENT KILINDINI.   PERSONNEL REMAINING PART OF CAPTAIN
SUPERINTENDENT ORGANIZATION AND AS SUCH PART OF C.IN C. E.FLEET
STAFF Ø WILL BE ADMINISTERED LOCALLY BY FLAG OFFICER IN CHARGE
KILINDINI (iv) NEW DELHI. 4 OFFICERS WORKING WITH D M I INDIA
TO DEAL WITH NAVAL ASPECTS JOINT INTELLIGENCE. F.O.C. R.I.N. IS
REQUESTED DEAL WITH LOCAL ADMINISTRATION MATTERS THE OFFICERS
REMAINING PART CAPT. SUPERINTENDENT ORGANIZATION AND C.IN C. E.FLEET
STAFF (v) SIGNALS AND CORRESPONDENCE CAPT. SUPDT. SHOULD CONTINUE
TO BE SENT COLOMBO(?) FOR THE PRESENT AND REPEATED KILINDINI ONLY
WHEN NECESSARY. NOMINAL LISTS NEW ARRANGEMENTS FOLLOW TO ADMIRALTY
(FOR D.N.I.) ONLY.

Distribution:

1st. N.M.
2nd. N.M.
D.S.C.
D.N.I.
S.I.B.
H. OF N.
C. RECS.

COPY OF MESSAGE.

²ᵒᵃⁿ/⁵⁷⁶ⁿᵛ

To ADMIRALTY 927 C. IN C., E.I. (R) A.C.N.B.; F.O.C., MALAYA;
C. IN C., FAR EAST

From C. IN C., EASTERN FLEET.

Method of Transmission WT {P/L. CODE. CONF. CODE. CYP.} FLAG

Date and Time Sent 27th December, 1941. 0951Z

Date and Time Received 28th December, 1941.

Originator's Number Time of Origin 0951Z/27

4074....

S E C R E T.

ADMIRALTY MESSAGE 1600A/21 TO C. IN C., EASTERN

FLEET ONLY. INTEND TO TRANSFER TO CEYLON THE NAVAL SECTION OF

F.E.C.B. (INCLUDING CAPTAIN ON THE STAFF (COMMA) Y AND SPECIAL

INTELLIGENCE) BY TRANSPORT RETURNING FROM SINGAPORE ABOUT 5th

JANUARY.

2.   INTERPRETERS WILL BE LEFT TO ASSIST ARMY AND AIR

SPECIAL INTELLIGENCE. INTELLIGENCE STAFF FOR F.O.C., MALAYA,

WILL COMPRISE A Y AND TWO OFFICERS ∅ ∅ F.E.C.B..

COMMANDER WISDEN ∅ WILL REMAIN BEHIND TO ASSIST IN TURNING

OVER. (MESSAGE ENDS).

Distribution :
1st N.M.
2nd N.M.
D.C.N.S.
D.N.I.
D.S.C.
S.I.B.
M. of M.
CONF. REC.

Appendix 6

THESE ARE SOME of the messages Admiral Yamamoto's headquarters in Tokyo sent to the Task Force before, and after, it sailed from Tankan Bay in the Kurile Islands, thus proving beyond any doubt that radio silence was broken after the fleet had assembled for the attack on Pearl Harbor.

The date of each message is shown at the top left. Immediately below is the code designator, JN-25, which was blanked out by the National Security Agency (NSA) because, when these decrypts were released in 1980, the NSA still refused to admit that any such a code had existed. At the bottom right-hand corner is the official date these messages were translated, which the authors of this book believe are false.

These messages were specially prepared by the U.S. Navy for the 1945–46 congressional Pearl Harbor investigation. They were never produced, because the subject of Japanese naval codes was only briefly mentioned by the U.S. Navy, and the inquiry team failed to appreciate their significance.

There are no JN-25 messages in any American archive dated prior to 20 November 1941, thus implying the U.S. Navy could not read the code until after the attack. (SRN series, RG-457, National Archives, Washington, D.C.)

(ed)

U MO 2   All Fleets
DE
HA FU 6   TOKYO Radio.
- SU U   W 77

- - - - - - - -   -- - - - - -

From: MO MI YU   HAINAN Guard Dist Chief of Staff.
Action: YU NO 893   Guard By TAKAO Radio
                MA SA MU   Garble
Info: NA RI 77   Combined Fleet CinC
                NI TO FU   Navy Vice Minister and Vice Chief of NGS
                FU TE RU   TAIHOKU Radio
                KU NU KE   SHANGHAI Radio
                SO HA ØØ
                KU NO 55   So Exp Forces CinC

1800/20 November 1941   (TOI 11/24 0737 G DX 16620 A) H

~~Garble~~   ~~I. .~~ 47300

              (HAINAN Guard District ?) DESOPORD # 68.

          1. Report of a factual case of leakage of secret
inf rmation regarding the concentration of our troops in HAINAN Island ~~[blacked out]~~
to a foreigner, has been brought to the attention of this office.

          Every section must further strengthen their efforts towards
prevention of espionage.

          2. Commencing November 24th and until further notice, no
one will be permitted to leave or enter HAINAN Island, unless they are MIlitary
~~xxxxx~~ Service, Military stores personnel or holders of special permits.

          3. From the same date, until further notice, all types
of communication from the island will be prohibited, unless specially
permitted by the Military.

                    (JAPANESE)

JN 5   0067 Z   (edg s) Navy Trans. 11/29/45

                                       ~~TOP SECRET ULTRA~~

F

(ed)

U MO 2   All Fleets
DE
HA FU 6   TOKYO Radio
- SU U   N 35

- - - - - - - - - - - - - - -

From: FU A U   TOKYO, Secretary to NGS.
Action: YU FI 549 Staff, Comm.Off. Cardivs, Combined Fleet.
Info: PO BE 249 Comb Fleet, Staff Comm Office.

1930/20 November 1941   (TOI 11/20.056 G TK 4155 A) H

~~Serial~~ 051

     350 copies of the Combined Fleet Special Call Sign List, and 50 copies
of the Combined Fleet "Number Date xix Table" (total weight 27 kilo) will be
sent to YOKOSUKA Air Group ▬▬▬ by noon 21 November. Arrange to take
delivery immediately.

Carded AUK
15 Jan 46

(JAPANESE)

JN 5   0104 Z   (adprs.) Navy Trans. 12/04/45

SRN. NO   115471

'ed)

```
U MO 2        All Fleets
DE
H. FU 6       TOKYO Radio
- SU U        W 34
- - - - - - - - - - - - - - - -

From:      O  RE 14   4th Fleet, Staff Comm Office
Action:    SI SI 649  Combined Fleet, Staff Comm Office
Info:      I  MU 3    3rd Comm Unit.
           O  SI Ø    SAIPAN Radio
           ME NU 1    6th Comm Unit.
           TO HE 3    4th Comm Unit.
           RU SI 2    ?????
```

1500/20 November 1941   (TOI 11/201642 S   MX 8310 A) H

▮▮▮▮   Serial 18400

Refer Combined Fleet Serial <u>570</u> (?)

1. Combined Fleet Secret OpOrd # 1 has not as yet been distributed
to units of the 4th fleet▮▮▮▮▮ and consequently they are unable to
participate. Please make suitable arrangements.

2. Distribution is expected to be completed▮▮▮▮Date 27
November!)

(GZ Comment: Another case of distributing written orders. Refer to GZ 0041 Z)

8AH

                          (JAPANESE)

JN 5   0043 Z   (RK) Navy Trans 11/27/45

SRN. NO   115403

(db)

U MO 2   All Fleets   ) *include*
DE:
HAFU 6   TOKYO Radio
U TU 3701 -SUU NR 406B7
W40

- - - - - - - - - -

From: KE RO 88   Comb Fleet CinC
To: YA KI 4   2nd Fleet
         E MU 6   Third Fleet
         O RE 1   4th Fleet
         SUYO 4   ~~Comb Air Force~~   *11ᵗʰ AIR FLEET*
         RI TA 3   CARDIVS, Comb Fleet
         RAA 2
         KI MU 9   SASEBO RDO
         KU MI 8   So. Exp Force
       (MI)NSI 3   (Less)~~Expo~~ex AirRon 6

11/202000/I 1941   (TOI 11/20 0720 KE G 16626A)H

━━━   *Serial 579*

This despatch is Top Secret.

To be decoded only by an officer.

This order effective as of the date within the text to follow.

TEXT:
        At 0000 on 21 November, repeat 21 November, carry out second
phase of preparations for opening hostilities.

JN-5 #0021-Z   (Japanese)   1/15/46   L. O. B.
                      (RK) Navy Tr. 11/26/45/Q

F   ~~TOP SECRET ULTRA~~

(ad)

U MO 2	All Fleets	
DE		
HA FU 6	TOKYO Radio	
- SU U	N 22	

- - - - - - - - - - - - -

From:	EO TE 33	to Exp Force CinC
Action:	EO SE 22	Comb Fleet CinC
	KO RE 44	2nd Fleet CinC
	WI KA ØØ	12th Air Group Commander.
	TA MA 55	YUKAZE Commanding Officer
Info:	GU YO 44	Comb Air Force CinC

1230/23 November 1941   (TOI 11/232007 G   CN 8310 A) H

██████ < ████ 981031

   MALAY Force DESORD # 1.

   2000, 21st.

   YUUKAZE ████████ is attached to Air Flot 22 ████████ until further

orders.

[GZ Comment: First appearance of MALAY Force in traffic.]

(JAPANESE)   L. D. D.

JN 5   0100 Z   (RK) Navy Trans 12/04/45

(ed)

FU WI 4   TAKAO Radio
DE
HA FU 6   TOKYO Radio
- SU U   W 172
- - - - - - - - - - -

From: I KA E   TOKYO Comm Office
Action: HO RO NO   All Nav List Chief of Staff.
        WU SE KU   All Guard List. Chief of Staff.
        SU FU 358   All Major Comds. Afloat, Chief of Staff.

1900/25 November 1941   **328**   (TOI 11/250032 G   JK   6520 A) H
                Serial 38312

PAGE	CALL	UNIT
3	HA — 5	E (MALAY) Force.
3	(———) 2	H (Dutch East Indies) Force.
3	RE YA 5	Attached Force (s).
3	SU TI 8 NO SE 4 TA HE 9	Striking Force
3	WI MA 5 SU YA 7	Air Force (Southern Force)
3	HO RI 6	South Seas Force
4	SU U 5	Submarine Force (Southern Force).
4	TE KI 6 KO RE Ø HA SA 2 TI E 5	Main Force
4	KU RA 2	Communications Force
6	TO WI 5	Commerce Destruction Unit.
7	NE SE 6 to KU MA 6 (6 calls]	Southern Force

(JAPANESE)

JN 5   0044 Z   (BROWN) Navy Trans 11/27/45

(ed)

```
- - - - - - -
DE
- - - - - - -
W 191        - SU U
- - - - - - - - - - - - - -
```

From: I KA E   TOKYO Comm Office, Chief.
Action: FU RA 949 Staff Comm Office Cardiv 4
Info: TE HI 356 RYUJO Comm Office

1910/ol December 1941   (TOI 1./011031 G &T 41551) H

JN 25 B   ~~~~~ 38600

            Revision of # 2 of Navy Call List # 10, effective December

1st.

PAGE	CALL	UNIT
3	▆▆▆ unident) YU 5	Submarine Force under 5th Fleet
4	▆▆▆ unident) 5	Submarine patrol force.
4	RI A 4	Communication Force.
6	TI HI 2	3rd Escort Unit.
6	TA I 7	4th Escort Unit.
6	FU NU 7	- - - - - - - - -
7	YA WI 7	Transport Division 3.
7	KE RI 3	Transport Division 4.
8	NU -- Ø	4th Fleet.

(with the exception of the following
Units; Base Force, Forces attached
to Base Force, 4th Civil Engineering
Dept., 4th Military Stores Dept.
4th Dept. of Supplies and Accounts
and 4th Weather Observation Post).

8   XEX RA RE Ø to   Southern Expeditionary Fleet
     ▆▆▆ unident) MU 2 (3 calls)

8   HE HO 1 to   Flagship of CinC of Southern
     TA TI 1 (3 calls)   Expeditionary Fleet.

JN 5   0055 Z   (Brown) Navy Trans 11/28/45

PAGE	CALL	UNIT
8	MU NI 3 to RO TO 9 (3 calls)	Ship-shore administrative offices of CinC Southern Expeditionary Fleet.
8	KO NA 3	———— attached to Southern Expeditionary Fleet.
14	——— 5	YAMATO. ← ———
14	████ unident) RO 4	AGANO.
14	——— NU 8	████ unident)
74	MI HE —— to YA NA —— (10 calls)	planes of KASUGA Maru.

(JAPANESE)

JN 5   0055 Z

F

(Brown) Navy Trans 11/28/45

SRN. NO   115420

(db)

WA SU Ø   Combined Fleet.   *include*
DE
ha FU 6   TOKYO Radio
Ŧ 30

- - - - - - - - - - - - - - -

From: YO WI ØØ   Combined Fleet, ClnC.
Action: SE TU 7   Combined Fleet.

12/021500/I 1941   (TOI 12/022100 S XT 4155 A) -H

~~████~~   Serial 676

     This despatch is Top Secret.

     This order is effective at 1730 on 2 December:

     ~~███~~ Combined Fleet Serial) # 10.

     Climb NIITAKAYAMA 1208, repeat 1208!

Comment: Interpreted freely, above means "Attack on 8 December". Explanation:
This was undoubtedly the prearranged signal for specifying the date for opening
hostilities. However, the significance of the phrase is interesting in that it
is so appropriately used in this connection.

     NIITAKAYAMA is the highest mountain in the Japanese Empire. To
climb NIITAKAYAMA is to accomplish one of the greatest feats. In other words
undertake the task (of carrying out assigned operations). 1208 signifies the
12th month, 8th day, Item time.

*GI Comment: Intercepted 2100, 2
Dec. 1941,*

£8H
F

                 (JAPANESE)

JN 5   0012 Z   (RK) Navy Trans ~~TOP SECRET ULTRA~~

(da)

KE SA 3		All Ships and Stations
MA SU Ø		Combined Fleet
DE		
HA FU 6		Tokyo Comm. Unit.
W 54		

From:	HA LO MA	Navy Minister
Action:	KI RO LO	All Nav Dist Cincs
	HA KI TE	All Guard Dist Cincs
	O U 11	All Fleets Cincs
	KA U SA	Manchuria RNO
	WI ME FU	Ihq Mission to F-1-C
	FU TE RU	TAIHOKU RNO
	WI YA SO	South Seas RNO
	NE U N*	Naval War College Chief

1520/02 December 1941   (TOI 12/022008 S NP 6520 A) H

▬▬▬▬▬   9020

   Starting 4 December 1941 additive system #8 of Naval

Code D will be used, and additive system # 7 will be discontinued.

   From Office of Naval Communication.

   As there are some communication units in Japan who have

not yet received additive list # 8, in communicating with them additive

list # 7 will be used.

JN 6   1370 Z   (JAPANESE)   carded LdD 3/13/46
AM DC   (es) Navy Trans. 3/1/44 ~~SECRET ULTRA~~

,ed)

FU LI 4   (NIKO Radio)
DE
HA FU 6   (TOKYO Radio)   Include
- SU U   NR 952
Z 86

- - - - - - - - - - - - - - -

From: RI TO ØØ   (4th Fleet)
Action: KURO 8   (Shore Activity) Maizuru #2 Spl. Land. Force.
         KE Nₐ 9   (CruDiv 6)
         YA KA ₐ2   (Ship Associated with CarDiv 2) COMDESDIV 23
         O U 5   (carrier) OBORO-DD
         MO FU 253   (4th Fleet All Command Officers)
         O SI ØØ   (SAIPAN Radio)
         I MU 33   (PALAO Radio)
         TO HE 33   (TRUK Radio)
         ME NU 11   (KWAJALEIN Radio)

12/041200/I 1941   (TOI 12/061848 G on 6565 A kcs)

            Serial 398

       SS South Seas Force Secret Instruction # 1.

    A special message on the occasion of the Declaration of War, to all
under my command.

        The critical time, which calls for your putting your strength to the
supreme test and for you to prove your unequalled loyalty to the throne, has at
last arrived. Operational plans have been perfected, all preparations have been
completed, every officer shall reassure himself on being thoroughly acquainted
with every phase of the previously issued instructions, fighting spirits must
soar and strict alert maintained in order to successfully carry out our plans.
Take the initiative against the enemy and be on your guard against attack from
the enemy. Obtain control and completely crush them by maintaining the closest
of cooperation between forces. Upon meeting the enemy, desperate strategy must
be applied, if it is found that counter to your expectation, advancing

                        (JAPANESE)

JN 5   0003 Z   Page 1   (edgs) Navy Trans 10/BLK5CRET ULTRA on or holding your line against the enemy is difficult.

Although giving one's life may be the means by which to pave the road to victory, remember that final victory is achieved by those possessing the spirit of endurance to fight through to the finish. It is strongly felt that in addition to the operations of this force being very wide and varied, reaching into many channels, the extent of success of each operation not only directly affects the Combined Fleet's operations, but will in the end have its effect on the whole outcome of the war.

Advance to strike, hold your own on guard, but in complete unity under the supreme command, always act in accordance with your deep loyalty to the Imperial throne, be a perfect soldier first, accomplish your duty and deprive yourself, thus earn the right to glory in victory.

G1 Comment: This message was intercepted 1848, 6 Dec., 1941

4/14/46

JN 5   0003 Z   Page 2   (JAPANESE)   (ed.s) Navy Trans ~~TOP SECRET ULTRA~~

DECLASSIFIED per E.O. 12065
by Director, NSA/Chief, CSS
1 June 1979   **SRN. NO**   115309

Appendix 7

SOME IDEA OF the paranoia and embarrassment that still grip intelligence agencies today fifty years after the start of the war in the Far East can be judged from these Central Bureau archives, finally released by Australia's Defence Signals Directorate (DSD) after an eighteen-month delay. It was claimed by the DSD that to acknowledge that Japanese codes were broken before December 1941 would not only upset a "foreign government," i.e., Britain and its GCHQ, but would also endanger Australia's security. It is hard to see what can be secret about the names of those who worked in the Central Bureau in 1941, since most of them are long dead.

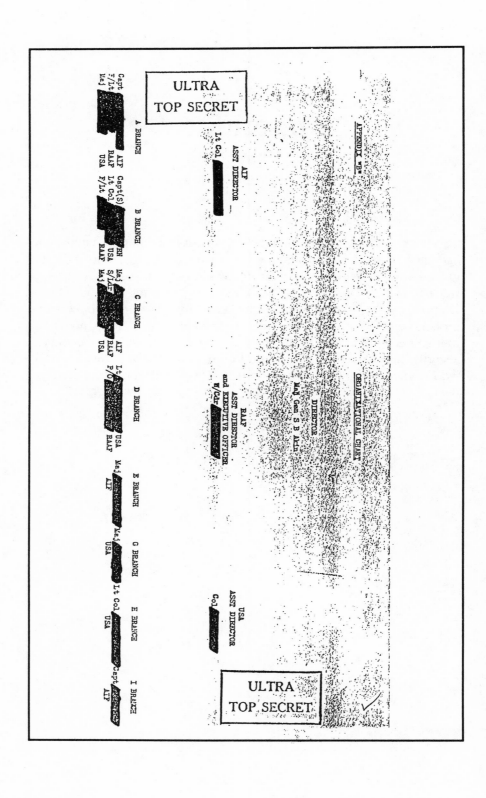

APPENDIX "B"

ORGANIZATIONAL CHART

DIRECTOR
Maj Gen S B Akin

AIF
ASST DIRECTOR
Lt Col

RAAF
ASST DIRECTOR
and EXECUTIVE OFFICER
W/Cdr

USA
ASST DIRECTOR
Col

A BRANCH
Capt AIF
F/Lt RAAF
Maj USA

B BRANCH
Capt(S) AIF
Lt Col RAAF
F/Lt USA

C BRANCH
Maj
S/Ldr USA
Maj RAAF

D BRANCH
Lt AIF
P/O RAAF
USA

E BRANCH
Maj
AIF

G BRANCH
Maj
USA

E BRANCH
Lt Col
USA

I BRANCH
Capt
AIF

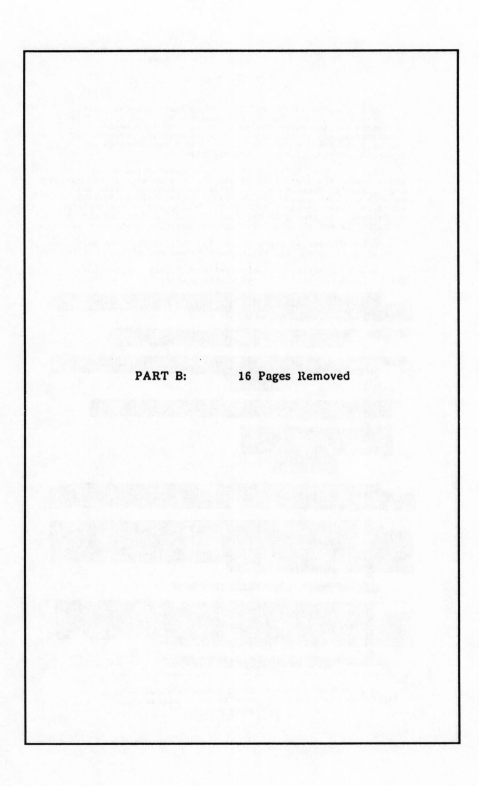

PART B: 16 Pages Removed

(11)

The invasion in the Philippines introduced a new aspect of the nature of the "Sightings" reported by Recce A/c. Prior to October 44 the recce duties on which they were employed consisted mainly of shadowing their own convoys, reporting to the base the position of the convoy they were covering, and reporting on the weather in the vicinity.

All messages, intercepted by our forward field units, which showed any indication of containing such convoy information were signalled "Immediate Ops" to Central Bureau. After the message had been worked on, as full a translation as possible would be passed to HQ of 7th Fleet. Subsequent to the transfer to Hollandia of the HQ of 7th Fleet, Field Units passed direct to Hollandia any derived intelligence regarding these convoys.

After October 44 recce A/c in the Philippines area were engaged on searching for Allied Task Forces and reinforcements.

From examination of a captured book it was evident that great stress was laid on recce of enemy carriers.

---

* 3 Enemy Battleships, 4 Cruisers, 4 Destroyers under weigh in Leyte Gulf, visibility poor, weather in the vicinity raining.

TOP SECRET

<u>Contents</u>.

TOP SECRET

Appendix 8

DEVELOPMENT OF ENIGMA AND TYPEX

ONE OF THE earliest cipher machines was designed by the Italian architect Leon Battista Alberti, who in the mid-1400s produced a pair of copper cipher discs on which were engraved two separate and movable rows of the alphabet which could be set to an infinitely large number of permutations known only to the holders of such a device.

The American statesman Thomas Jefferson invented his wheel cipher machine around 1790, consisting of up to thirty-six separate discs on a central spindle, each of which was engraved with the complete alphabet producing the staggering number of thirty-six factorial combinations or 371,993,326,789,901,217,467,999,448,150,835,200,000,000 permutations. Although never used at the time, Jefferson's wheel was rediscovered in 1922 and, slightly modified, became the U.S. Army's code machine M-94, which used twenty-five discs on a spindle just over four inches long and remained in service until World War II. But these cipher wheels were slow and awkward to use and not suited for handling large volumes of traffic between many different units.

It was hardly surprising, therefore, that by 1927 a large number of different inventors had registered nearly 200 patents for various forms of rotor cipher machines. But of all these only three names have found a place in history: Edward Hebern in America, Arthur Scherbius in Germany, and Arvid Damm in Sweden. All three used a system of interchangeable rotors, but the machines produced by Hebern and Scherbius displayed their output on twenty-six glow lamps, thus requiring an operator and assistant, while Damm's machine (the B-211, for example) printed out the cipher or plain text on a strip of gummed paper.

Inevitably, the Enigma cryptograph is by far the best-known, and its history is well documented, some of the best accounts being *Intercept*, Josef Garlinski; *Enigma*, Wladyslaw Kozaczuk; *Top Secret Ultra*, Peter

Calvocoressi; *The Hut Six Story,* Gordon Welchman; and *Machine Cryptography & Modern Cryptanalysis,* C. A. Deavours and Louis Kruh. All these books contain a wealth of highly technical detail showing how Enigma keys (rather than the machine itself) were broken. Welchman's account is particularly valuable, since it is the only firsthand account of someone at GCCS during the war, and its publication greatly upset GCHQ, who for some quaint reason still believe such revelations endanger Britain's security today.

German interest in machine cryptography had begun as early as 1915 but was halted in 1918 following the Armistice. But with the rebirth of militarism under the Weimar Republic, work on machine cryptography restarted, and interest centered on the ideas of Arthur Scherbius, an engineer who lived at Wilmsdorf in Berlin. Scherbius had constructed a rotor cipher machine he called Enigma (after Sir Edward Elgar's *Enigma Variations,* in which each of Elgar's friends is described by a different piece of music), but he lacked the financial resources to develop it further. Scherbius therefore joined forces with Willie Korn, who owned a company called Enigma Chiffriermaschinen AG in Berlin and improved Scherbius's original design, adding the important feature of interchangeable rotors that the prototype did not have. He then exhibited the improved Enigma at the 1923 International Postal Exhibition in Berlin as a means of protecting business secrets.

His poor sales record was shared by others. In America, Edward Hebern, born 1869, designed one of the world's first enciphering machines when in 1915 he linked two electric typewriters so that the plain text was typed into the first and emerged as cipher text from the second. The system possessed certain cryptographic flaws, and Hebern then turned to the design of a five-rotor cryptograph which he patented (U.S. Patent #1638072) in 1921; and he founded Hebern Electric Code, Inc., that same year. In order to publicize his cryptograph, Hebern advertised a piece of unbreakable cipher text in a magazine and invited readers to try and solve it. Miss Agnes Meyer, then working for the U.S. Navy did so, and Hebern was so impressed that he came to see her (and later hired her away). He also showed the U.S. Navy his machine.

Fired with enthusiasm for his new invention, Hebern spent far too much money on building a grandiose new factory in Oakland, California, to manufacture his cryptographs, with the result that by 1924 he was in severe financial difficulties because he had only sold two machines at $600 each to the U.S. Navy, two to the U.S. Army, seven to a shipping company, one to the Italians, and one to GCCS in London. The company went bankrupt in 1926, but Hebern started all over again and founded the International Code Machine Company in Reno, Nevada.

In 1928, Hebern managed to sell four five-rotor machines for $750 each to the U.S. Navy in San Francisco, who put them to use handling their top-secret communications. The Navy was evidently satisfied with these trial machines and in 1931 placed an order for thirty-one more machines at a total cost of $54,480. Some of these were later renovated and were still in service in 1942. However, in 1934 Hebern suddenly fell out of favor and the Navy decided not to buy any more machines from him; and until he died in 1952 at the age of eighty-two, Hebern was involved in unsuccessful litigation against the American government to obtain compensation for his work in protecting the nation's secrets. Six years after his death, the government paid his estate $30,000 in settlement of his claim of $50 million.

A similar fate nearly befell Arvid Damm in Sweden, until his company was rescued by Dr. Emanuel Nobel and his close friend Karl Wilhelm Hagelin. To protect their investment, Hagelin's son Boris, was put in charge of the company and proved so successful that he ended up owning it. During the prewar years, Hagelin produced a large range of cryptographs, some small enough to slip into a pocket while others were about the size of a portable typewriter like the Enigma. Hagelin sold his machines to virtually every major country in the world—excluding Britain, whose armed forces showed no interest—selling 5,000 of his Type C-36 to France alone.

But it was in America that Hagelin had his greatest success, and after a trial with fifty of his machines, the American government persuaded Hagelin and his wife to come to New York in 1940. In the requisitioned L. C. Smith & Corona typewriter factory at Groton, New York, Hagelin mass-produced 400 of his small hand-operated M-209 cryptographs daily, which were used by the U.S. armed services throughout World War II. In the process, Hagelin became a millionaire (the only cryptograph inventor to make money from his invention). After the war, he founded Crypto AG in Zug, Switzerland, which to this day is one of the leaders of modern microchip cryptographic technology.

But one country had no doubts about the value of machine enciphering. Convinced that secure communications for their armed services lay with Enigma, in 1926 the German Navy made the quantum leap forward by officially adopting it as their main encoding system. In 1928, the German Army followed suit (and gave it the title of Model G), and the Air Force in 1934. Later military intelligence (Abwehr), SS units, the secret state police (Gestapo), the Nazi security and political intelligence service (Sicherheitsdienst), and even the state railways all adopted Enigma.

From 1926 onward, development of Enigma was firmly under the control of the German government, and the machine disappeared from the commercial market altogether. Security of the machine was further improved by the addition of a plugboard (called a *stecker*), and a static reflecting rotor (called the *umkerwalze*), which reversed the path of the electrical signal passing through the three active rotors. Subsequently, the German Navy, who were very security conscious over their cipher traffic, added a fourth rotor, making the machine even more complex.

The basic military Enigma, known as Model 1 (*Eins*), although sometimes called Type W (for Wermacht Enigma), first went into service with the Army on 1 June 1930 and offered 200 quintillion different setting positions. It formed the cornerstone of the seemingly unbreakable German cipher communications system.

A few commercial Enigmas were used by the Germans in Spain during the Spanish Civil War (1936–39), and some of their messages were broken by GCCS. But GCCS never realized the improvements that were being made to Enigma thereafter and was unable to break any messages sent via the military Enigma until Polish codebreakers showed them how to do it in 1939. This aspect of the Enigma story was, until recently, carefully concealed by many histories of British intelligence during World War II in order to convey the impression that GCCS broke Enigma on its own.

There was no secret about the Enigma cryptograph that Scherbius widely advertised for sale at $200 a machine as a means of protecting commercial secrets. Scherbius filed American patent #1,584,660 on 11 May 1926 and British patent #267,472 for his Enigma on 11 August 1927. Several countries bought commercial versions of the Enigma. The U.S. Signal Corps, the Japanese, and GCCS each bought two, and the Italians bought one. The Japanese immediately began to copy the Enigma rotor system and produced a very cumbersome version with the rotors mounted on top of the machine, which the Americans later codenamed Green. However, very few of these were produced before Yardley's revelations in his book (see Chapter 4) became public knowledge and spurred the Japanese on to construct even more secure cryptographs for their secret messages.

As long ago as 1936, Lord Louis Mountbatten, then Fleet Wireless Officer with the Mediterranean Fleet, had recommended that the Royal Navy adopt a machine cryptograph for enciphering all its radio traffic as the German Navy had been doing since 1926 with the Enigma. The two Enigmas GCCS had bought in 1928 had lain idle while the Inter-Departmental Committee on Cipher Machines, formed in 1926, debated how best to use machine cryptography. But at the end of six years they had been unable to come to any decision. (Air 2/2720, Avia 8/355 & 8/356, and ADM 1/11770, PRO, Kew.)

In 1934, Group Captain O. G. Lywood, a Royal Air Force signals officer, asked GCCS if he could borrow one of the Enigmas, and he took it to the RAF's Wireless Establishment at Kidbrooke, in southeast London. Together with Flight Lieutenant Coulson; Mr. E. W. Smith, the workshop foreman; and Sergeant Albert Lemon, he set about building a copy of the Enigma using mainly parts from commercial teletypes then in service with the RAF.

The quartet busied themselves for three years and eventually produced a cumbersome machine they called the RAF Enigma with Type-X Attachments. Unlike the Enigma, which was the size and weight of a portable typewriter, Lywood's machine was huge and consisted of a standard Creed teletype with an Enigma rotor basket grafted on the front, which was machined from solid brass and alone weighed ten pounds. The entire machine weighed over 120 pounds and needed a 230-volt AC power supply, unlike Enigma's battery system. The only advantage Typex had over Enigma was that it was able to print out the cipher and plain texts simultaneously on paper tape at fifty words per minute, whereas Enigma showed the text by means of lettered glow lamps that had to be recorded by the operator's assistant.

Lywood proudly demonstrated his brainchild to the Cipher Committee in 1937. They were unimpressed and refused to authorize any money to finance further development. Fortunately, the RAF decided to continue on their own and allowed Lywood to take his prototype to Creed & Company at Croydon, in south London, a small family firm run by the deeply religious Creed brothers, who led the work force in prayers before each day's work began.

Creed's main business was the production of electromechanical teletypes for the British Post Office (the forerunner of today's British Telecom). Since 1929 it had been owned by the ITT Corporation of America, but it seems that details of their work on Lywood's copy of Enigma did not get passed back to their American parent.

With the help of Mr. F. E. Brake, Creed's managing director, and Mr. Kirk, their chief designer, twenty-nine machines were built based on Lywood's prototype. These were called Type-X Mk I (the name Enigma having been quietly dropped) and were used to equip the main RAF headquarters. Creed then made a number of improvements and by 28 May 1937 had produced a much better machine they called Typex Mk II. This was shown to the Cipher Committee on 14 June, and they immediately approved an order for 350 Mk II machines at a cost of £107.8.0 each, which was enough to equip the entire RAF down to station level.

A later attachment enabled Typex Mk II to produce punched tape using the standard five-unit Baudot code (invented by the Frenchman Jean Baudot in the nineteenth century), but the Mk II could not work on line with other Typexes.

As orders grew, Creed transferred production to a new secret factory at Treforest in Wales. By September 1941, 3,232 Mk II machines had been produced at a cost of over £300,000. The Mk III Typex was hand-operated and, although much smaller, still far more cumbersome than Enigma. Typex Mk IV was built around the Creed Model #7 teletype and printed out the text on rolls of message forms. Typex Mks V, VI, and VII were all experimental models and never went into production. Typex Mk VIII was the first model capable of interfacing with other Typexes sending and receiving Morse code transmissions and automatically converting them into printed plain text. In 1942, after America entered the war, Typex Mk VIII was modified by Commander Don Seiler, USN, to interface on line with the American M-134 cryptograph known as ECM to the U.S. Navy and Sigaba to the U.S. Army. With the Typex converter, these became known as Communications Security Publications CSP-1700 or more usually as the Combined Cipher Machine (CCM). The reason for Seiler's converter was that U.S. regulations prohibited any foreign personnel from handling or seeing American cipher machines.

Typex Mk II used five active rotors plus one static rotor (similar to the Enigma's *umkerwalze* or reflector). The two entrance rotors, IV and V, were stators and, once initially set, did not move during encipherment. With its three moving rotors, two stators, and a reflector, Typex was plainly a copy of Enigma and infringed their patents. A long correspondence between the Whitehall bureaucrats began as to who would have to pay royalties to the Berlin factory. This was still going on when war began.

What Typex did not have was, of course, the *stecker* or plugboard, because that had been added only to the military version of Enigma and no one at GCCS had ever heard of this improved model. GCCS had refused to cooperate with French and Polish codebreakers before the war, and it was not until 25 July 1939 that members of GCCS visited the Polish codebreaking center near Warsaw and for the first time saw their copy of the German military Enigma.

The Army took thirty machines from the RAF order for field trials, most of which they left behind on the beaches at Dunkirk in 1940. Fortunately the Germans saw they were copies of the old commercial Enigma and simply took them into service, as they interfaced without difficulty with their older Enigmas; and as they believed Enigma was unbreakable, they made no attempt to see if Typex could be broken.

If properly used, the Enigma was unbreakable, and indeed several keys were never penetrated by GCCS throughout World War II; but the machine suffered from three basic problems. First, by the time World War II began its hardware technology was already ten years out of date, so that, for example, the most secure version—that used by the German Navy—came with a set of eight rotors, four of which were used at a time. But by 1941, the U.S. Army's Sigaba cryptograph (called ECM by the U.S. Navy) used fifteen rotors, ten to create the electrical maze and five for the mechanical linkage. It was not until late into the war that the Germans introduced their ten rotor *Geheimschreiber* cryptograph. The second problem with Enigma was the software, particularly the initial keying procedure, which required a three-letter group to be repeated twice, and it was this flaw that enabled Polish codebreakers to first enter the system. The third problem was that because some 10,000 Enigmas were in use, they became so commonplace that bored code clerks began taking shortcuts so that, for example, they would run their fingers diagonally down the keyboard producing repetitive three-letter combinations like QAZ or WSX. All this was in addition to the fact that the rigid hierarchical command structure of Germany's armed forces produced endless stereotyped messages which were easily identifiable.

The Royal Navy refused to even experiment with Typex, let alone use it in their ships, because it was beneath their dignity to use a machine designed by the RAF, which they considered the junior service, and they were also highly displeased that a junior officer like Mountbatten should have told them the Navy's cipher security was no good. Nor did the Navy make any effort to try some of the smaller cryptographs then on the market such as the Hagelin, which the U.S. armed forces used extensively.

So although the history books have concentrated on showing how clever the British and American codebreakers were at penetrating the German and Japanese code systems, the truth is that the Royal Navy had just as insecure codes as did the Japanese and for several years into the war suffered badly from their refusal to accept modern cipher technology.

Appendix 9

THIS IS SIR Robert Craigie's report on the Far East situation in 1941. His views so infuriated Churchill that Sir Robert was obliged to rewrite his report, eliminating some of his more extreme disagreements with British policy toward Japan, but even so, the sanitized version was not circulated until 1943.

When Sir Robert finally got back to Britain in 1942, he was invited (as is customary for British ambassadors) to lunch with King George VI at Buckingham Palace. During the meal, Sir Robert mentioned his report to the king who said he had never seen it and, it later transpired, although a copy of the original version had been sent to the palace, Churchill had seized it back before the king could see it.

Sir Robert was so upset at the way in which his views had been suppressed that he tried to resign from the Foreign Service, but Churchill refused to let him do so saying "it would be unpatriotic in wartime." Instead, Sir Robert was sent on leave "to await a new appointment," but this never came and, because he was still in government service, Sir Robert was prevented from making any public comment. Sir Robert was not employed by the Foreign Office again until 1945 when, following Churchill's defeat, he was offered a job by the new Labor government.

(Letter from Robert Craigie, 3 December 1991, and Crown copyright material, reproduced with the permission of the Controller of Her Majesty's Stationery Office, FO/371 35957, Public Record Office, Kew.)

F

Sir R. Craigie, following upon a talk with
Sir A. Cadogan, has been engaged in making some
amendments to his official report on his period
in Tokyo. It will be recalled that it was decided
on F.730 that the despatch should not be circulated
until the departmental memorandum on events
leading up to the outbreak of war with Japan
could be circulated with it. Sir R. Craigie
was, I believe, made aware of this decision at
the time.

A copy of Sir R. Craigie's report, with
the amendments which he has now made, is attached
below. In leaving this with the Department
Sir R. Craigie said that he had gone as far
as he considered he could to remove or amend the
more controversial parts. He asked me to say
when resubmitting the despatch that he greatly
hoped it would now be found possible to print it
as it stands, pointing out that he had been asked
by one or two people, including The King, when
his report would be available.

The changes do not alter the fundamental
thesis of the despatch, but nevertheless it may
be thought that the risk of arousing controversy
is now less real and that the despatch might now
be printed, as revised, for limited circulation
here (i.e. excluding the Dominions).

6th February, 1943.

Sir R. Craigie has eliminated some of the
more extreme expressions of disagreement with
the policy of H.M.G. But the report is still
open to the criticisms contained in Sir A.
Cadogan's minute of 31st October.

As expurgated (and having regard to recent
events in the war situation as a whole) the
circulation of the report is less open to objection than when first considered. But it would
still/

Minutes.

still be desirable to circulate at the same time,
if possible, the Department's memo edited to
make it suitable for printing. I will try and
produce this during the coming week when the
doctor obliges me to be away from the Office.

(Initialled) H.A.C.

7th February 1943.

Sir R. Craigie's amendments
are a matter of degree rather
than of principle.

I think we had better
see the Dept. memo. — and
perhaps let Sir R. Craigie
see it also — before we
consider reversing the previous
decision.

8.2

Yes. Now that we have waited so long,
and the Departmental Memo. is on the
point of being ready, it wd. be unwise to
launch Sir R. Craigie's dep. alone.

A.C.   16. 2. 1943.

Nothing to be Written in this Margin.

now see F2602
8.21

SECRET.   Copy No 37

DOCUMENTS RELATING TO

THE OUTBREAK OF WAR WITH JAPAN

12045 [25495]

Sir R. Craigie to Mr. Eden.

Old Possingworth Manor,
Sir,   *Blackboys, Sussex, 4th February.* 1943.

I HAVE the honour to transmit herewith an account of developments in Japan's relations with Great Britain and the United States during the six months immediately preceding the outbreak of war with that country, together with an introductory outline of events since my appointment to this post and of my own connexion therewith. In the absence of confidential archives, all of which were burnt on the 8th December, some inaccuracies on points of detail and as regards dates may have crept into an account compiled from memory. Furthermore, my knowledge of what was occurring elsewhere—and particularly in Washington— was often far from complete and sometimes derived exclusively from Japanese sources. Nevertheless, it has seemed to me useful to furnish, while my memory of them is still fresh, a chronicle of events during these critical months as seem from the angle of His Majesty's Embassy at Tokyo and in the light of such knowledge as I possessed of what was happening behind the scenes in Japan. I have also taken the opportunity to explain, more fully than was possible at the time by telegram, the underlying reasons for the various recommendations on points of policy which I made during those last months. My comments are made in the full realisation that only a part of the picture has been visible to me here and that there may have been reasons for this or that step taken in other parts of the world which have not been apparent in Tokyo.

2. In the annals of history it would be difficult to find a more flagrant instance of a base and treacherous attack than that which Japan delivered against Britain and the United States in the early hours of the 8th December, 1941. There have, of course, been numerous cases in which one country has attacked another without a previous declaration of war or the presentation of an ultimatum—indeed, this has been the common practice of the Axis Powers during the present war. Moreover, Japan herself set the classic example of an attack delivered in time of peace when her destroyers fell upon the Russian fleet in Port Arthur at the outset of the Russo-Japanese war in 1904. But in the present case the Japanese descended to a particularly low level of treachery. Negotiations between the United States and Japan were still proceeding at Washington when the blow fell and it was not until several hours after the attack on Hawaii that Mr. Togo informed Mr. Grew and myself, still without any mention of war, that the Japanese Government had decided to terminate them. Furthermore, at the very moment of the attack, an exchange of friendly telegrams was proceeding between the President of the United States and the Emperor of Japan, the latter's encouraging reply to the President's message having been handed to my United States colleague at 7.30 A.M. on the 8th December. This was some five hours after the Japanese surprise attack on Hawaii which, by Japanese time, must have taken place about 2 A.M. Again, it would not be easy to find a parallel for a Foreign Minister discoursing affably with an Ambassador on matters of current interest. as Mr. Togo did with me, several hours after a treacherous attack had been delivered on the territory of that envoy's country. Such instances of duplicity show the lengths to which the Japanese Government were prepared to go in their efforts to secure the full effect of their surprise attack.

3. Despite these elaborate efforts of the Japanese Government to conceal their real purpose, both His Majesty's Government and the United States Government were fortunately aware that war might come at any moment. They probably did not know whether the first blow would be delivered directly against British or American territory or indirectly through Siam and the Netherlands East Indies; but they were well aware that Japanese preparations for a further southward move were in an advanced stage and that, ever since the imposition of the "freezing" measures, Japan stood poised for an attack which, whatever its direction, would mean war at least for the British Empire. More than once I had reported, on the basis of reliable information available to me, that the Japanese Government would not be able to continue the Washington conversations for more than a very limited period after the assumption of the premiership by General Tojo, adding that I regarded these negotiations as the last barrier against war. Indeed throughout the year 1941 the general burden of the warnings sent from

this post had been that a Japanese attack, if not averted by diplomatic means, would be on a greater scale and take place at an earlier date than many British authorities appeared to anticipate. Although, judging from telegrams received by me during October and November, you were disposed to consider that the warn- .gs reaching me from Japanese sources were part of the Japanese "war of nerves," it was nevertheless clear that His Majesty's Government realised that further aggressive action by Japan might be expected at any moment, and particularly after the despatch of the final United States communication to the Japanese Government of the 26th November. From the report of the Judicial Commission sent to enquire into the causes of the Hawaiian disaster, we know that on that same day (the 25th November American time), the United States authorities in Hawaii had been warned of the danger of a Japanese attack. I also know that the 3rd December the United States Naval Attaché (though not the ambassador) received instructions to destroy all his cyphers. Finally on the 7th December came the report from the C.O.I.S., Singapore, that Japanese protected convoys had been sighted on the 6th December by a British recon- naissance plane heading west and north-west from Indo-China across the Gulf of Siam—a movement which could only imply warlike intentions. Thus the British authorities concerned were aware that an attack was impending, though probably not of the precise point or points at which it would be delivered. Judging from such indications as can be gleaned from the Japanese press, our forces in Malaya were, in fact, at their battle stations and prepared for the Japanese attack when it was delivered at dawn on the 8th December.

4. One point which it is important to establish is the date on which the Government of Japan finally decided upon war. Early in October there had been a noticeable increase in the severity of the emergency restrictions on travel by foreigners in Japan, particularly in the area of the Inland Sea, and an almost complete withdrawal of Japanese shipping from the long-distance trade routes still remaining open; there had also been observed a marked diminution in the amount of Japanese coastal shipping, a great increase in the movements of transports and an apparent cessation of all refits of naval units. In mid- November the mobilisation measures which had been put into effect during July and August were further intensified. These were all signs—duly reported at the time—that a further stage had been reached in Japan's war preparations, and they corresponded to the increasing tension in American-Japanese relations; but they did not necessarily imply that a final decision had as yet been reached to go to war. On the 26th November the concluding American communication in the Washington negotiations was received by the Japanese Government—a communi- cation which rejected the Japanese compromise proposal of the 20th November and restated in some detail the British and American conception of a "new order" in Eastern Asia. Immediately after the receipt of this communication in Tokyo an important Cabinet meeting was held, followed by consultations with the Emperor. In the light of these developments and of the corroborative evidence outlined in the two following paragraphs, I consider the decision to go to war was taken on or about the 27th November. We may, however, assume that even then no definite date would have been set by the Cabinet for the actual attack, a decision on this vital point falling within the prerogatives of the Imperial Headquarters and the Chiefs of the Army and Navy General Staffs.

5. Apart from the fact that the concluding American communication was received on the 26th November, the following indications point to the final Japanese decision having been taken about that time. In the first place there is the interesting report, which forms enclosure 2(') to this despatch, of the Japanese commander of an air unit which took part in the attack on Hawaii early on the morning of the 8th December (Japanese time). This officer speaks of the aircraft carrier to which his unit was attached having, at the moment of the attack, completed a voyage across the Pacific of 4,000 miles, which would be the distance from Japan to Hawaii if, as is probable, a circuitous northern route had been followed. If we place the speed of the aircraft carrier at 400 miles a day, she must have sailed from Japan about the 28th November, i.e., the day after the important Cabinet consultations mentioned in the preceding paragraph.

6. Another indication of the date of the Japanese decision is to be seen in the change—barely perceptible though it was—in the attitude and bearing of the Minister for Foreign Affairs during our interview of the 5th December (see paragraph 54 of enclosure 1)—a change to which in retrospect I attach more

(') Not printed.

B 2

importance than I did at the time. A further confirmation that the decision took place some time between the 19th November and the 1st December is provided by the record (enclosure 3)(¹) of the interesting conversations which Lady Craigie had on those two dates with Mrs. Togo, the German-born wife of the Japanese Minister for Foreign Affairs. At the first interview Mrs. Togo, who was in highly emotional state, spoke of the great strain upon her husband and of my duty as British Ambassador here to intervene in order to prevent a breakdown. In the interview on the 1st December, however, Mrs. Togo's demeanour had completely changed. She spoke of the situation as being "past worrying about," adding that "no one on earth could prevent wars nowadays—it was just a state of mind into which countries got and which seemed inevitable." Lady Craigie left with the impression that Mr. Togo had finally decided to throw in his lot with the extremists and so informed me on her return to the Embassy. At that time I regarded my wife's report as one of the many indications that things were going from bad to worse; but, in retrospect, I think it can be accepted as supporting my thesis that the decision to declare war on the United States and Great Britain was taken on or about the 27th November.

7. The important question now arises whether any further steps could or should have been taken by the United States or Great Britain to prevent the outbreak of war with Japan. This is a subject on which divergent opinions are necessarily held. On the one hand there is a school of thought which holds that war between the Democracies and Japan was inevitable; that ever since the outbreak of the Sino-Japanese conflict the militarists had been steadily turning Japan into a totalitarian State, fully equipped for war on the largest scale and subjected internally to that intensive and mendacious propaganda which is the hall-mark of all such States; that for the last ten years—to go back no further— the minds of the Japanese people had been poisoned against us and steadily prepared for the necessity of waging war "to defend Japan's position as the stabilising Power in East Asia"; that this process had been greatly accelerated by the frontal clash of interests throughout the period of the Sino-Japanese conflict; and, finally, that physical as well as "spiritual" preparation for a major war had reached such a scale by the late summer and autumn of 1941 that, while the outbreak of war could be delayed, it could no longer be averted.

8. There is much to be said for this view, though I personally consider the word "inevitable" to be too strong. Had war not broken out in Europe and had there been, therefore, no prospect of an early destruction of Germany's military power, we should, it is true, have had to face a steady increase in the strains and stresses of the Far Eastern situation until some day an important restraining link might have snapped. In the actual world situation of December 1941, however, there were elements which might well have given pause to the Japanese Nationalists. After two and a quarter years of struggle, Great Britain and her Allies appeared to us in Tokyo to be at length slowly gaining the upper hand over Germany; the Russian armies were pressing steadily forward towards the German frontier; our armies in Libya were pushing beyond Benghazi; from the United States we were already receiving a magnificent contribution in material and that type of active naval assistance which was most vital to us, namely, the convoying of ships across the Atlantic and an "undeclared" war on German submarines and surface raiders. So far as could been seen from Tokyo we were on the way to winning the battle of the Atlantic and were passing from the defensive to the offensive on the other fronts. The war had thus reached the stage at which, for the first time, even to the prejudiced eyes of the Japanese, the prospects of German victory began to be doubtful. Admittedly this was a dangerous phase, for the Japanese militarists would know that their last chance of effective intervention must come before German offensive power showed definite signs of collapse. During this transition stage the risk of Japanese intervention was at its greatest. Thereafter, as the certainty of an Allied victory became more and more apparent, the risk might be expected steadily to diminish until a point would be reached when the danger of a direct Japanese attack could, for all practical purposes, be discounted. I consider, therefore, that, had it been possible to reach a compromise with Japan in December 1941 involving the withdrawal of Japanese troops from South Indo-China, war with Japan would not have been inevitable.

9. According to a second school of thought, American participation in the war with Germany was so vital to the Allied cause that it must be secured even at the price of Japan's entry on the other side. With the limited knowledge

(¹) Not printed.

of the whole strategic position, which was at my disposal in Tokyo, I do not pretend to offer any authoritative opinion on this point. All I would say is that, looking at the matter primarily from the point of view of the situation in the Pacific and in Eastern Asia, this theory has always appeared to me to be ، ghly questionable. In endeavouring to controvert it I have, at different times, drawn attention to the strength and high morale of Japan's armed forces, the determination, courage and endurance of the Japanese people and, finally, the failure of the Sino-Japanese war to make any serious inroads on Japan's military strength and economic stability. I argued that, in the event of an American-Japanese war, the attention and resources of the United States would have to be so fully devoted to resisting a powerful Japanese attack in the Pacific that, for a time at least, American material aid to us, both in and across the Atlantic, was bound to be seriously curtailed. The goal at which I suggested our diplomacy should aim and which, given a less uncompromising attitude toward Japan during the concluding stages of the Washington conversations, might well have been achieved, was American participation in the war coupled with continued Japanese neutrality.

10. It is a sound maxim, particularly in time of war, that policy should conform to strategy. If we leave on one side for a moment the place of the United States in our strategical calculations, it will readily be agreed that the needs of British Imperial strategy have, during the last five years, demanded the neutralisation of Japan, at least until such time as it became clear either that war with Germany could be avoided or that, war with Germany having broken out, an Allied victory was definitely assured. The details of our naval, military and air preparations have lain outside my province and, quite rightly, I was not informed of the strength and disposition of our forces in the Far East. I had urged from time to time that we should send to the Far East reinforcements of men, planes and ships to the utmost extent of our capacity; but I recommended this step rather as an additional deterrent against a Japanese attack than in the belief that anything we could spare at that time from other fronts would be adequate to resist a full-scale Japanese onslaught on British territory. In February 1941 I sounded a note of warning against applying the "Maginot Line" mentality to our situation at Singapore. We could neither effectively reinforce Singapore without seriously weakening other fronts, nor hope, alone, to hold out in the Far East against a Japanese attack for more than two or three months. Such being our situation, the requirements of strategy seemed to me to demand the continuance during 1941 of those Fabian tactics which, in recent years, had enabled us to turn many a difficult corner in our relations with Japan.

11. Turning now to the place of the United States in our Far Eastern strategy, it has always seemed unwise in the extreme to place undue reliance on active United States assistance in the early stages of a war with Japan. If the first Japanese attack were not actually delivered against American territory, delays must be expected to occur while Congress debated the question of American intervention. Even assuming American entry into the war from the outset, it was never clear how the United States, with its main fleet based as far away as Hawaii, could be expected to throw into the region of the South-Western Pacific that overwhelming naval and air strength which would be necessary to check, in its early stages, a Japanese attack on Malaya. Taking my stand on these assumptions, I urged that we should not rely on the United States for the defence of British territory in the Far East, but should base our own policy toward Japan primarily on the requirements of our own strategical position. This seemed the more necessary in that the United States Government had been at pains to make it clear that they could not commit themselves in advance to any promise of active resistance in the event of a Japanese attack on Siam, the Netherlands East Indies or British territory in the Far East.

12. Up to the date of the Tripartite Pact of September 1940, Anglo-American policy towards Japan was firm, without being uncompromising. From that date onwards, the United States increasingly took the lead in the enunciation and prosecution of policy, British policy tending to follow American policy along parallel lines. This, in itself, was an excellent development, corresponding as it did to a natural shift in responsibility from British to American shoulders as our own preoccupations and commitments in Europe increased. Its principal manifestation was the imposition in July 1941 of measures for the "freezing" of Japanese assets as an answer to the Japanese entry into Southern Indo-China, thus demonstrating clearly to Japan that deeds would be answered by deeds. Such action, of course, involved a risk of immediate war, but it averted

what was at that time an even greater risk, namely, that the Japanese Government should be left to assume that they could proceed with complete impunity along their path of territorial aggrandisement in South-Eastern Asia. It also had the merit of removing from the minds of the more responsible Japanese leaders the lingering hope that any further southward advance could be nu without the virtual certainty of war with the United States.

13. But this new phase of American leadership had its dangers. American methods in the conduct of diplomacy often err on the side of rigidity and formality, whereas the situation in the Far East called for a more delicate touch and reasonable elasticity in diplomatic technique. Impressed by the undoubted effectiveness of their economic sanctions, the United States Government appeared to be convinced that they had Japan " on the spot "; that Japan's economic situation would oblige her to yield if a Far Eastern settlement, involving peace with China, were now to be resolutely enforced upon her; and, finally, that Japan, exhausted by four years of war in China, was in no condition to risk war with the United States. I know that these views were being urged in Washington by the Chinese Government; I know also that they were at variance with the advice and information furnished by my United States colleague to his Government. So far as my own reports were concerned I had frequently drawn attention to the resiliency of the Japanese economic structure; to the fact that the Japanese Government were progressively concentrating all available economic resources upon the building up of the Japanese war potential; and to the fallacy of regarding the hostilities in China as monopolising or even curtailing Japan's capacity for striking elsewhere. I had, moreover, given it as my considered opinion in October 1941 that Japan's former desire to avoid war with the United States at almost any cost could no longer be counted upon as a factor in the situation should Japan feel herself to be finally driven into a corner.

14. Realising that things were going from bad to worse at Washington during the summer of 1941, and that if war with Japan was to be avoided a change at least in method and technique was essential, I begged His Majesty's Government on more than one occasion to keep themselves informed of the details of the negotiations in order that they might exercise a moderating influence both in Washington and Tokyo, as occasion demanded. As reported by me at the time, Admiral Toyoda had suggested that His Majesty's Government should take a more active interest in the American-Japanese negotiations—an idea which was pressed even more insistently by his successor, Mr. Togo, who stated that my own intervention and suggestions would be welcome. Your reply on each occasion was to the general effect that, having complete confidence in the conduct of the negotiations by the United States Government, His Majesty's Government intended to leave the matter entirely in their hands. By acting thus, His Majesty's Government obviated the risk of Anglo-American friction in connexion with Far Eastern affairs; they moreover ensured that the United States must necessarily be involved if a breakdown of the negotiations should lead to war—a vitally important consideration. As against these advantages, there can be no doubt that the absence of any British moderating influence, whether at Washington or at Tokyo, increased the chances of that breakdown which eventually occurred.

15. This was the situation when the Japanese made their compromise proposal of the 20th November (paragraph 42 of enclosure 1), which, with its offer of the evacuation of Southern Indo-China, aimed at the virtual restoration of the *status quo ante*. I urged strongly upon His Majesty's Government that, subject to certain amendments which I had reason to believe could be secured from the Japanese Government, a *modus vivendi* on these lines should be concluded. In my view the withdrawal of Japanese troops from Southern Indo-China and the limitation of their number in Northern Indo-China to one or two divisions would have meant so complete a dislocation of the Japanese army's plans for an attack on Malaya, or, indeed, for any further southward advance, that it would have been well worth purchasing at the cost of the supply to Japan of oil and other raw materials in quantities insufficient to add materially to Japan's war potential. Mr. Hull did, indeed, prepare a draft answer to Japan along the above lines which, subject to certain essential modifications of form, could have been made acceptable to the Japanese Government; this constructive counter-proposal was never submitted to the Japanese Government, owing, it would appear, to the opposition of the Chinese Government.

16. If an arrangement with Japan on the above lines would have constituted " appeasement," as claimed by General Chiang Kai-shek, it is at least clear that

7

Japan, by withdrawing from a position long coveted by the Japanese army and navy, would have been doing her fair share of the "appeasing." With every day that passed Japan's preparations for war were gaining momentum and the essential thing at that moment was to arrest this momentum before it passed beyond control. From information which has reached me subsequently to the outbreak of war, and which I regard as entirely reliable, I learned that, before making their proposal of the 20th November, the Japanese Cabinet had secured from the Japanese army and navy an absolute assurance that, should an agreement be reached on that basis, all preparations for an attack on Britain and the United States would immediately be suspended.

17. If it be objected that Japan's withdrawal from Southern Indo-China might only have been temporary, I would reply that our own counter-measures could have been reimposed with equal rapidity in the event of any breach of faith by Japan. If it be urged that the Japanese Government—or at least the Japanese army—never meant this offer seriously, I submit that such an assertion is of little value unless supported by concrete evidence and that for my own contrary view I have the support of the evidence which reached me at the time through my local contacts as summarised in paragraphs 43 and 44 of enclosure 1 to the present despatch. This Japanese offer was, in fact, the last throw of the Emperor and the moderates in their effort to avert the disastrous war into which the Japanese army were seeking to project their country.

18. The concluding move in the Washington negotiations was the presentation of the American proposals which reached Tokyo on the 26th November. This document, which is summarised in paragraphs 48 and 49 of the enclosed memorandum, laid down with admirable clarity and precision a settlement of the whole Far Eastern problem based on the principles of equity, justice and equality as between all the nations concerned. But, wittingly or unwittingly, it ignored the fact that for some years past Japanese foreign policy had ceased to be founded on such principles; it required Japan to abandon once and for all the objectives in China for which she had been fighting during the the past four years; and it contained stipulations, such as those relating to the renunciation of the Tripartite Pact and the abandonment of the Nanking régime, which Japan regarded as derogatory to her national honour. Entirely just and legitimate as such a proposal was, it is difficult to understand how anyone with any knowledge of contemporary Japan—powerful, arrogant, proud, self-seeking—could have believed that it had even the slightest chance of acceptance in the circumstances obtaining in November 1941. Only after the defeat of Germany could we have hoped or expected to effect, without recourse to arms, a settlement with Japan on such terms.

19. If I have ventured, with all respect, to sketch the alternative procedure by means of which war with Japan could have been postponed and perhaps averted, it is not because I find anything to defend in the acts and policies of that country. Here was a nation controlled by a powerful, ruthless and ambitious military caste, a nation police-ridden to an extent only comparable with Germany and indoctrinated during the past ten years with those very theories of conquest and national aggrandisement which we are engaged in fighting in Europe. During that period Japan has passed from one planned aggression to another in her expansionist drive towards her goal of political paramountcy and economic self-sufficiency in Eastern Asia. Of Japanese militarism it may be truly said, as George Meredith said of Napoleonism, that it aims at "the infliction of wrongs and outrages on other nations for the glory and increase of their own." Nothing can excuse either Japan's attack on China or the conduct of the Japanese military in China during the progress of the operations. On purely ethical and ideological grounds, therefore, the attitude assumed by the United States Government during the Washington negotiations and by His Majesty's Government towards those negotiations can be justified up to the hilt. But the burden of my advice during the years 1937 and 1941 has been that we could not afford to follow a purely idealistic policy or to deal with Japan according to her merits so long as we remained under the threat of war with Germany—a proposition which became still more obvious after the actual outbreak of war in Europe, followed by the collapse of France. It was the Pétain Government's betrayal of the Allied cause by refusing to continue the fight from the French colonies which, more than any other single event, created in the Japanese mind the belief in the certainty of a German victory and led to the conclusion of the Tripartite Pact. This pact appears to have been regarded in London and Washington as committing Japan irretrievably to ultimate intervention in the war—a view which I have never

shared, but which may, I fear, have unduly influenced the United States Government's attitude during the course of the Washington conversations. Pact or no pact, I considered that the day of reckoning with Japan should be postponed by every honourable means open to diplomatic technique until a time of our own choosing—our time, that is, not Hitler's. Had that been done, our final settlement with Japan, following upon the defeat and disruption of Germany, might never have required an actual recourse to arms.

20. So much for the past. We are now engaged on a titanic struggle in the Far East, of which the first phase has resulted in the Japanese armies pushing forward to the gates of India, to the shores of the Indian Ocean, and to within a few hundred miles of Australia. Given the possibility of holding the Japanese approximately on their present line while an Allied offensive develops against Germany, our reverses in the South-Western Pacific should not be irreparable. Should the campaigns of the present year result in a further appreciable weakening of Germany's military position and bring with it the certainty of her ultimate defeat, the effect on the Japanese Government and ultimately on the Japanese people would be enormous. Japan's lines of communication are now spread out over a vast area in the South-Western Pacific and the Bay of Bengal and, once we are in a position to spare adequate air and naval forces for the purpose, a determined joint Anglo-American attack on these far-flung communications should render Japan's position in the Netherlands East Indies, the Mandated Islands, and even Singapore, virtually untenable. We have witnessed the effects of a Japanese surprise attack, with all its initial advantages. We have seen what Japanese forces, possessing virtual command of the air, can do on the offensive against troops inferior in numbers and equipment. We have seen the excellence (both in design and execution) of Japanese staff work based on plans worked out during many years in the utmost detail and with great ingenuity. It has yet to be seen what will be Japan's performance when placed on the defensive, subjected to intensive attacks from the air, obliged to improvise plans at short notice, and faced with attacks from unexpected directions. Since Japan's emergence from seclusion during the Meiji era, her military record has been one of uninterrupted success, but in earlier Japanese history there are instances of expeditions to the continent of Asia which have failed lamentably when the tables were turned on the Japanese forces. Moreover, a morale based on the theory of the utter invincibility of Japanese arms and of the marked superiority of the Japanese soldier and sailor over those of all other nations may conceivably prove to be of that brittle type which cracks when the day comes to face serious reverses. The care with which the Japanese censorship and propaganda machine withholds from the Japanese public all reliable news of Japanese losses, even when these must be known to the enemy, denotes an unhealthy disinclination to trust the people with any real knowledge of the sacrifices which Japan must still face in order to satisfy the fevered ambitions of her military leaders. True, some of the more responsible Ministers, unlike the newspapers, have warned the country of the stupendous nature of the task ahead of it, but even they foster the notion of complete Japanese invincibility and imperviousness to serious loss. Shortage of merchant shipping may well prove to be Japan's Achilles' heel, at which we may assume that the Allied forces will be striking with ever-increasing vigour. Even though the Japanese authorities may succeed in keeping from the people a knowledge of their actual losses in naval and merchant vessels, the resulting shortage of shipping is something which cannot be hidden, and which, when it becomes gradually known, is bound to have a demoralising effect on public opinion. So far as raw materials are concerned, Japan is now presumably in a position to secure adequate supplies of rubber and tin from occupied territory; but in oil she might begin to face a deficiency if by the end of this year she has been unable to place the Netherlands East Indies and Burma wells (presumably all destroyed or seriously damaged) in full production again; while in iron and steel Japan's shortage must be a continuing one and it is difficult to believe that her existing stocks, coupled with what she can derive from occupied territory, will satisfy her enormously increased requirements for more than a year ahead.

I have, &c.

R. L. CRAIGIE.

Notes

INTRODUCTION, pp. 25–28

1. Longfield Lloyd was a member of a small team studying Japanese codes at Sydney University. The three others were Professor T. G. Room (professor of mathematics), R. J. Lyons (lecturer in mathematics), and A. P. Treweek (lecturer in Greek). In January 1941, Eric Nave went to Sydney University and examined the work they had been doing, which had not been very successful, and he decided to incorporate the four of them into his new team with the Navy Department at Melbourne. Longfield Lloyd's father was the first Australian High Commissioner in Japan. (Kenneth Smith, Sydney University Archivist, letter 17 June 1987, Ref: 45/016, and Australian Archives CRS A816/43/302/18.)

2. Churchill, *The Second World War,* vol. 3, p. 537.

3. John G. Winant, *A Letter from Grosvenor Square* (London: Hodder & Stoughton, 1947), pp. 198–99.

4. *The Second World War,* vol. 3, p. 539.

1: THE BROADWAY EAVESDROPPERS, pp. 29–45

1. No official history of GCCS has, of course, ever been published, but by some bureaucratic error a report by Alastair Denniston (GCCS's first chief) managed to find its way into a public archive. *Denniston Papers,* 2 December 1944, *A Report on the Work and History of GCCS* (Cambridge: Churchill College Library), and also Nigel West, *GCHQ* (London: Weidenfeld & Nicolson, 1986). Although there is a fundamental difference between a code and a cipher, it is unimportant in the context of this book. In simple terms a code is where a word or complete phrase is replaced with a word or group of numbers, whereas with a cipher each letter is replaced with another letter, group of letters, a single figure, or group of figures. For anyone interested in these technicalities, David Kahn, *The Codebreakers* (New York: Macmillan, 1967) remains the finest definitive work, now in its eleventh edition.

2. Minute Paper 16/5262. Australian Archives MP 472, File #5/18/8562; Australian Archives MP472, File #5/18/8562. Confidential letter 116/8368. Australian Archives MP 472, File #5/18/8562, and Letter 18/8562, File #684, HMAS *Tingira*

records, Sydney. Australian Archives MP 472 File #5/18/8562. In return for being sent to Japan, Eric Nave agreed to remain in the RAN up to the age of thirty. Long before that happened, Nave had been borrowed by the Royal Navy and never returned to the RAN.

3. Arthur Purves Shaw entered the Royal Navy on 15 July 1913 and had continuous service until he retired on 28 September 1950 with the rank of captain. He spent most of his time after returning from Japan with GCCS. He was awarded the CBE in 1942 and the American Legion of Merit in 1948. He died on 23 September 1952. (Information kindly supplied by Miss H. R. Martin, Ministry of Defence, London, 1989.)

4. The main purpose of the visit was to thank the people of Australia and New Zealand for their generosity following the disastrous earthquake of 1 September 1923, which had devastated Japan, killing more than 100,000 people. The commander of one of the ships in the squadron, the *Yakumo*, was Captain Yonai Mitsumasa, a naval intelligence officer who was later to become C-in-C of the Japanese Fleet, Foreign Minister, and finally Prime Minister of Japan.

5. Bowden archives, 18 February 1924 (Nave private papers).

6. Naval cipher message 805(N), 30 May 1925 (Nave private papers).

7. Acronyms abound in the world of intelligence, largely in order to make it seem more mysterious and important. Sigint is an overall designation that includes:

> *Comint,* Communications Intelligence: the collection, processing, decoding, and analysis of foreign communications sent by any means.
>
> *Elint,* Electronic Intelligence: the collection, processing, decoding, and analysis of foreign non-communication electromagnetic intelligence, the most common of which is an enemy's radar.
>
> *Telint,* Telemetry Intelligence: the interception, processing, and analysis of telemetry sent back, for example, by rockets.

Other useful acronyms to bear in mind are *Humint,* Human Intelligence, the common spy or traitor, and *Imaginint,* Imaginary Intelligence, which is invented to please politicians and thus secure increased funding of the agency's operations.

8. Joseph Mazzini complained to the Secretary of State, Sir James Graham, that his letters had been opened and the contents passed to the Neapolitan government. James Bamford, *The Puzzle Palace* (Boston: Houghton Mifflin, 1982), p. 328.

9. Today the Government Communications Headquarters (GCHQ), the successor to GCCS, together with America's National Security Agency (NSA), intercept all Britain's international communications traffic (telephone, telex, cable, facsimile, and computer data) entering and leaving the country, and any internal trunk circuits they choose from a number of jointly owned tapping centers such as Morwenstow in Cornwall and Menwith Hill in Yorkshire. The legality for doing any of this is very dubious and for that reason has never been debated in

Britain's Parliament. James Rusbridger, *The Intelligence Game* (London: The Bodley Head, 1989).

10. Modern technology now allows transponder pods to be placed over undersea cables so that the signals can be monitored. The U.S. Navy and the NSA have in recent years done this to Russian cable systems off their coasts in Operations Barnacle, Holystone, and Ivy Bells, all of which were compromised by a traitor working within the NSA. *The Intelligence Game,* pp. 231–32; William Burrows, *Deep Black* (New York: Bantam, 1988), p. 139; David Wise, *The Spy Who Got Away* (New York: Random House, 1988), p. 246; and Bob Woodward, *Veil* (New York: Simon & Schuster, 1987), pp. 448–49.

11. West, *GCHQ,* pp. 36–37.

12. Patrick Beesly, *Room 40* (London: Hamish Hamilton, 1982).

13. The first of these was the German naval codebook *Signalbuch der Kaiserlichen Marine (SKM),* which had been recovered from the cruiser *Magdeburg* by the Russians, then Britain's ally, who handed it over to the Admiralty on 10 October 1914. The second was a copy of the German *Handelsverkehrsbuch* codebook used by German merchant ships and some warships. It was seized by the Royal Australian Navy from the German steamer *Hobart* in August 1914. The third was a copy of the German *Verkehrsbuch* found in the nets of a British trawler in the North Sea on 30 November 1914. Beesly, *Room 40.*

14. Patrick Beesly, *Very Special Intelligence* (London: Hamish Hamilton, 1977), pp. 2–5; and Kahn, *Codebreakers,* pp. 272–73.

15. Sinclair's nickname "Quex" was derived from Sir Arthur Pinero's play first performed in 1900, *The Gay Lord Quex,* about "the wickedest man in London" (although the expression "gay" did not have the same meaning it has acquired today). Although Sinclair was not wicked, while serving in the Royal Navy he had had a stormy personal life, which ended in divorce in 1920, just after he was made ADC to King George V. Despite the very strict rules about divorce in those days, the King liked him so much that he kept him on his staff. Sinclair became head of MI6 on 14 June 1923 and remained a director of GCCS.

16. Several books have been written about the history of Cable & Wireless, a good one being Hugh Barty-King, *Girdle Round the Earth* (London: Heinemann, 1979), but all carefully sidestep the matter of cable interception by GCCS. However, Denniston's report is very frank about the arrangement, which makes it all the more surprising that it was not suppressed by MI6.

17. U.S. Senate, Committee on Interstate Commerce. *Cable Landing Licenses.* 66th Congress, 3rd Session, 1921 (Washington, D.C.: Government Printing Office), and also Bamford, *Puzzle Palace,* pp. 329–31.

18. RG 457, SRH-012, National Archives, p. 110.

19. Problems in Ireland and fears of a Bolshevik-style revolution in England encouraged by the depression and high unemployment continually occupied the minds of the government and the intelligence services at the time. The revolution never came, but terrorism in Northern Ireland remains. As a result, today all communications between England and the Republic of Ireland and Northern Ireland are intercepted by GCHQ.

20. The OSA first came into existence in 1911, when frivolous and bogus spy scares were much in fashion. The Act has since been replaced by the Official Secrets Act of 1989, which looks to be as useless and contentious as the old one. Legally speaking, everyone in Britain is subject to the OSA and could be prosecuted for passing on secrets without authority. Signing the OSA does nothing more than remind a person of his responsibilties. David Hooper, *Official Secrets* (London: Secker & Warburg, 1987).

21. RG 457, SRH-012, National Archives, p. 112.

22. *Denniston Papers,* p. 18.

23. Robert J. Lamphere and Tom Shachtman, *The FBI-KGB War* (New York: Random House, 1986), p. 81.

24. The security of the OTP system is naturally vulnerable to human error and theft, as occurred with the *Venona* intercepts that the Federal Bureau of Investigation had made of Russian messages from New York to Moscow in 1948. In the early part of World War II, U.S. intelligence agents had obtained from a battlefield in Finland part of a Russian OTP codebook. In 1944, the Russians made the fatal error of sending out to their New York Trade Delegation office random sheets that had been used before. The FBI burgled the office and photographed these random pads and the plain texts of messages that had been sent. With these three components they could then work out the additive tables for past messages. *The FBI-KGB War,* pp. 78–86; Peter Wright, *Spycatcher* (New York: Viking, 1987); *Newsweek,* 19 May 1980, p. 32; and correspondence with Robert Lamphere, 1986–88.

Such a combination of basic error and opportunity for theft is extremely rare. An example of the efficiency of the OTP system is shown by the case of the Czechoslovakian spy Erwin von Haarlem, whom Britain's Security Service (MI5) had under close surveillance over a long period of time as he received his coded OTP messages by commercial radio from Prague. But when MI5 finally arrested Haarlem on 2 April 1988, they were unable to reconstruct any of these because he had destroyed all the used random pages.

25. Russian covert operations were largely financed by diamonds illegally smuggled into Britain. John Costello, *The Mask of Treachery* (New York: William Morrow, 1988), chapter 5.

26. In America, a similar trade organization was called the American Trading Organization, or Amtorg. Its true purpose was the same as Arcos. Amtorg also used the OTP system for communicating with Moscow, and the American codebreakers were unable to read any of this traffic. (Sinkov interview, January 1990.)

27. CAB 23/55, PRO, Kew; and Hansard, Official Report of the Proceedings of the British Parliament, 5th Series, vol. CCVI, 26 May 1927.

28. Intelligence and politics make uneasy partners. On the one hand, intelligence agencies please their political paymasters by giving them the sort of information they know will suit their policies (for example, President Reagan's hatred toward Libya). But there are occasions when itelligence fails to reach the right politician because it conflicts with the bureaucrats' line of thinking. Britain's Pearl Harbor occurred on 2 April 1982, when the British Prime Minister

and her cabinet awoke one fine spring morning to discover that the Falkland Islands had been captured by Argentina.

It was later claimed that British intelligence had no advance warning of the invasion, but subsequently a retired deputy director of MI6 stated that GCHQ and MI6, through their American partners, the NSA and CIA, had been given a very detailed summary of the Argentinian plans and knew all about the invasion. But since the Foreign Office controlled both MI6 and GCHQ, and was busily engaged in trying to give the Falkland Islands away to Argentina, only to be frustrated by the annoying patriotism of the islanders, the intelligence summaries that the Foreign Office gave the Joint Intelligence Committee were so diluted that by the time they reached ministerial level their findings were ambivalent and therefore ignored. Rusbridger, *Intelligence Game,* Introduction.

29. Domvile retired as DNI in 1930, by which time he had become an ardent admirer of Hitler and was his guest at the Nuremberg rally in 1936. In 1937, Domvile founded the pro-Nazi organization in London called The Link, which, together with the Anglo-German Fellowship, by 1939 had thirty-five active branches and a membership of 4,500, mainly drawn from the wealthy upper classes. Another of Domvile's friends at the time was the British spy for Russia Guy Burgess, who defected to Moscow after the war. In 1940, Domvile was among those arrested and interned under the Section 18b regulations and was not released until 1943.

2: OTHER GENTLEMEN'S MAIL, pp. 46–61

1. There are many good histories of Ameria's foreign espionage activities, among them being Anthony Cave Brown, *The Last Hero: Wild Bill Donovan* (New York: Times Book, 1982); Thomas F. Troy, *Donovan and the CIA* (Maryland: 1981); Dr. Rhoderi J. Jones, *The CIA and American Democracy* (New Haven: Yale University Press, 1989).

2, Kahn, *Codebreakers,* chapter 7.

3. Joseph C. Grew, *Ten Years in Japan* (New York: Simon & Schuster, 1944); Robert Dallek, *Franklin D. Roosevelt and American Foreign Policy—1932–1945* (New York: Oxford University Press, 1979); Jeffrey M. Dorwart, *The Office of Naval Intelligence: The Birth of America's First Intelligence Agency,* 1865–1918 (Annapolis: U.S. Naval Institute Press, 1979).

4. David Kahn, *Kahn on Codes* (New York: Macmillan, 1983), p. 257.

5. Noel Barber, *Sinister Twilight* (London: Collins, 1968); Stephen Howarth, *Morning Glory* (London: Hamish Hamilton, 1983), pp. 148 and 199.

6. Fletcher Pratt, *Sea Power and Today's War* (New York: 1939), pp. 175–79.

7. Apart from copying western aircraft, the Japanese engaged the services of well-known designers such as Herbert Smith, who had been a member of the team that produced the famous World War I Sopwith Camel fighter. Smith produced the original design for the Japanese A5M fighter, the forerunner of the famous Zero, or A6M Reisen, which completely surprised the west by its performance. An indication of how bad British intelligence was about Japanese air-

craft design occurred on 10 December 1941, when Admiral Sir Tom Phillips on board HMS *Prince of Wales,* which was accompanied by HMS *Repulse,* came under air attack from the Japanese off the coast of Malaya. When a lookout reported that Japanese torpedo-carrying aircraft were about to attack, Phillips angrily replied; "Don't be silly, they don't have any." Within less than an hour both ships had been torpedoed and sunk, with the loss of 47 officers and 793 men. Martin Middlebrook, *Battleship* (London: 1977).

8. Columbia Films, 1957, Sam Spiegel.

9. Kahn, *Codebreakers,* chapter 12; Bamford, *Puzzle Palace,* pp. 27–35; Herbert Yardley, *The American Black Chamber* (Bobbs-Merrill, 1931); and Herbert O. Yardley, *A History of the Code and Cipher Section During World War I.* SRH-030, Record Group 457, National Archives, Washington, D.C.

10. It was Dr. James C. Heburn, an American medical missionary who had spent many years in Japan, who first established the Heburn system of romanization of the Japanese *kana* ideographs into roman letters.

11. Yardley conceived the idea whereby the Military Intelligence Division in Washington would ask the Japanese military attaché at their embassy to forward a routine request for information on some seemingly mundane matter to the Japanese War Office in Tokyo. Such a message would first have to be encoded, and as Yardley would know the original plain text he could then compare that with the intercepted cipher text. The message would contain some western names that would not be in the Japanese code dictionary and therefore the attaché's code clerk in Washington would have to spell each one out letter by letter in *kana.* Since these parts of the cipher text would show up easily, Yardley could then reconstruct the rest of the message around them. (Yardley, *Black Chamber,* pp. 266–68.) In the world of codebreaking this is known as a crib, an expression used in schools and colleges to describe an illicit list of answers used during an examination. Codebreaking cribs can appear in several forms. When Rear Admiral Karl Doenitz was promoted to full admiral on 14 March 1942, German naval headquarters sent an identical message announcing this to every U-boat at sea. Thus it was not hard for the codebreakers to guess the message's contents.

In wartime, it is possible for codebreakers to ask that a particular target be attacked and then wait for the attack report to be sent by that enemy position back to their headquarters. In peacetime, typical cribs can be found when diplomats, anxious to impress their superiors, send back long verbatim reports of speeches or political reports whose text lengths can easily be identified. The Japanese were in the habit of sending out identical long flowery messages to all their diplomatic missions on special occasions such as the Emperor's birthday. Good code clerks overcome cribs by padding out the message with bogus text that alters the length.

12. The problem with *kana* is that each character has two meanings, depending upon whether it is spoken as hard or soft. CHI, a hard sound as in CHINA, is followed by the *nigori* suffix, whereas SHI, the soft sound as in SHIP, is

followed by the *hanigori* suffix. When sending *kana* in Morse code the *hanigori* and *nigori* sounds had to be denoted as separate signals (see Appendix 1).

13. Kowalefsky had been invited to Japan to give a series of lectures on cryptography, and among his group of students was Commander Risaburo Ito, who had served with the Royal Navy in the Mediterranean, then Japan's allies, in World War I. Like Yardley, Ito had enjoyed himself breaking the British naval codes then in use and went on to become one of Japan's foremost code experts. Because Kowalefsky told the Japanese about the German Enigma, they bought copies, and Ito based his first cryptograph on its multirotor system. But although Ito helped invent two of Japan's main cryptographs, it fortunately never occurred to him to use them throughout the Japanese Navy, which continued to rely on book codes.

14. As with most countries, Japan had numerous scares that their codes were being broken. In September 1938, the Japanese naval commander in China reported that he suspected his code was no longer secure. (Record Group 457, SRH-355, p. 319, still partly censored, National Archives.) On 5 May 1941, the Foreign Ministry warned the Washington Embassy that their Purple messages were being read by the Americans. (SRDJ 011563, JD/09, National Archives.) In September 1942, the Japanese were given Ultra material seized by the Germans from the Australian steamer *Nankin* which showed that their naval code JN-25 had been broken by the Americans and had been the cause of their defeat at the Battle of Midway in June 1942. (James Rusbridger, "The Capture of the *Nankin*," *Encounter*, May 1985.) In each case, although junior officers knew the truth, they could not, or dared not, convince their superiors.

15. Yardley, *Black Chamber*, pp. 289–90.

16. RG 457, SRH-029, National Archives, p. 9.

17. In Britain, the question of foreign intelligence gathering has always been a very sensitive subject. The Secret Intelligence Service, MI6, although controlled by the Foreign Office, does not officially exist, in the quaint belief that this will persuade foreign countries to accept that Britain does not spy on them. MI6's offices at Century House, 100 Westminister Bridge Road, in London are officially called a research department. Since the mid-1970s, GCHQ, the successor to GCCS, has officially existed, but its role is never publicly discussed by the government, since much of what it does is illegal, and therefore the less politicians know about such activities the fewer lies they have to tell.

18. RG 457, SRH-029, National Archives, p. 10.

19. Kahn, *Codebreakers*, p. 360.

20. Yardley, *Black Chamber*.

21. *Secret Inks*, 4 April 1931, vol. 203, #40; *Codes*, 18 April 1931, vol. 203, #42; *Ciphers*, 9 May 1931, vol. 203, #45; and *Cryptograms and Their Solution*, 21 November 1931, vol. 203, #45. SRH-012, RG 457, vol 2 (National Archives, Military Reference Section, Washington, D.C.).

22. Peter Wright had been a member of Britain's Security Service, MI5, and retired to Australia believing that the agency had been deeply penetrated by the

Russians and that the director-general, Sir Roger Hollis, was himself a spy. Besides this allegation, Wright's book contained a wealth of hitherto unpublished detail of MI5's illegal activities, all of which embarrassed the government. As a result, they foolishly embarked on hugely expensive litigation throughout 1987–88 in Britain, Australia, and elsewhere (but sensibly not in America), which not only ended in defeat but a legal bill in excess of £3 million and enhanced the book's world sales to over 1.8 million rather than the more likely 20,000 copies had it been left to its own devices.

23. Cooperation and exchange of Sigint between America and Britain was first formally discussed at a meeting in April 1940 between President Roosevelt and William Stephenson, head of MI6's office in New York, the British Security Coordination (BSC), and followed by another meeting on 8 July 1940 between the British ambassador in Washington, Lord Lothian, and President Roosevelt. Exchanges of information and equipment continued until the BRUSA agreement of 17 May 1943 was signed, which established on a permanent basis future cooperation. This was replaced by the secret UK-USA Agreement of 1947, which not only linked GCHQ and the NSA but also the Sigint agencies of Canada, Australia, and New Zealand. The history of the agreement has not always been smooth, especially when the NSA discovered its secrets being passed to the Russians by spies in the heart of GCHQ, resulting in their refusing to share further information. New Zealand has dropped out in recent years because of its anti-nuclear stance but is now building satellite surveillance systems (similar to NSA's Rhyolite) in the south island, jointly funded by the Government Communications Security Bureau (GCSB), Australia, and GCHQ in order to provide an alternative non-American system. One valuable advantage with the UK-USA Agreement is that it enables GCHQ to tap American communications and the NSA to do the same in Britain, thus allowing both governments to deny any illegal domestic interceptions such as Operation Shamrock and Minaret. Ronald W. Clark, *The Man Who Broke Purple* (London: Weidenfeld & Nicolson, 1977); Jeffrey T. Richelson and Desmond Ball, *The Ties That Bind* (Australia: Allen & Unwin, 1985); Bamford, *Puzzle Palace*; Rusbridger, *Intelligence Game;* and private information, New Zealand, 1990.

24. RG 457, SRH-029, National Archives, p. 12.

25. Ironically, in the fall of 1944, while campaigning as the Republican candidate for the presidency, Dewey himself became involved in a bitter row over American codebreaking secrets. Dewey had intended making public the fact— then known only to a few high officials—that Roosevelt had been reading Japanese codes prior to Pearl Harbor and that they had contained details of the forthcoming attack. Although this was quite untrue, it conveniently bolstered Dewey's claim that Roosevelt had deliberately allowed the attack to happen in order to get America into the war. When news of this reached Washington, General George C. Marshall, the Army Chief of Staff, wrote Dewey a personal letter without telling Roosevelt, as he wished to keep the matter non-political. Marshall explained the background of the prewar codebreaking of diplomatic messages (but did not deal with the prewar breaking of Japanese naval codes,

presumably because Marshall knew nothing about it), and asked Dewey to refrain from making any further public statements that would jeopardize the safety of American forces in the Pacific. Reluctantly Dewey agreed.

26. Yardley's banned manuscript was found by David Kahn in 1968 in the National Archives, RG 60, Department of Justice File 235334. Though not able to publish this book, Yardley went on to publish several others, which included *Yardleygrams* (1932), *The Blonde Countess* (1934), *The Red Sun of Nippon* (1934), *Crows Are Black Everywhere* (1945), and *The Education of a Poker Player* (1957). In 1935, Metro-Goldwyn-Mayer bought the film rights to *The Blonde Countess* and made it into a film called *Rendezvous*, starring William Powell.

Yardley died at the age of sixty-nine on 7 August 1958 and was buried with full military honors at Arlington Cemetery. To make certain that neither Yardley nor anyone else privy to such secrets would be in a position to embarrass the government again, an act was passed on 10 June 1933, becoming Public Law 37, which made it illegal for anyone employed by the U.S. government to divulge codebreaking secrets. Today the act is known as Section 952 of Title 18 of the United States Code. Nevertheless, unlike Britain, the American government has retained a sensible attitude to those retired intelligence officers who wish to write their memoirs. There is a perfectly simple procedure by which manuscripts are submitted in advance to the agency for which the author worked, and any sensitive material can be deleted without problems arising later. For example, when Robert Lamphere, a retired FBI employee, wished to write about his work breaking Russian codes (the Venona decrypts) in *The FBI-KGB War*, he agreed to remove sensitive passages about the FBI burgling the Russian Trade Delegation offices. Anyone in America who tries to publish such a book without having it vetted not only runs the risk of prosecution but automatically has the profits sequestered. In Britain the new 1989 Official Secrets Act has yet to be tested in court.

27. Yardley, *History of the Code & Cipher Section;* Kahn, *Codebreakers,* pp. 369 et seq; William F. Friedman, *A Brief History of the Signal Intelligence Service,* 29 June 1942, RG 457, SRH-029, National Archives; and Bamford, *Puzzle Palace,* pp. 27 et seq.

28. The rank of colonel was an honorary one conferred on him in 1915 by the governor of Kentucky. RG 457, SRH-030, National Archives, p. 4.

29. Sinkov interview, Phoenix, Arizona, January 1990.

30. Laurence F. Safford, *A Brief History of Communications Intelligence in the United States,* 21 March 1952, RG 457, SRH-149; and *Historical Review of OP-20-G,* 17 February 1944, RG 457, SRH-152, National Archives.

31. RG 457, SRH-029, para. 10, National Archives, p. 13.

32. OP-20-G was also known as Station N or Negat because it was located in the Navy office. OP-20-G's first problem—just as had faced Yardley and GCCS—was how to find some Japanese naval material to decode. In 1923, instructions were sent out to U.S. Navy ships in the Pacific and the USS *Huron,* which was then at Shanghai, for their radio operators to start recording any Japanese naval

cipher messages they intercepted in much the same way that Nave was to start doing two years later for the British. Then in 1924, an intercept station was established at the U.S. Consulate in Shanghai, and a year later, in 1925, the 14th Naval District at Pearl Harbor assigned one operator at the naval radio station at Wailupe, east of Honolulu, to monitor any Japanese radio traffic he could find. In 1927 another intercept station was established at the U.S. Embassy in Peking. The first set of Japanese naval messages was decrypted on 23 October 1924.

33. Captain J.S. Holtwick, USN, *Naval Security Group History to World War II,* June 1971, SRH-355, National Archives.

34. Only one of these RIP-5 machines appears to have survived the war and, still in working order, is now in the private museum of the U.S. Navy Security Group headquarters in Washington, D.C. The authors are particularly grateful to Commander Newman and George Henrikson, special assistant for security, for allowing it to be inspected and providing unique photographs for this book.

3: STRAWS IN THE WIND, pp. 62–74

1. In fact, GCCS spent a lot of its time breaking American diplomatic codes, which work continued until 1942, when an embarrassed Winston Churchill wrote Roosevelt on 25 February 1942 saying that he had ordered his codebreakers to stop such work. PSF Safe File, Boxes MR/162 & PSF/5, Roosevelt Library, New York.

2. Safford, *Communications Intelligence,* SRH-149, RG 457, National Archives. Some parts of this report, mainly to do with the JN-25 code and details of intercept stations, are still censored in 1991 by the NSA.

3. Ibid., p. 10.

4. Ibid., p. 10.

5. Holtwick, *Naval Security Group History,* p. 82.

6. In *The Broken Seal,* p. 39, Farago calls him Dr. Emerson J. Haaworth, a former Quaker missionary in Japan and teacher at Tokyo University. His wife acted as secretary because she was the only person who could read his writing.

7. It was also known as JN-1, as it was the first Japanese Navy code to be broken by the Americans.

8. SRH-149, p. 6.

9. Ibid., p. 21.

10. Ray Schmidt, "First Lady of Naval Cryptology," *U.S. Naval Security Group Bulletin,* 1982.

11. *And So Was I,* personal notes by Captain Duane Whitlock, USN (unpublished 1986), p. 1.

12. Recently brought up to date by the Diplomatic Privileges Act of 1964, which Britain has signed. But GCHQ (GCCS's successor) still intercepts the communications of every foreign embassy in London. Britain is also a signatory of the International Telecommunications Convention, which is supposed to guarantee the secrecy of all international communications, but this does not stop GCHQ, with the NSA, from monitoring every communication entering and leaving Britain. Rusbridger, *Intelligence Game,* pp. 21–22.

13. Throughout the 1920s and 1930s, Japan ordered large quantities of specialized military equipment from European manufacturers, including Rolls-Royce aero engines and Barr & Stroud range finders from Britain, so that their own designers could copy them. In 1934, a large Japanese naval mission led by Admiral Matsushita visited Germany, where they were received by Hitler and allowed to inspect factories, dockyards, military installations, and all the latest warships. Details of all these visits and orders subsequently placed were sent back to Tokyo via their naval attachés and were thus read by GCCS. In particular, the ability of GCCS to intercept and read the prewar messages from the Japanese Embassy in Berlin (which included diplomatic and attaché) gave an incredible insight into Germany's most secret plans, which they were willing to discuss with Japan in order to bring them into closer cooperation, eventually resulting in the Tripartite Pact signed on 27 September 1940. Thereafter, and continuing throughout World War II, the messages flowing between Berlin and Tokyo by direct beam radio provided the Allies with their most important source of intelligence about the Germans. The messages went in a variety of different code systems. Diplomatic messages between 1931 and 1937 were encoded on the Type 91, or Red, cryptograph. After 1937, they were encrypted on the Type 97, or Purple, cryptograph, broken by the Americans on 25 September 1940. Attaché traffic was encrypted in either a book code or later on the Coral cryptograph. Although the Germans could not read these messages (because they never broke the Japanese Purple code), they must have had a good idea of their content but did nothing to stop them, or to warn the Japanese, even though, as early as 1940, German intelligence knew that the Americans were reading these high-grade Purple messages. Canaris memorandum to Foreign Minister Ribbentrop, *Chef Abwehr I No. 24/40 Chefs,* 25 April 1940 (Freiburg: Bundesarchiv); Ladislas Farago, *The Game of the Foxes* (New York: McKay, 1971); and Clark, *The Man Who Broke Purple.*

14. Malone died on 25 February 1965.

15. See also State Department report 29 August 1940. American Embassy, London, Files 820.67 and 820.02, National Archives, Washington.

16. MI6, generally known as the Secret Intelligence Service, operates only outside Britain, while MI5, the Security Service, is responsible for security within Britain. The demarcation lines are not always absolute, and MI6 has occasionally been involved in domestic operations, usually with disastrous results. Rusbridger, *Intelligence Game,* chapter 2.

17. Considering it was the RAN who after long debate had arranged and paid for Nave to go to Japan to learn the language, it is remarkably odd they never inquired why he should have been on such an extended loan with the Royal Navy merely as an interpreter. During the interwar years, the RAN had no codebreaking agency of their own able to intercept and read Japanese signals, and it is clear from their proposed posting for Nave that they had no plans to use his talents in that direction.

18. SRH-355, p. 85.

19. Rear Admiral J. F. W. Nuboer, Royal Netherlands Navy, *A History of Afdel-*

ing 1, Intelligence, Naval Staff, Batavia, translated by Robert Haslach; and Robert Haslach, *Nishi no Kaze, Hare* (Holland: Uniboek BV, Weesp, 1985), available only in Dutch. The authors are indebted to Howard Baker and Dr. L. G. M. Jaquet for having provided expert translations from this valuable book on the little-known history of Dutch cryptographic work, since all Kamer 14's archives were destroyed in 1942 before the arrival of the Japanese.

20. SRH-355, pp. 247–48.

21. By December 1941, the Japanese had built forty Type A or Red machines. OP-20-G built only five copies of the Red machine. One was kept in Washington, one went out to Station Hypo in Pearl Harbor, and a third to Station Cast in Cavite. The remaining two were given to GCCS in January 1941, who sent one to FECB in Singapore. The German codebreakers at their Foreign Office codebreaking bureau Pers Z who were monitoring the cable traffic between Berlin and Tokyo also broke the Red machine. The work of the German Foreign Office codebreaking section had begun in 1919 and was first known as Referat I Z. In 1936 it was renamed Pers-Z, the Z section of the Personnel and Administrative Division. It was a deliberately meaningless title to conceal the true nature of the work. The first Red machine messages were broken by Pers-Z in April 1938, the solution time of each intercept being fourteen days. By September, the solution time was down to about two hours. Curiously, although Pers-Z knew that the Red machine was based on their own Enigma, it never occurred to them that if they could break the Japanese cryptograph, others might be able to break Enigma. Indeed, when detailed evidence that Britain was reading Enigma was passed to the Germans in August 1943 by Colonel Masson, head of the Swiss secret service, junior intelligence officers found it impossible to convince their seniors of the facts. Colonel Masson got his information from a Swiss-American working in the U.S. Navy Department in Washington who had several times visited Britain as a member of an official delegation. Masson's report of 18 August 1943 stated: "The English have in their 'Intelligence Naval Office' [actually the Admiralty's Operational Intelligence Centre] a quite outstanding aid in the struggle against the U-boats. A special office since the outbreak of war has concerned itself exclusively with the decipherment of German codes. For some months past it has succeeded in reading all orders sent by the German navy to the U-boat commanders, something that has tremendously simplified the hunt against the U-boats." *OKW/Abwehr I/MTB 1663/43 Kdos & OKM 4/Abt/Skl Operation Geheimaltung 1941–1944* (Freiburg: Bundesarchiv); and Dr. J. W. M. Chapman, *Deutschland-Japan Historische Kontakte* (Bonn: Bouvier Verlag Herbert Grundmann, 1984), pp. 231–32.

22. Deavours, *Machine Cryptography,* p. 225.

23. Layton, *"And I Was There,"* pp. 58–59, and SRH-355, pp. 353–55.

24. On 10 May 1942 the Australian steamer *Nankin* was captured by the German surface raider *Thor* while en route from Fremantle in Australia to Colombo in Ceylon with a crew of 180 and 162 passengers, including 38 women and children. Among the *Nankin*'s cargo the Germans found 120 sacks of mail,

which included some secret mail from the Combined Operations Intelligence Centre (COIC) at Wellington, New Zealand, intended for FECB in Colombo. Among the COIC documents were Numbers 12, 13, 14, and 15 of their "Most Secret" weekly summaries of intercepted Japanese messages encoded in JN-25 covering the period 21 March through 20 April 1942, which gave the latest dispositions of Japanese warships in the Pacific that had been obtained from breaking their cipher traffic in the weeks before the Battle of Midway. Fortunately the documents did not reach Japan until 29 August, and it was not until they were handed over at a meeting on 3 September by the German naval attaché in Tokyo, Admiral Wenneker, who had been responsible for handing over the *Automedon* documents in 1940 (see Chapter 5) that the Japanese Navy first realized that their general naval code JN-25 had been fully penetrated by the Americans and that this had lost them the Battle of Midway in June 1942. Although the Japanese tried to improve their code security and, ironically, even belatedly ordered 500 Enigma cryptographs from the Germans, it was impossible to re-equip the entire Japanese Navy with a new code system. Nor was anyone brave enough to tell Yamamoto the truth, with the result that he was killed in April 1943 when details of his visit to the Solomon Islands sent in JN-25 were intercepted and decrypted by the Americans. James Rusbridger, "The Capture of the *Nankin*," *Encounter,* May 1985. Long after the war, and despite the public revelations at the 1945–46 Pearl Harbor inquiry, the Japanese refused to believe that their Red and Purple cryptographs had been broken by the Americans by cryptanalysis alone, and argued that either machines had been stolen by the Americans or their secrets betrayed by a traitor. This refusal to accept the skills of codebreakers like Friedman and his team is probably one reason why the NSA still keeps the relevant files so heavily censored.

25. Arthur Purves Shaw entered the Royal Navy on 15 July 1913 and had continuous service until his retirement on 28 September 1950 with the rank of captain. He was awarded the CBE in 1942 and the American Legion of Merit in 1948. He died on 23 September 1952. (Information kindly supplied by Miss H. R. Martin, Ministry of Defence, London.)

26. #65-174, FBI Archives, Washington, D.C. Kuehn's spying activities were not detected by the FBI or U.S. Navy counterintelligence until two days after the Pearl Harbor attack, when he was arrested and charged with espionage. On 19 February 1942, Kuehn was tried in secret before a military court in Hawaii and, on 21 February found guilty on eight counts of spying and sentenced to death by firing squad. The trial was so secret that Francis Biddle, the U.S. Attorney General, told Roosevelt on 4 March that it was the Japanese consul, Kita, who had been sentenced to death, which caused considerable alarm at the White House. Sumner Welles warned President Roosevelt that if Kita was shot, the Japanese would certainly take reprisals against American diplomats still in Japan. Eventually, J. Edgar Hoover managed to explain to the President what had happened, but it was still thought unwise to execute Kuehn because of the number of American nationals still held in Germany and Japan. On

26 October 1942, Kuehn's sentence was commuted to thirty years' imprisonment by the Army, who forgot to advise the FBI, who still thought he had
been shot. It was not until June 1943 that any public announcement about
the trial was made. Kuehn's wife and children were held in detention until
January 1945, and were repatriated to Germany after the war ended. Kuehn
left Leavenworth Penitentiary in 1948 and returned to Germany and died there
in 1956.

4: A TOUCH OF MAGIC, pp. 75–88

1. Edda Mussolini married Count Galeazzo Ciano in 1930, thereby guarantee-
ing his future career. He was chief of the press bureau in 1933 and Under
Secretary of State for Press and Propaganda in 1934. After commanding a
bomber squadron in Ethiopia in 1936, he returned to Rome and became Foreign
Minister. His policies proved ambivalent, and toward the end of World War II
he urged a separate peace with the Allies and eventually took part in the depos-
ing of Mussolini. However, the dictator was rescued by the Germans, and Mussolini set up a new regime in northern Italy, where Ciano was arrested and shot
on 11 January 1944.

2. Rushbrooke retired from the Navy in 1946 with the rank of vice admiral
after forty-one years of service, and his honors and awards included the CBE
and DSC. Beesly, *Very Special Intelligence*, p. 258, and information kindly supplied by Mrs. L. C. Unwin, Ministry of Defence.

3. The generally accepted version is that while Japanese and Chinese troops
were facing each other across the bridge, one of the Japanese soldiers went off
into some bushes to relieve himself. His colleagues suspected he had been
abducted by the Chinese, and shots were exchanged. Before order or sense
could be restored, war had erupted. Howarth, *Morning Glory*, p. 212.

4. In July 1937, the Japanese Navy Air Force had 219 aircraft: 48 land-based
bombers, 51 carrier-based dive-bombers, 54 carrier-based attack and torpedo
bombers, and 66 carrier-based fighters. The carrier-based air force totaled ninety
aircraft divided among the carriers *Ryujo, Hosho,* and *Kaga.* Of the three, *Kaga*
was by far the largest, at 33,600 tons, capable of carrying twelve each of fighters,
dive-bombers, attack bombers, and torpedo bombers. *Morning Glory*, p. 212.
Through British human intelligence (Humint) and Sigint, FECB had been able
to piece together much of this information, but it received little attention in
London.

5. U.S. Navy Director of Naval Communications, *Memoranda on the Congressional Investigations of the Attack on Pearl Harbor,* SRH-233, RG 457, National
Archives, p. 7.

6. Due to lack of staff and equipment, the two outlying stations, Hypo and
Cast, did little or no Japanese codebreaking until 1940–41. All of that was done
at Negat or OP-20-G. The growth in naval codebreaking personnel is shown
below, in addition to which there was also the U.S. Army's team at SIS:

Date	Officers	Enlisted	Civilians	Total
1925	1	2	4	7
1926–35	Net increase of about 10 men per year			
1936	11	88	10	109
1940	12	121	15	147
1941 (Jan.)	44	489	10	543
1941 (Dec.)	75	645	10	730

7. The Purple machine did not use the German Enigma rotor system as had the Red machine. It was a radically new design using a combination of Strowger-type rotary telephone selector switches (also known as steppers or uniselectors), which were designed to work the automatic telephone systems of the 1930s invented by Almon B. Strowger. A Kansas City undertaker, Strowger first patented his automatic telephone system on 12 March 1889 in order to frustrate his business rival's wife, who worked as a telephone operator and used to put his clients through to her husband.

The function of a stepping switch is to divert incoming current at an input terminal to one of a number of output terminals arranged in a fan-shaped arc. Contact is made by a wiper. In the Purple machine, each selector unit had six levels of twenty-five steps each. At a given level the signal from the input terminal could be sent to any of the twenty-five outputs by stepping the wiper for that particular output. There was nothing particularly advantageous from a cryptographic viewpoint in using stepping selectors in place of rotors. In fact, rotors offered far more permutations than did selectors, which are fixed and cannot be varied. Exactly why the Japanese chose selectors in place of rotors is unclear, but despite its apparent complexity, Purple offered only very modest cipher security. It would have been a far better machine had Ito stayed with the rotor system and increased the number, as the Americans did with their Sigaba or ECM cryptograph, which used ten rotors. It also does seem quite amazing that, although an officer in the Japanese Navy, Ito never suggested that either of his cryptographs should be used throughout the fleet. He was apparently content to let them continue using old-fashioned book codes of a type which he knew the Americans had broken twenty years earlier.

Purple still retained the same input and output typewriter arrangement of the earlier Red machine and its twenty-six-plug board arrangement, but the actual cryptographic element was achieved by the banks of selector switches instead of rotors. The other difference was that Purple worked on roman letters, not *kana*, so it could encode English words as well as *romanji*. Deavours, *Machine Cryptography*, pp. 226–39.

8. SRH-159, National Archives.

9. Sinkov interview.

10. SRH-149 and Layton *"And I Was There,"* pp. 80–81.

11. Farago, *Broken Seal,* p. 200.

12. Unlike Churchill, who had an intimate knowledge of the technology of codebreaking dating back to his days at the Admiralty in World War I and the work of Room 40, and during World War II visited Bletchley Park and talked directly to the codebreakers. Gordon Welchman, *The Hut Six Story* (New York: McGraw Hill, 1982), p. 128.

13. S. B. and S. H. Vardy, *Society in Change* (New York: Columbia University Press, 1983), pp. 103–17.

14. Commander M. S. L. Burnett, OBE, RN (known to his friends as "Bouncer"), joined the Royal Navy on 15 May 1918 and had continuous service until he retired on 22 September 1949. He was a close friend of Eric Nave, who was his best man at his wedding in Scotland. Burnett was mentioned in dispatches for gallantry and devotion to duty in Singapore in December 1941 and was awarded the Legion of Merit for services as communication intelligence officer with various British units in the Southwest Pacific and later as liaison officer with U.S. Navy units from May 1941 to September 1945. Burnett was awarded the OBE in January 1957 and his death occurred on 17 July 1984. (See also Preface, p. 5.)

15. Layton, *"And I Was There,"* p. 77.

16. SRH-149, National Archives, p. 14.

17. Laurence F. Safford, "Rhapsody in Purple," *Cryptologia,* July 1982, p. 220.

18. SRH-355, RG 457, National Archives, p. 417.

19. So far as is known, this is the first page from a JN-25 additive table ever released by the U.S. Navy. When the authors asked in January 1990 if they could have additional pages so as to show more clearly the method of penetration, this was refused on the grounds that it would endanger the security of the United States today.

20. Laziness among code clerks was not confined to the Japanese. In early 1942, the Admiralty (which was still using codes similar to JN-25) sent a very secret warning to senior Far East code officers that with monthly traffic running at over nine million groups, analysis had shown that clerks were becoming lazy and using the same pages in the additive tables far too frequently, with the result that some messages could now be read by the enemy within a week. The warning continued: "An ordinary [additive] table of 100 pages can carry 30,000 groups with safety. After that it becomes progressively weaker. Most of our tables with the exception of submarine and Flag Officers' tables are over the safety limit."

There then followed a detailed analysis of how many times clerks had been using the same pages. Fortunately for the British, the Japanese were too preoccupied with success to be bothered about codebreaking. (Secret Naval File 8/10/20, National Archives, New Zealand.)

21. Bletchley Park (officially known as Station X during the war) is a large vulgar Victorian country house built by Sir Herbert Leon around 1885. Today most of it is used by British Telecom as a training center, but GCHQ still retains ownership of some of the buildings around the main house, which are used for training purposes. West *GCHQ*, p. 105; and private information from GCHQ.

5: THE NAIL IN THE HORSE'S SHOE, pp. 89–106

1. The passenger liner was sunk by the *U-30* with the loss of 128 lives. Highly embarrassed by the attack, which was in contravention of Hitler's orders, the Germans put out a crude piece of disinformation claiming the British had destroyed the liner themselves.

2. Costello, *Pacific War*, p. 66.

3. Chamberlain wanted his successor to be Lord Halifax, who was also the preferred choice of King George VI and most of the Conservative Party. More important, Halifax also had the support of the Labour Party in opposition, including Clement Attlee, Hugh Dalton, and Herbert Morrison, none of whom liked Churchill. However, in the end, Halifax refused to accept the job as Prime Minister because as a peer he would have been unable to sit in the House of Commons, and thus he allowed Churchill to take on the role. Nevertheless, for several months after Churchill became Prime Minister, he was received with only lukewarm enthusiasm by Parliament, and some Conservatives began to regret that they had ousted Chamberlain. It was only after Chamberlain's death from cancer in October 1940 that Churchill became leader of the Conservative Party and was fully accepted.

4. Morgan, *FDR*, p. 520.

5. Others who were alleged to share these anti-war views included Queen Mary (who was of German descent), the Duke of Windsor (who had visited Hitler before the war), the Aga Khan, the Dukes of Buccleuch and Westminster, and Lords Londonderry, Rushcliffe, and Philimore. The Duke of Buccleuch was the brother-in-law of the Duke of Gloucester (King George VI's brother) and a senior member of the royal household but was later removed from these duties by Churchill. Adding to the confusion, there was a spy in the American Embassy in London known only as "The Doctor," who was passing on top-secret information to Rudolf Hess's office in Berlin. According to Sir Dick White, former head of Britain's MI5 and MI6, "The Doctor" was never caught, though it is generally believed he was either Joseph Kennedy or someone on his staff and may have contributed to the surprising and embarrassing arrival of Hess in Britain in 1941, which continues to intrigue historians. Not surprisingly, little about these embarrassing affairs appears in the files at the PRO, as the Foreign Office continues to refuse their public release. It was perhaps fortunate for Churchill that Hitler was slow in taking advantage of this anti-war feeling, for had he proposed a peaceful settlement that would have left Britain and its empire intact, Churchill might not have been able to persuade his War Cabinet to reject it.

6. Philip Goodhart, *Fifty Ships That Saved the World* (New York: Doubleday, 1965).

7. Because of their poor condition the Admiralty insisted that every vessel be given a complete refit, which resulted in only twenty-nine being in service by mid-1941. A further complication was a shortage of crews and the need to retrain them to use American-style equipment. In the end it was more of a

symbolic arrangement, drawing America nearer the war in Europe, than one with any significant military advantages to Britain. In return, America acquired a valuable network of overseas bases from which to defend itself.

8. *The Diaries of Sir Alexander Cadogan: 1938–1945* (New York: Putnam, 1972). Alan Brooke was appointed Churchill's Chief of the Imperial General Staff (CIGS) in December 1941.

9. Mortimer interview, December 1989.

10. As far as can be ascertained, only Eric Nave and Lieutenant Commander Mortimer survive from the original members of FECB.

11. As the work at Bletchley Park grew, numerous wooden huts were built on its grounds. Hut 8 handled naval codebreaking and Hut 4 naval intelligence analysis.

12. Information kindly supplied by Ralph Erskine, and also Beesly, *Very Special Intelligence,* pp. 68–69.

13. Joint Chiefs of Staff records, RG 225 on microfilm Locator M-1421, #10-207, reels 301–302, National Archives, Washington, D.C.

14. Commander C. R. L. Parry was in the USS *West Virginia,* Lieutenant Commander C. C. Martell in *Boise,* and Lieutenant Commander D. C. Cairns in *Sterrett.*

15. Safford, "Rhapsody in Purple," p. 204.

16. Ibid., p. 222.

17. Typical of these was the Most Secret message #610 from the Secretary of State for Dominion Affairs to the Australian Prime Minister dated 2 September 1941. MP 1049/5, File 1877/10/37, Australian Archives, Victoria.

18. Letter from Captain Duane Whitlock, USN (Ret.), quoted by Graydon Lewis, editor of *Cryptolog* magazine, in letter 23 November 1986. Captain Whitlock had trained as a Sigint radio operator with Class 20 of the "On-the-Roof Gang" in Washington between November 1937 through March 1938. In 1941, Whitlock was a chief petty officer (traffic analysis) at Station Cast in Cavite and may not have known the exact details of any cryptographic exchanges. According to Safford's report (Pearl Harbor Liaison Office, CNO Documents, RG 80, National Archives, Washington D.C.), there appear to have been at least some exchanges of intercepted material between Cast and FECB.

19. Interview, December 1989.

20. On the morning after the Pearl Harbor attack, there was such shock at FECB that the Americans had been caught unprepared that Commander T. P. Wisden, who had joined FECB in 1940, held a meeting to satisfy himself that everything FECB had known about the attack from reading JN-25 had been passed on to CINCPAC. Like Lieutenant Commander Mortimer, Wisden was not allowed to attend the 1945–46 Pearl Harbor inquiry. (Mortimer interview.)

21. Throughout the late 1930s and long into the war, British governments held to the naive belief that the economic blockade of Germany was Britain's key to victory and would soon bring Hitler to his knees. The prewar Industrial Intelligence Centre (IIC), which was supposed to monitor Germany's economic position, consistently got its facts wrong and underestimated Germany's ability

to overcome the blockade and later the RAF's bombing raids. Even in late 1941, German factories were still only working one shift per day, employed far fewer women than in Britain, possessed far more modern machine tools, and were producing luxury goods for the domestic market that had long disappeared in Britain. Any equipment shortages suffered by the German Army were the result of bureaucratic maladministration, not of any shortage of manufacturing capacity or raw materials. Between 1939 and 1942, RAF's Bomber Command absorbed about one-third of Britain's total industrial resources yet, as the Butt Report of August 1941 showed, navigation was so poor that only two bombers in five came within five miles of the target on full-moon nights, and only one in fifteen on moonless nights. As a result, little or no damage was being done to the enemy's industrial capacity, and British bombers had been killing Germans no faster than the Germans had been killing highly trained aircrews. The Admiralty were quick to seize on the report and argue that the same resources would have been far better spent on the Royal Navy defending the vital convoy routes. It was the shock of the Butt Report that led to the introduction of area bombing, a euphemism for dropping bombs at random over towns and cities. CAB 47/15, Public Record Office, Kew; Wesley K. Wark, *The Ultimate Enemy* (Oxford: Oxford University Press, 1986), chapter 7; A. J. P. Taylor *The Second World War* (London: Hamish Hamilton, 1975), p. 129; Max Hastings, *Bomber Command* (London: Michael Joseph, 1979), chapter 4; Denis Richards, *The Royal Air Force 1939–1945* (HMSO, 1953); and Sir Charles Webster and Noble Frankland, *The Strategic Air Offensive against Germany* (HMSO, 1961).

22. Costello, *Pacific War*, p. 68.

23. Ibid., p. 72.

24. Arthur Marder, *Old Friends, New Enemies* (Oxford: Oxford University Press, 1981), pp. 36–41.

25. CAB/65/8, COS (40) 592, 31 July 1940, now CAB 66/10, Public Record Office, Kew.

26. Bernhard Rogge and Wolfgang Frank, *Schiff 16* (Hamburg: Stalling Verlag, 1955); Ulrich Mohr, *Atlantis* (London Press, 1955); Edwin Hoyt, *Raider 16* (Ohio: World Publishing, 1970); and August Muggenthaler, *German Raiders of World War II* (London: Robert Hale, 1978).

27. The Italians had begun the penetration of British naval codes during the increased activities of the Royal Navy during the Abyssinian campaign in 1935, and they passed on their knowledge to the Germans. The Germans captured a great deal of cipher material from various British embassies and consulates in Scandinavia in April-May 1940, and a complete set of current codebooks from the submarine HMS *Seal*, which surrendered off the German coast in 1940. *Seal* had been minelaying off the German coast on 4 May 1940 and was on her way back to England when the submarine struck a mine, which flooded part of the vessel. *Seal* managed to get back to the surface, but her engines had seized, and at 0400 hrs on 5 May she was spotted by a German seaplane, which landed and accepted *Seal*'s surrender. The captain and a petty officer were taken off by the seaplane, and the rest of the crew waited two hours before a German trawler

arrived. Why the codebooks were not thrown overboard is unclear, and details of this incident are not available, as court-martial records are closed in Britain for seventy-five years. (Undated letter from Ernest Trueman, who was an engine room artificer on *Seal*, courtesy of the Imperial War Museum, London.)

28. *Report of Commission of Inquiry on the Loss of Certain Vessels by Enemy Action and the Alleged Leakage of Information and Sinking of* Commissaire Ramel *by German Raider* Atlantis *in September 1940.* (Files I/61/2/7 and MPI/587/22/153S, Australian Archives, Canberra.)

29. Stephen Roskill, *The War at Sea: 1939–45,* Volume 1 (London: HMSO), p. 282, and report by Samuel Harper, the *Automedon's* fourth engineer. After being taken prisoner, Harper and the rest of the crew from the *Automedon* were later transferred to the German vessel *Storstad* and eventually arrived at Bordeaux in France in January 1941. Some weeks later, while the crew were being taken across France to a German prisoner-of-war camp, Harper jumped from the train at night and started making his way across France. By a series of fortunate coincidences, he met with friendly Frenchmen who passed him on from one group to another, until on 18 March 1941 he reached Marseilles. On 9 April, he was taken across the Pyrenees by a party of smugglers and reached Madrid, where with the help of the British Embassy he went on to Gibraltar, arriving on 31 May 1941. In Gibraltar, Harper was closely questioned by Naval Intelligence as to the fate of the *Automedon* and the mail, and he was able to confirm that all the mail had been seized. (Common Services Records Centre, Liverpool.)

30. The Japanese were coming under increasing pressure to assist the German Navy in their fight against Britain, which viewpoint was skillfully put by the German naval attaché in Tokyo, Admiral Paul Wenneker, an officer of great maritime experience and much personal charm that enabled him to tread a highly successful path between his naval duties and the rather formal social and diplomatic life in Japan. The Japanese were, as always, eager to learn. The Germans, for their part, needing an ally in the Far East, were anxious to help, always provided the Japanese would reciprocate with facilities useful to their naval forces. Japan's official war history, *Senshi Sosho,* draws a discreet veil over the extent of the aid Japan provided Germany for its submarine and surface raider operations in the Far East, but they did allow the Germans to establish secret refueling depots in the Mandated Islands. The war diary of Wenneker from 1939 to 1943 has been translated and edited by Dr. John Chapman of Sussex University and published as *The Price of Admiralty.*

31. Report by Samuel Harper, Blue Funnel Line Archives, Liverpool.

32. John Chapman, *The Price of Admiralty,* vol. 2 and 3 (London: Saltire Press, 1984).

33. 209/40-212/40 gKdos, OKM signal log, Military Reference Section, National Archives, Washington, D.C.

34. SRNA 0020, RG 457, National Archives, Washington, D.C. This intercept was among some 130,000 similar messages declassified in 1979 under Executive Order 12065.

35. An open-cockpit single-engined biplane torpedo bomber made by Fairey

Aviation which entered service with the Royal Navy's Fleet Air Arm in 1936. It had a top speed of 139 mph, a range of 770 miles, and could carry an eighteen-inch torpedo or a 1,500-pound mine or bombs. Affectionately known as the Stringbag, it had one advantage: it flew so slowly that it frequently confused enemy gunners.

36. Taranto Report, Churchill papers, 3/468, Folio 23, Public Record Office, Kew.

37. Martin Gilbert, *Finest Hour* (London: Heinemann, 1983), p. 906.

38. Taranto Report, Churchill papers, 3/468, Folio 23, PRO, Kew.

39. It was Gronau's report that prompted the Germans to arrange for one of their spies called Popov (who was in fact a double agent working for the British) to visit America and establish a network of agents.

40. Wenneker's diary, 12 December 1940, in Chapman, *Price of Admiralty*. In his notes, Dr. Chapman comments:

> The Japanese Navy was clearly aware that British naval forces in the Far East were steadily being transferred westward in the second half of 1940, but the defiant position adopted by [the British] had served to cover up the extent of British weakness. With this A1 intelligence about the real position, it is hardly surprising that subsequent efforts by Churchill and Eden to influence the Japanese position prior to Pearl Harbor were rather less than credible. From 1922, Japanese navy planners had had to contend with the likelihood of a two-power threat in the Pacific. From the end of 1940 it is now evident that the . . . [Japanese] naval staff . . . could concentrate with single-minded equanimity on the US Pacific fleet.

See also John Chapman, *Forty Years On,* vol. 5, part 1, pp. 69–86, *British Association for Japanese Studies,* 1980.

41. Report from Naval Intelligence, Singapore, 14 November. (Australian Archives MP 1049/5, 2021/5/552.)

42. ADM/1135, Public Record Office, Kew.

43. Historical Section, Cabinet Office, London, letter to author 23 August 1984.

44. Private correspondence, August 1984, with Colonel Brian Montgomery, author of *Shenton of Singapore* (London: Leo Cooper in assoc. with Secker & Warburg, 1984), and Hugh Humphrey, CMG, OBE, who was Sir Shenton's private secretary in 1940. After the war Brooke-Popham inquired what had happened to his copy of the Chiefs of Staff report and was told that the ship carrying it had been sunk by a submarine. (Letter from Squadron Leader G. H. Wiles, Air Ministry, 15 July 1948.)

45. Churchill, *Second World War,* vol. 4.

46. Prime Minister's personal minute to Chiefs of Staff, D4/2, Churchill papers, 20/67, PRO, Kew.

47. General Sir Archibald Wavell, one of Britain's ablest military com-

manders, had fallen afoul of Churchill while in command of the forces in North Africa in 1941 because he had dared argue against Churchill's repeated demands that he should launch fresh attacks while the bulk of his forces had gone to fight a useless campaign in Greece. Wavell's famous telegram that "a big butcher's bill is not necessarily the sign of success" so infuriated Churchill that Wavell was sent to India as C-in-C and replaced by General Claude Auchinleck. Following the attack on Pearl Harbor and knowing Singapore and Malaya were already doomed, Churchill and Roosevelt agreed on 28 December 1941, during the Arcadia Conference in Washington, to establish the American, British, Dutch, and Australian (ABDA) Command with Wavell at its head. Despite the rhetoric, it was no more than a cosmetic attempt to revive sagging morale, and Wavell, with no extra forces at his disposal, was simply the fall guy to distract attention away from Churchill. The ABDA Command was dissolved on 25 February 1942.

48. Page had served as Deputy Prime Minister of Australia from 1934 to 1939, and had briefly been Prime Minister in April 1939. From 1941 to 1942 he was Australia's representative in London, attending War Cabinet meetings before returning to Australia to take up his duties with the War Cabinet in Canberra.

49. Curtin was so angry that he included in his message to Churchill the sentence "Without any inhibitions of any kind, I make it quite clear that Australia looks to America, free of any pangs as to our traditional links or kinship with the United Kingdom."

Although Curtin later regretted the statement, it certainly showed the resentment and suspicions that existed between Churchill and the Australian government under Curtin. Had the Australian people known about the *Automedon* affair, there would have been a far greater outcry. (PREM 4/50/7A, 5 February 1942, and PREM 4/50/6, 29 March 1942, PRO, Kew.)

50. Rogge and Frank, *Schiff 16;* and Mohr, *Atlantis.* These concentrated on the buccaneering aspect of the raiders' exploits.

51. Roskill, *War at Sea*, vol. 1, p. 282.

52. Under Executive Order 12065 authorized by President Carter. All the decrypts were heavily censored by the National Security Agency, often to the point of rendering them useless to any historian.

53. Costello, *Pacific War,* p. 608.

54. Military Reference Section.

55. (London: Collins, 1981), p. 614.

56. Letter from author dated 18 April 1983.

57. Foreign Office letter, 9 August 1983.

58. Permanent Under Secretary's Department, Foreign & Commonwealth Office, letter 2 February 1984.

59. Maclean was recruited by the Russians while at Cambridge University before the war and despite being an alcoholic and a homosexual joined the Foreign Office. In 1944, he was posted to Washington, where he passed on information about the atomic bomb to the Russians, thus explaining Stalin's lack of surprise when first told about it by President Truman in Potsdam. Mac-

lean later told Moscow of Truman's orders to General MacArthur not to carry the Korean War into China. Maclean came under suspicion in May 1951 but was warned, and together with another spy, Guy Burgess, fled to Moscow.

60. W292/39/49, Y67/67/650, and Y2380/84/650.

61. Letter from Library & Records Department dated 10 January 1985.

6: THE UNEASY RELATIONSHIP, pp. 107–29

1. The Johnson Act of 1934 prevented any country that had defaulted on repaying its debts to America after World War I from raising further funds in the United States. As the British had defaulted in 1932, they were automatically debarred and therefore had to pay for any purchases in cash.

2. Morgan, *FDR*, p. 579.

3. Although the public image of Lend-Lease showed it to be a very friendly and casual arrangement, in reality the Americans extracted a very high price from the British government for their help, causing enormous bitterness. Clive Ponting, *1940: Myth and Reality* (London: Hamish Hamilton, 1990), chapter 10.

4. Safford, *Rhapsody in Purple*, p. 211; *The History of the U.S. Signal Corps in World War II*, pp. 192–93; Farago, *Broken Seal;* and Clark, *Man Who Broke Purple*. Naturally no copy of the letter is available in any British archive, because the British government refuses to admit having received Purple and Red machines from the Americans with which to read Japanese codes.

5. Early radar operated in metric wavelengths, but shorter centimetric wavelengths were needed to obtain more accurate information. At the same time, high power was needed for maximum range, and these two requirements could not be handled by any existing transmitting valve. The American Klystron valve was an improvement but still could not handle enough power. In 1938, the Air Ministry asked Professor Marcos Oliphant of Birmingham University to find a means of generating radio wave pulses less than 50cms long. By 1940, his team of scientists had developed a cavity resonator, or Magnetron, which functioned as a transmitting valve and could handle all the power needed. Disclosing this invention to the Americans was not a real sacrifice, because the British electronics industry was so badly equipped that, like the machine tool industry, wartime production depended upon American mass-production technology.

6. Sinkov interview, January 1990.

7. Lord Cadman was born in 1877 and spent his early career in the mining industry. In 1923, he joined the board of the Anglo-Iranian Oil Company, becoming chairman in March 1927. At the time of the Americans' visit to Bletchley, Cadman was a tired, sick man. He never recovered from his illness and, after returning from Wales to Shenley Park, died on 31 May 1941 at the age of sixty-four. (Information very kindly supplied by Miss Janette Harley, Archivist, BP International.)

8. Throughout the war, Oshima's long, detailed reports to Tokyo provided GCCS and the Americans with a remarkable insight into Hitler's thoughts and plans. Oshima and his staff were allowed to move about Germany, freely in-

specting defenses and seeing tests of new weaponry. As German intelligence knew that the Americans had broken Purple, it remains a mystery why they did not warn the Japanese.

9. Safford, *Communications Intelligence,* p. 217.

10. It has never been explained why OP-20-G did not photograph the JN-25 codebooks and send copies only to GCCS.

11. London Embassy secret files, Box #15, File #820.020/A-Z, Record Group 84, National Archives, Washington, D.C.

12. Churchill, *Second World War,* vol. 3, p. 532.

13. WO 208/882, PRO, London. It is interesting to note the different style used by British BJ's and American Purple. In America they were typed up on normal message forms, but in Britain it appears that the raw decrypt with the translation attached was written up by hand, so that only the one copy would be made.

14. PREM 3/485/6, Folio 18, PRO, Kew.

15. Apart from the security classification, Ultra (or in the case of FECB, Zymotic) messages derived from codebreaking also contained phrases like "Special Intelligence" or "Most Secret Sources," while messages sent to those not privy to the Ultra secret contained expressions like "reliable source" or "reliably reported" in order to conceal their true source.

16. Morton had first met Churchill on the Western Front in World War I, where Morton won the Military Cross. From 1929 to 1939, Morton had been head of the Industrial Intelligence Centre, the cover name of a government agency responsible for discovering the true nature of Germany's war plans, and had covertly —and illegally—fed Churchill throughout the 1930s secret information about the Nazis so that he could harass the government. Ronald Lewin, *Ultra Goes to War* (New York: McGraw Hill, 1978), Chapter 7.

17. File N30/68/3, National Archives, New Zealand.

18. According to the official history, OP-20-G had recovered about 2,000 values by January 1941, which would have been enough to break quite a lot of messages, especially if the Japanese code clerks were lazy and used the same place in the additive table too often. SRH-355, p. 398, National Archives, Washington, D.C.

19. Francis L. Lowenheim, ed., *Roosevelt and Churchill: Their Secret Wartime Correspondence* (New York: Saturday Review Press, 1975), p. 129. The "drifting straws" were of course the Black Jumbo messages being decrypted by GCCS and FECB.

20. Cipher Telegram 125, Ambassador Grew to State Department. File 711.94/ 1935, FS/FF, National Archives, Washington, D.C.

21. Farago, *Broken Seal,* p. 135.

22. Costello, *Pacific War,* p. 83.

23. Ibid., p. 99; Layton, *"And I Was There,"* p. 75; and Howarth, *Morning Glory,* p. 247.

24. Layton, *"And I Was There,"* pp. 146–47.

25. From March through December 1941, American codebreakers intercepted and decoded 223 Purple messages passing between Tokyo and Washington.

(SRDJ Series, RG 457, National Archives, Washington, D.C.) On 11 October 1941, a joint Army-Navy Intelligence Committee was authorized, but the committee did not have its first meeting until after 7 December.

26. Layton, *"And I Was There,"* pp. 116–17.

27. Ruth R. Harris, "The Magic Leak of 1941," *Pacific Historical Review* #50, February 1981, pp. 77–96.

28. John Costello *Mask of Treachery* (New York: William Morrow, 1988).

29. Morgan, *FDR,* p. 598.

30. Layton, *"And I Was There,"* pp. 134–37.

31. Records of Joint Army and Navy Boards, 4 September 1941. RG 225, Microfilm Locator M-1421, #10-207, reel 301, National Archives, Washington, D.C.

32. Churchill, *Second World War,* vol. 3, pp. 527–28.

33. Cabinet Papers 65/24, #112, 12 November 1941, PRO, Kew.

34. Hansard, *Official Report of the Proceedings of the British Parliament,* 27 January 1942, p. 593.

35. Ibid., p. 602.

36. Ibid., pp. 606–607.

37. Ibid., p. 607.

38. Hopkins papers, 21 February 1942, PSF File, Great Britain (Roosevelt Library).

39. Martin Gilbert, *Winston S. Churchill: The Wilderness Years* (London: Macmillan, 1981).

40. Morgan, *FDR,* pp. 600–603.

41. Michael Korda, *Charmed Lives* (New York: Random House, 1979), pp. 146–47. The film in question was *That Hamilton Woman,* starring Laurence Olivier and Vivien Leigh, which included a long speech written by Churchill in which Lord Nelson (Olivier) pleads with the British Admiralty not to trust Napoleon: "Napoleon can never be master of the world until he has smashed us up—and believe me, gentlemen, he means to be master of the world. You cannot make peace with dictators, you have to destroy them."

The America First Committee secured the help of Senator Gerald Nye, a powerful isolationist, to have the Senate Committee on Foreign Relations investigate the work of "British agents" like Korda in the American film industry. Korda received a subpoena to appear before the committee on 12 December 1941. Fortunately, the Japanese intervened and instead he became a premature patriot. For his work in America, Churchill bestowed a knighthood on Korda.

42. Costello, *Pacific War,* p. 94.

43. Admiral Karl Doenitz, commander of Germany's U-boats, later C-in-C of the German Navy.

44. General (later Field Marshal) Sir Archibald Wavell, one of Britain's finest military commanders, who as C-in-C Middle East was responsible for the first victories in North Africa. A taciturn man, Wavell refused to be bullied by Churchill and as a result was removed from his command and sent to India.

45. General Erwin Rommel, Hitler's mercurial commander in North Africa

who nearly defeated the British and in the process acquired almost legendary powers of brilliance (including the nickname "The Desert Fox"), which were, in fact, almost entirely due to his codebreakers' ease at reading British operational signals because they were still using obsolete code systems, a point carefully omitted from British postwar histories.

46. Costello, *Pacific War*, p. 112.

47. Hirohito read out a poem, or *tanka*, written by his grandfather Emperor Mutsuhito, which read:

> Since all the seas of the world are brothers,
> Why do winds and waves of strife
> rage so violently?

48. The most powerful battleship ever built, *Yamato*, the ancient name for Japan, was 862 feet long, displaced 72,000 tons, had a speed of over twenty-seven knots, and three turrets (each weighing 2,800 tons), each holding three 18.1-inch guns capable of firing a shell weighing 3,200 pounds. (Previously, the largest warship in the world was the British battle cruiser HMS *Hood* of 42,000 tons.) Although four Yamato-class ships were planned, only one other, the *Musashi*, was completed. Both were sunk during the war and never took part in any ship-to-ship battles. The third vessel, *Shinano*, was completed as an aircraft carrier, while the fourth was scrapped during construction. Overall, the project was a waste of scarce resources, although the ships were an excellent example of the technical skill of the Japanese. Admiral Isoruko Yamamoto was particularly critical of the entire project, stating, "These ships are like elaborate religious scrolls which old people hang up in their homes. They are of no proved worth. They are purely a matter of faith—not reality."

49. Minutes of the Defence Committee, 12 December 1939. (File CRS/816, Item 43/302/18, Australian Archives, Belconen.)

50. Letter #88 N8/1, Menzies to Secretary of State for Dominion Affairs. (File CRS/816, Item 43/302/18, Australian Archives, Belconen.)

51. Captain Nave's report is now part of File 1937/2/415 of MP 1185/8, Australian Archives, Brighton. When after many months this file was finally declassified to the authors under a Freedom of Information Application (FOIA), most of the pages had been blanked out by the Defence Signals Directorate at the request of GCHQ, who had told them that to release them even after fifty years could "be reasonably expected to damage relations between Australia and the United Kingdom." (Letter from Mr. F. T. Bryant, Regional Director, Australian Archives, Victoria, 2 February 1988.) Likewise, the minutes of this meeting were also unavailable for fear of "damaging the security of the Commonwealth," but fortunately a copy had been misfiled in the Prime Minister's secret correspondence records, MP 1185/8, File 1945/2/6, Australian Archives, Victoria.

52. Or it may have been part of the deliberate policy to conceal from anyone, including the Australians, the full extent of FECB's achievements.

53. SIO opened for business with a staff consisting of Lieutenant K. S. Miller,

RAN; Lieutenant A. R. "Jim" Jamieson, MSc, RAN; Major A. P. Treweeke, BA; Professor T. G. Room, MA, FRS; R. J. Lyons, MA; and Lieutenant Ian Longfield Lloyd; together with three civilian clerical staff: Miss Robertson, Miss Eldrige, and Miss Shearer.

54. After Pearl Harbor Nave helped establish the Central Bureau, Australia's first properly integrated Sigint organization, which was staffed by an Australian-American team of codebreakers, including Abraham Sinkov, throughout the war working closely with General Douglas MacArthur in Brisbane. An FOIA request to see the Central Bureau records for this period resulted in a long eighteen-month battle with the Defence Signals Directorate under Australia's complex archive access legislation. Despite the protests of GCHQ, eventually some files were declassified, but they had been made virtually useless from a historical viewpoint because each page was heavily censored, even to the point of removing the indexes and names of serving officers, all of whom are long dead. To demonstrate the bizarre paranoia that persists in agencies like the DSD and GCHQ, some pages are reproduced in Appendix 7.

55. Conversations with Captain Frank Lloyd; also Baron Burkhard von Mullenheim-Rechberg, *Battleship Bismarck* (London: Bodley Head, 1981); Beesley, *Very Special Intelligence*, p. 81; Peter Calvocoressi, *Top Secret Ultra* (London: Cassell, 1980).

56. Lowenheim, *Roosevelt and Churchill*, p. 163; and Warren F. Kimball, *Churchill and Roosevelt: The Complete Correspondence* (Princeton: Princeton University Press, 1984), p. 265.

57. PREM 3, 163/3, 16 November 1941, PRO. Smuts was proved right when both ships were sunk by Japanese aircraft off the Malayan coast on 10 December 1941, with the loss of forty-seven officers and 793 men.

58. Churchill, *Second World War*, vol. 3, p. 528.

7: THE INFAMOUS DAWN, pp. 130–50

1. SRDJ-015549, SRH-118, RG 457, National Archives.

2. Interview Captain Forrest Biard, USN (Ret.), Long Beach, January 1990. Captain Biard was a codebreaker working at Station Hypo at Pearl Harbor in 1941 and was fluent in Japanese.

3. SRH-210, RG 457, p. 21, National Archives.

4. Biard interview, 1990.

5. SRDJ-015589, SRH-118, RG 457, National Archives.

6. SRDJ-017188, SRH-118, RG 457, National Archives.

7. The title of the Pearl Harbor operation was chosen in honor of the signal flag used by Admiral Togo at the Battle of Tsushima in 1905. Layton, *"And I Was There,"* p. 111.

8. A copy of this order was recovered from the wreck of the Japanese cruiser *Ca Nachi* in 1944.

9. Michael Montgomery, *Who Sank the Sydney?* (Australia: Cassell, 1983).

10. Montgomery, *Shenton of Singapore*, p. 3.

11. London had promised Malaya that by the end of 1941 they would have 366 first-line aircraft. In fact, they had seventeen Lockheed Hudsons, thirty-four Bristol Blenheims, twenty-seven ancient Wildebeeste torpedo bombers, forty-one Brewster Buffaloes, ten Blenheim night fighters, three Catalina flying boats, four Swordfish, and five Sharks. There was not a single first-line fighter, although one squadron of Hurricanes did eventually reach Malaya but were destroyed on the ground before they could be used in battle.

12. Only 163 F2As were ever built, entering squadron service with the U.S. Navy in 1939. Proving quite useless, they were cheaply sold off to the Finnish Air Force, Holland, and the RAF in the Far East.

13. Richard Hough, *The Death of a Battleship* (New York: Macmillan, 1963), p. 153; and Barber, *Sinister Twilight,* p. 42.

14. This is the translation of the message made by Nave and his team at the SIO. It differs slightly from the American translation of the same intercept (#2353), which reads:

> Regarding the broadcast of a special message in an emergency.
> In case of emergency (danger of cutting off our diplomatic relations), and the cutting off of international communications, the following warning will be added in the middle of the Japanese language short-wave broadcast.

The key "execute" phrases were the same as in the Australian version, but the final paragraph reads:

> This signal will be given in the middle and at the end as a weather forecast and each sentence will be repeated twice. When this is heard please destroy all code papers, etc. This is as yet to be a completely secret arrangement. Forward as urgent intelligence.

It will be seen that there is a conflict in these instructions, because it first says that the key "execute" phrases will appear in the middle of the broadcast, and then in the last paragraph says they will appear in the middle and at the end.

However, despite these differences in translation, which highlight the problem of turning Japanese *kana* into English, the purpose of the message and the manner in which the key phrases were to be used are the same. Pearl Harbor Hearings 1945, vol. 27; Robert A. Theobald, *The Final Secret of Pearl Harbor* (New York: Devin-Adair, 1954), pp. 135–36; Australian Archives CRS A5954; and SRDJ-017205, SRDJ-016994, RG-457, SRH-118, National Archives.

15. This was Australia's first interservice Sigint and codebreaking organization, formally established on 28 November 1941, although it had been operating for some months previously. On 15 April 1942, it became the Central Bureau and was a joint Australian/American operation throughout World War II. In late

1945, it changed its name to the Defence Signals Bureau, and in October 1977 to the Defence Signals Directorate, by which name it is known today, with its headquarters at Victoria Barracks in Melbourne (although by 1992 it will have moved to new offices in the military complex outside Canberra). Its current director is Mr. Tim James. The DSD works closely with Britain's GCHQ and America's NSA and is a signatory to the 1947 UKUSA Treaty. Australian Archives CRS 816, Item 43/302/18, MP 1185/8, File 1937/2/415, parts of which are still classified; and Jeffrey T. Richelson & Desmond Ball, *The Ties That Bind* (Australia: Allen & Unwin, 1985), pp. 36–37.

16. Kahn, *Codebreakers,* p. 16.

17. Hewitt Inquiry report, SRH-210, RG 457, National Archives, Washington, D.C.

18. Commodore J. W. Durnford, RN, second naval member of the Australian Naval Board. Department of Defence, Canberra, letter 20 January 1988.

19. Australian Archives ACT CRS A/5954, Box 558.

20. Sir Frederick Geoffrey Shedden, KCMG, Secretary, Department of Defence, 1937–56. The Shedden papers are jointly held by the Australian Archives (MP 1217) and the Department of Defence and cover the period 1901–71. The index to the papers is over 250 pages long. In 1987, the copy of the Winds message together with the "execute" portion was found in CRS A/5954, but the rest of the Shedden papers are still undergoing declassification, a process being made unduly protracted by the interference from GCHQ at Cheltenham, who object to anything connected with codebreaking being released. So strong have their protests been that some papers already released into the public domain have been reclassified again.

21. This was an expression used to denote intelligence derived from codebreaking.

22. SRH-210, RG 457, National Archives, Washington D.C., p. 32.

23. In the SRN Series, RG-457, Military Reference Branch, National Archives.

24. Secret cypher files #41, National Archives, New Zealand.

25. SRN 115403 and SRN 115471, RG 457, National Archives.

26. SRN 115385, RG 457, National Archives. This copy shows that it was not translated until 26 November 1945.

27. Mortimer interview, and Marder, *Old Friends, New Enemies,* p. 400. The whereabouts of Mortimer's charts today are a mystery. They are not in the PRO, and the Naval Historical Branch say they have never seen them (letter from John Brown, D/NHB/9/2/33, 13 November 1989). But as they also showed information derived from reading JN-25, it seems likely they are held by GCHQ.

28. The text of this message is only available from documents recovered from the wreck of the Japanese cruiser *Ca Nachi,* National Archives, Washington D.C., although the Dutch codebreakers at Kamer 14 claimed to have intercepted the same message.

29. FO 371, File 35957, 22 August 1943, PRO; and also D.C. Watt, "Was the War with Japan Necessary?" *The Daily Telegraph,* 15 July 1972. Craigie's report,

now in the PRO, is a sanitized version of his original report, and he evidently toned down some of his comments because of Churchill's anger. The Foreign Office cannot now find the original version of the report.

30. FO 371, File 35957, 19 September 1943, PRO.

31. Churchill, *Second World War*, vol. 3, p. 530.

32. Ibid., p. 530, and also Churchill papers, 20/45, personal telegram T-871.

33. U.S. Embassy file 701, Telegram #5670, RG 84, National Archives.

34. PREM 3, Group 252, Section 5, PRO.

35. Pearl Harbor Hearings, part 3, p. 1444.

36. Pearl Harbor Hearings, part 32, p. 732.

37. Ibid.

38. Pearl Harbor Hearings, part 3, pp. 1404–14, and part 5, p. 2304.

39. SRDJ 017036, SRH-118, RG 457, 26 November 1941, National Archives.

40. Layton, *"And I Was There,"* p. 201. There are two versions of Stimson's diary in the Pearl Harbor Liaison Office files at the National Archives, Washington, D.C., one in an abbreviated form, and the other a full version. Apart from very minor textual variations, the content of both is the same.

41. Ibid.

42. Stimson Safe File, 25 November 1941, and British Joint Intelligence Committee report. (Pearl Harbor Liaison Office file, National Archives, Washington, D.C.; and *"And I Was There,"* p. 544.)

43. Anthony Cave Brown, *The Secret Servant* (London: Michael Joseph, 1988), p. 375.

44. Churchill also communicated with Roosevelt through a secret channel he had established with William Stephenson at MI6's offices at 630 Fifth Avenue in New York, which used the cover name of British Security Coordination (BSC), and whose telegraphic address was "Intrepid, New York," a codename that has often been inaccurately bestowed on Stephenson himself. Churchill instructed Stephenson to get as much military aid from Roosevelt, and at the same time help to "bring them in." Stephenson enlisted the help of a New York lawyer, William Donovan, who later created America's Office of Strategic Services (OSS). Stephenson told Churchill, "Donovan exercises controlling influences over Knox, strong influence over Stimson, friendly advisory influence over [the] president and Hull. There is no doubt we can achieve infinitely more through Donovan than any other individual."

It is claimed that neither Anthony Eden, Britain's Foreign Secretary, nor Hull knew anything about this secret arrangement. In turn, Roosevelt used his son, Colonel James Roosevelt, as his personal courier for his messages to Churchill via Stephenson.

On the afternoon of November 26, James made a special trip to BSC in New York with a message from the President for Churchill which read "Negotiations off. Services expect action within two weeks" (Layton, *"And I Was There,"* p. 203). As no copy of this message exists in any archive, it is impossible to assess its full text, but the quoted extract certainly does not suggest that Roosevelt had suddenly acquired knowledge of the Task Force's sailing from his codebreakers at OP-20-G reading JN-25, otherwise he could have been far more precise. Stephenson's own postwar accounts of his work at BSC are so full of inaccuracies and deliberate distortions that it would be most unwise to place any credibility upon claims made about his alleged closeness to Churchill or Roosevelt.

45. Pearl Harbor Liaison Office files, Box 45, 27 November 1941, National Archives.

46. SRN 116741, RG 457, National Archives. Officially this was not decoded until 13 March 1946.

47. SRN 115376, RG 457, National Archives.

48. Mortimer interview.

49. ADM 119/1185, PRO.

50. In April 1941, the Dutch naval liaison officer at FECB was Captain L. G. L. Van der Kun, and the military liaison officer Major J. M. J. Wegner (RG-225, Microfilm, Locator M-1421, #10-207, reels #301–302, National Archives, Washington, D.C.). Later that year Lieutenant Tony Leland, RNVR, who had originally worked for the British firm of Harrison & Crossfield in Java, worked at FECB and was consulted on any aspects of Ultra and JN-25 that affected the Dutch (Mortimer interview). This information conflicts with Wylie's dismissive comments that the Dutch codebreakers produced nothing of importance, but is perhaps a good example of the prima donna stance all codebreakers seem to adopt about their abilities.

51. Letter from General ter Poorten to Major H. A. Long, U.S. Army, 23 July 1960, Royal Netherlands Army Archives, The Hague, Holland.

52. Louis de Jong, *The Kingdom of the Netherlands in World War II* (Official History, vol. IIa); L. G. M. Jaquet, *Aflossing van de Wacht*, p. 126; and report by Captain J. W. Henning, chief codebreaker Kamer 14, dated 11 March 1965, Royal Netherlands Army Archives. The authors are most grateful to Lieutenant Colonel H. L. Switzer, of the Royal Netherlands Army Archives, for his expert translations of this material.

53. Over the years there has been much confusion about the type of transmission used. Captain Safford's account states that it was in Japanese *kata kana* Morse code. But the Japanese government sent out their daily "General Information Broadcasts" as well as *Domei News* broadcasts to its diplomatic and consular missions around the world in both voice and Morse code. Each mission had its own shortwave receiver and operator to handle these broadcasts. Briggs received his "execute" signal in *kana* Morse code, while the Japanese in Washington and the RAN and FECB received their versions as a voice broadcast. (SRH-210, RG 457, Military Reference Section, National Archives, Washington, D.C.; and *Cryptolog*, December 1988, kindly made available by the editor, Graydon Lewis.)

54. Both parts of the Winds message were received by Lieutenant Charles Dixon, RNZVR, a codebreaker stationed at Stonecutters Island in 1941. After the

surrender of Hong Kong, on 25 December 1941, Dixon was a prisoner of war with other officers, including Lieutenant Cedric Brown, RNVR. Dixon told Brown of receiving both parts of the message, and how surprised he was that the Americans were caught unprepared at Pearl Harbor because of the information he had been receiving and decoding in Hong Kong on behalf of FECB, which he assumed was being passed on to the Americans. Charles Dixon died in New Zealand on 10 June 1985 at the age of seventy-seven. Cedric Brown was the senior naval officer on the C-in-C's staff in charge of codes and ciphers. (Interview 21 September 1988.)

55. John Toland, *Infamy* (New York: Doubleday, 1983), pp. 346–47.

56. Interview with Ralph Briggs in Las Vegas, April 1988, and SRH-051, RG 457, National Archives.

57. Class 20 convened in November 1937 and graduated in March 1938. Their instructor was Chief Radioman Walter McGregor. Other members of the class included Henry E. Ethier, Glen E. Evans, James H. Johnson, Elliott E. Okins, Pearly L. Phillips, Charles A. Walters, and Duane L. Whitlock. In fact, the training period for this particular class was shortened by the dramatic sinking by the Japanese of the USS *Panay* in December 1937 and the sudden demand for trained radio operators. The On-the-Roof training courses spanned a period of about fifteen years, from 1926 to 1941, during which time twenty-six marines and 150 sailors were trained in radio interception duties. The first instructors were self-taught and included Harry Kidder, who was affectionately referred to as "Pappy" of the outfit, Dorman A. Chauncey, and Malcolm W. Lyon. By early 1941, the demand for radio intercept operators had increased so greatly that training operations were transferred from the old Navy Building to Bainbridge Island in the state of Washington.

58. SRH-210, RG 457, p. 66.

59. Safford also sent Cheltenham a bunch of flowers, which caused much amusement. For some time they remained on Wigle's desk, but when some of the men started teasing him he took them home for his wife. (Briggs interview, Las Vegas, April 1988.)

8: CHURCHILL'S WAR, pp. 151–54

1. Churchill, *Second World War,* vol. 3, p. 533.

2. SIS 25552, RG 457, National Archives, shows that the Admiralty sent it to OP-20-G at 3:30 P.M. on 1 December 1941.

3. SRDJ-017349, SRH-118, RG 457, National Archives.

4. SRDJ-017357, SRH-118, RG 457, National Archives.

5. *The Second World War,* vol. 3, p. 537.

6. Halifax diary, 7 December 1941. By 4:30 P.M. local time, Halifax had also called Canadian Prime Minister Mackenzie King to tell him of Roosevelt's call.

7. *The Second World War,* vol. 3, p. 537.

8. BBC Written Archives, Caversham.

9. *The Second World War,* vol. 3, p. 539.
10. Mortimer interview.

9: DRAWING THE BLINDS, pp. 155–80

1. Figures kindly supplied by the U.S. National Parks Service, May 1988.
2. The museum and its bookshop are staffed by men and women of the National Parks Service. Frequently naval veterans who served in ships at Pearl Harbor in December 1941 are also present, and they can vividly recreate the emotions of that day.
3. In 1956, the C-in-C 14th Naval District asked the Pacific War Memorial Commission to sponsor a public campaign to build a memorial worthy of the memory of the *Arizona.* Hawaii's delegate to Congress, J. A. Burns, introduced legislation which the 85th Congress approved on 15 March 1958, authorizing construction of a suitable memorial. A bill appropriating $150,000 was passed by the 87th Congress and signed by President John F. Kennedy. A further $100,000 came from the State of Hawaii and the balance of $250,000 from public donations. The American Veterans Association contributed the carillon and also paid for the Italian marble used in the shrine. Total cost of the memorial was $532,000, and it was opened in 1962. Ironically the architect, Alfred Pries, was interned as an enemy alien in 1941. The memorial is in the shape of an enclosed bridge, 184 feet long and thirty-six feet wide, which spans the wreck without touching it and enables more than 200 people at a time to view it.
4. The oldest relic of the ship, first placed on her on 17 October 1916.
5. Following the fleet order made by Admiral Redford, C-in-C U.S. Pacific Fleet on 7 March 1950.
6. Briggs interview, 1988.
7. First heavily censored American newspaper reports claimed the Japanese had sunk only an "old" battleship and one destroyer, while American forces had inflicted "heavy casualties" on the Japanese. In Britain, the equally heavily censored newspapers gave the impression that Pearl Harbor was a great American victory, with the *Daily Express* reporting on its front page for 8 December, "Jap Plane Carrier and Four U-Boats Sunk."
8. No history of FECB has been allowed to appear in any official record, although in ADM 199/1185, Public Record Office, London, a list of FECB personnel for October 1941 has somehow slipped past the censors. In ADM 199/1472A, PRO, London, section #280 headed "Transfer of FECB from Singapore to Colombo" has been cut out of the volume, and a handwritten note added: "Contents of this section intelligence sensitive but not of historical importance. Dated: 1/11/71." However, copies of the Admiralty messages detailing the evacuation and transfer of FECB from Singapore to Colombo, in late December 1941, can be found in MP 1185/8, File 1937/2/159, Australian Archives, Victoria, so the excision at the PRO is pointless but serves to highlight the paranoia existing at GCHQ even today.

9. ADM 119/1185, Public Record Office, London. This page also seems to have escaped the notice of the censors. Details of the radio links can also be found in ADB Conversations, RG 225, Microfilm Locator M-1421, 10-207, reels #301-302, National Archives, Washington, D.C.

10. NA 016/12/30, National Archives, Wellington.

11. As used in SRMN-006, National Archives, Washington, D.C.

12. Wigle's statement was made to the U.S. Naval Security Group in Washington, but not produced at the 1945 inquiry. The statement became public knowledge only when, ironically, Ralph Briggs found it when he was working at the U.S. Naval Security Group headquarters some thirty years later.

13. Layton, *"And I Was There,"* p. 265.

14. Briggs interview, 1988.

15. After the war, in November 1945, attempts were made by the Americans to try and trace the originals of both parts of the Winds messages in the Japanese Foreign Ministry archives. The investigation was protracted, because the Americans did not want to admit to the Japanese that they had been reading their J-19 consular code in 1941. In the end, the investigators found that all pertinent records had been burned prior to 14 August 1945, and no individual could be traced who would even admit to sending the first part of the message (#2353), about which there was no dispute. So it was hardly surprising that no one was found who would admit to sending the second, or "execute" portion. (SRH-177, RG 457, National Archives.)

16. SRH-210, p. 54.

17. SRH-355, National Archives, p. 398.

18. Executive Order #12065.

19. SRN series, RG-457, Military Reference Division, National Archives.

20. SRH-355, RG 457, National Archives.

21. This would particularly apply to those messages that continued to be sent also in the old Blue Book code.

22. SRH-149, RG 457, National Archives.

23. Ibid., p. 221.

24. Cate was born in Japan of missionary parents and had lived there for most of his life.

25. Pearl Harbor Liaison Office, CNO Documents, RG 80, National Archives, Washington, D.C.

26. Letter dated 8 May 1989, Serial 5750, GHD/0256.

27. Mr. Henrikson not only most courteously showed one of the authors around the U.S. Navy's fascinating codebreaking museum but has supplied many photographs and other valuable information for this book. His inability to supply any information about pre–Pearl Harbor JN-25 material was again repeated at a meeting in January 1990.

28. There have been persistent—although unconfirmed—reports that large quantities of U.S. Navy records from the Pearl Harbor period have been illegally shredded in recent years without first being properly declassified and offered to the National Archives as part of America's national heritage. Since the U.S. Navy

will not admit that the records existed in the first place, it is obviously difficult for them to admit they have destroyed them.

29. If one accepts the official version that JN-25 was not broken until after Pearl Harbor, then one would expect to find decoding dates of at least mid-1942, by which time JN-25 was being freely read, and there was enough staff to spare to look back through pre–Pearl Harbor material.

30. Letters dated 20 July 1988, Serial 5511 GH/0598, and 26 January 1989, Serial 5750 GHD/0042.

31. Letter dated 9 March 1989, Serial J9723A. However, as explained in the Preface, p. 6, at the Nimitz Conference at Hawaii in December 1991, Mr. Frederick Parker, the NSA's historian, after consultation with GCHQ, issued a statement that both American and British codebreakers had broken JN-25 prior to the attack.

32. Interview with Lieutenant Commander W. W. Mortimer, RNR (Ret.), 13 December 1989. The authors are greatly indebted to Commander Mortimer for the information and primary wartime documents he kindly provided that have provided so much useful information about FECB and its work.

33. After the war, there was an Anglo-American agreement not to reveal any details about the breaking of the German Enigma, because both the British and Americans were busily selling reconditioned Enigmas to many third-world countries at bargain prices, assuring them that all their messages would be secure, whereas in fact, both countries' Sigint agencies were able to read all such traffic for many years until 1974, when the story began to leak out.

34. Mortimer interview, December 1989.

35. Ibid.

36. The last conversation with the Foreign Office was on 11 December 1989, with Mr. R. Newton, Permanent Under Secretary's Department, who again confirmed that the authors could not see any FECB material.

37. Francis H. Hinsley, *British Intelligence in the Second World War* (Cambridge: Cambridge University Press, 4 volumes, 1979–90).

38. Naval File N/8/10/20, National Archives, New Zealand.

39. National Archives, New Zealand.

40. SRMN-006, RG 457, National Archives.

Bibliography

Agawa, Hiroyuki. *The Reluctant Admiral: Yamamoto and the Imperial Navy* (New York: Harper & Row, 1979).

Andrew, Christopher. *Secret Service* (London: Heinemann, 1985).

Ball, Desmond. *A Suitable Piece of Real Estate* (Sydney: Hale & Iremonger, 1979).

Bamford, James. *The Puzzle Palace* (Boston: Houghton Mifflin, 1982).

Barber, Noel. *Sinister Twilight* (London: Collins, 1968).

Barty-King, Hugh. *Girdle Round the Earth* (London: Heinemann, 1979).

Beesly, Patrick, *Very Special Intelligence* (London: Hamish Hamilton, 1977).

Berle, Adolf A. *The Adolf A. Berle Diaries: 1937–1971* (New York: Franklin D. Roosevelt Library, 1973).

Burkhard, Baron von Mullenheim-Rechberg. *Battleship Bismarck* (London: Bodley Head, 1981).

Burrows, William. *Deep Black* (New York: Bantam, 1988).

Cadogan, Sir Alexander. *The Diaries of Sir Alexander Cadogan: 1938–1945* (New York: Putnam, 1972).

Calvocoressi, Peter. *Top Secret Ultra* (London: Cassell, 1980).

Cave Brown, Anthony. *Bodyguard of Lies* (London: W. H. Allen, 1976).

———. *The Last Hero: Wild Bill Donovan* (New York: Times Books, 1982).

———. *The Secret Servant* (London: Michael Joseph, 1988).

Chapman, John. *The Price of Admiralty* (London: Saltire Press, 1984–90).

Churchill, Sir Winston S. *The Second World War*, 6 Volumes (London: Cassell, 1948–54).

Clark, Ronald. *The Man Who Broke Purple* (London: Weidenfeld & Nicolson, 1977).

Collier, Basil. *The War in the Far East, 1941–45* (New York: Morrow, 1969).

Connell, John. *Wavell: Scholar and Soldier* (London: Collins, 1964).

Costello, John. *The Pacific War* (London: Collins, 1981).

———. *The Mask of Treachery* (New York: William Morrow, 1988).

Craigie, Sir Robert Leslie. *Behind the Japanese Mask* (London: Hutchinson, 1945).

Cruikshank, Charles. *Deception in World War II* (Oxford: Oxford University Press, 1979).

Dallek, Robert. *Franklin D. Roosevelt and American Foreign Policy: 1932–1945* (New York: Oxford University Press, 1979).

Deavours, C. A., and Louis Kruh. *Machine Cryptography & Modern Cryptanalysis* (Dedham, Mass.: Artech Books, 1985).

Dobson, Christopher, and Ronald Payne. *The Dictionary of Espionage* (London: Harrap, 1984).

Dorwart, Jeffery M. *The Office of Naval Intelligence: 1865–1918* (Annapolis: Naval Institute Press, 1979).

Falk, Stanley. *Seventy Days to Singapore* (New York: 1975).

Farago, Ladislas. *The Broken Seal* (New York: Random House, 1967).

———. *The Game of the Foxes* (New York: David McKay, 1971).

Garlinski, Josef. *Intercept* (London: Dent, 1979).

Gilbert, Martin. *Finest Hour* (London: Heinemann, 1983).

———. *Road to Victory* (London: Heinemann, 1986).

Glees, Anthony. *The Secrets of the Service* (London: Cape, 1987).

Goodhart, Philip. *Fifty Ships That Saved the World* (New York: Doubleday, 1965).

Grew, Joseph C. *Ten Years in Japan* (New York: Simon & Schuster, 1944).

Handel, Michael, ed. *Strategic and Operational Deception in the Second World War* (London: Frank Cass, 1987).

Harris, Ruth R. "The Magic Leak of 1941," *Pacific Historical Review*, February 1981.

Haslach, Robert. *Nishi no Kaze, Hare* (Holland: Uniboek BV, 1985).

Hastings, Max. *Bomber Command* (London: Michael Joseph, 1979).

Hinsley, Francis H., *British Intelligence in the Second World War* (Cambridge: Cambridge University Press, 1979–90).

Hodges, Andrew. *Alan Turing: The Enigma* (London: Burnett, 1983).

Hoehling, A. A. *The Week Before Pearl Harbor* (New York: Norton, 1963).

Holmes, Wilfred. *Double-Edged Secrets* (Annapolis: Naval Institute Press, 1979).

Hooper, David. *Official Secrets* (London: Secker & Warburg, 1987).

Hough, Richard. *Death of a Battleship* (New York: Macmillan, 1963).

Howarth, Stephen. *Morning Glory* (London: Hamish Hamilton, 1983).

Hoyt, Edwin. *Raider 16* (New York: World, 1970).

Hudson, W. J., and H. J. W. Stokes, *Documents on Australian Foreign Policy 1937–49*, Volume V, July 1941–June 1942 (Canberra: Australian Government Publishing Service, 1982).

Jong, Louis de. *The Kingdom of the Netherlands in World War II* (Netherlands Official History, Volume IIa).

Kahn, David. *The Codebreakers* (New York: Macmillan, 1967).

———. *Kahn on Codes* (New York: Macmillan, 1983).

Kennedy, William V. *The Intelligence War* (London: Salamander, 1983).

Kimball, Warren F. *Churchill and Roosevelt: The Complete Correspondence* (Princeton: Princeton University Press, 1984).

Kirby, Stanley W. *Singapore: The Chain of Disaster* (London: Cassell, 1971).

Knightley, Phillip. *The Second Oldest Profession* (London: Deutsch, 1986).

Korda, Michael. *Charmed Lives* (New York: Random House, 1979).

Kozaczuk, Wladyslaw, *Enigma* (London: Arms & Armour Press, 1984).

Lamphere, Robert, and Tom Shachtman. *The FBI-KGB War* (New York: Random House, 1986).

Layton, Edwin T., with Roger Pineau and John Costello. *"And I Was There"* (New York: William Morrow, 1985).

Lewin, Ronald. *Ultra Goes to War* (New York: McGraw-Hill, 1978).

Lord, Walter. *Day of Infamy* (New York: Holt, Rinehart, 1957).

――――. *Incredible Victory* (New York: Harper & Row, 1967).

――――. *Lonely Vigil* (New York: Viking, 1977).

McLachlan, Donald. *Room 39: Naval Intelligence in Action: 1939–45* (London: Weidenfeld, 1968).

Marder, Arthur J. *Old Friends, New Enemies* (Oxford: Oxford University Press, 1981).

Middlebrook, Martin. *Battleship* (London: Heinemann, 1977).

Mohr, Ulrich. *Atlantis* (London: London Press, 1955).

Montgomery, Brian. *Shenton of Singapore* (London: Leo Cooper, 1984).

Montgomery, Michael. *Imperialist Japan* (London: Christopher Helm, 1987).

――――. *Who Sank the* Sydney? (Australia: Cassell, 1983).

Morgan, Ted. *FDR* (New York: Simon & Schuster, 1985).

Muggenthaler, August. *German Raiders of World War II* (London: Robert Hale, 1978).

Popov, Dusko. *Spy/Counterspy* (New York: Grosset & Dunlap, 1974).

Prange, Gordon W. *At Dawn We Slept* (New York: McGraw-Hill, 1981).

Pratt, Fletcher. *Sea Power and Today's War* (New York: 1939).

Richards, Denis. *The Royal Air Force: 1939–1945* (London: HMSO, 1953).

Richelson, Jeffrey, and Desmond Ball. *The Ties That Bind* (Sydney: Allen & Unwin, 1985).

Robertson, John. *Australia at War* (Melbourne: Heinemann, 1981).

――――, and John McCarthy. *Australian War Strategy 1939–45: A Documentary History* (Australia: University of Queensland Press, 1985).

Roskill, Stephen W., *British Naval Policy Between the Wars* (London: W. H. Allen, 1968 and 1976).

――――. *The War at Sea: 1939–45* (London: HMSO, 1953, vol. 1).

Rusbridger, James. "The Sinking of the *Automedon,* the Capture of the *Nankin,"* *Encounter,* May 1985.

――――. "The Winds of Warning," *Encounter,* January 1986.

――――. *The Intelligence Game* (London: The Bodley Head, 1989).

Stripp, Alan. *Codebreaker in the Far East* (London: Frank Cass, 1989).

Tansill, Charles C. *Back Door to War* (Chicago: Henry Regnery, 1952).

Taylor, A. J. P. *The Second World War* (London: Hamish Hamilton, 1975).

Taylor, John, and Kenneth Munson. *History of Aviation* (London: New English Library, 1978).

Theobald, Robert. *The Final Secret of Pearl Harbor* (New York: Devin-Adair, 1954).

Toland, John. *Infamy* (New York: Doubleday, 1982).

Vardy, S. B. and S. H. *Society in Change* (New York: Columbia University Press, 1983).

Waller, George M. *Pearl Harbor: Roosevelt and the Coming of the War* (Boston: Heath, 1965).

Wark, Wesley. *The Ultimate Enemy* (Oxford: Oxford University Press, 1986).

Webster, Sir Charles, and Noble Frankland. *The Strategic Air Offensive Against Germany* (London: HMSO, 1961).

Welchman, Gordon. *The Hut Six Story* (New York: McGraw Hill, 1982).

West, Nigel. *GCHQ: The Secret Wireless War 1900–86* (London: Weidenfeld & Nicolson, 1986).

————. *A Matter of Trust: MI5 1945–1972* (London: Weidenfeld & Nicolson, 1982).

————. *MI5: British Security Service Operations 1909–1945* (London: The Bodley Head, 1981).

————. *MI6: British Secret Intelligence Service Operations: 1909–1945* (London: Weidenfeld & Nicolson, 1983).

Winterbotham, F. W. *The Ultra Secret* (London: Weidenfeld & Nicholson, 1974).

Wise, David. *The Spy Who Got Away* (New York: Random House, 1988).

Wohlstetter, Roberta. *Pearl Harbor: Warning and Decision* (Stanford: Stanford University Press, 1962).

Wright, Peter. *Spycatcher* (New York: Viking, 1987).

Yardley, Herbert. *The American Black Chamber* (New York: Bobbs-Merrill, 1931).

Index

About the Authors

JAMES RUSBRIDGER WAS born in 1928 and began his career working in the naval design office at Vickers Armstrong on a variety of conventional and nuclear weapons systems. Later, as an international commodity broker, he worked for Britain's Secret Intelligence Service in Eastern Europe. Since his retirement, he has specialized in researching and writing books and television documentaries about intelligence affairs. His first book, the highly acclaimed *The Intelligence Game* (The Bodley Head/New Amsterdam Press) was published in 1989, followed by his equally controversial World War II investigation, *Who Sank Surcouf?* (Random Century). James Rusbridger is unmarried and lives in Cornwall in southwest England.

ERIC NAVE was born in 1899, and in 1917 he joined the Royal Australian Navy. Because of his expertise in learning the Japanese language, in 1925 he was loaned to the Royal Navy to start their first codebreaking activities against Japan. In 1928, Eric Nave joined the Government Code & Cipher School in London as head of the Japanese naval codebreaking department. Transferring to the Royal Navy in 1930, he went out to the Far East Combined Bureau in Singapore in 1937, where he continued his codebreaking work. Later, in 1942, Eric Nave founded Australia's Central Bureau, continuing his codebreaking work until the end of the war in 1945, and in 1972 was awarded the OBE. In 1947, Eric Nave joined the Australian Security Intelligence Organisation, finally retiring in 1959 after a forty-two-year career in codebreaking and intelligence for the British and Australian governments. Eric Nave is married and lives in Melbourne, Australia.